Trail of Story, Traveller's Path

Trail of Story, Traveller's Path

Reflections on Ethnoecology and Landscape

by Leslie Main Johnson

AU PRESS

© 2010 Leslie Main Johnson

Published by AU Press, Athabasca University
1200, 10011 – 109 Street
Edmonton, AB T5J 3S8

Library and Archives Canada Cataloguing in Publication

Johnson, Leslie Main, 1950-
    Trail of story, traveller's path : reflections on ethnoecology and
landscape / Leslie Main Johnson.

Includes bibliographical references and index.
Also available in electronic format (978-1-897425-36-7)
ISBN 978-1-897425-35-0

    1. Landscape ecology–Canada, Northern. 2. Traditional ecological
knowledge–Canada, Northern. 3. Indians of North America–Ethnobiology–
Canada, Northern. 4. Landscape–Canada, Northern. I. Title.

GN476.7.J64 2010   304.2089'970719   C2009-901827-6

Cover and book design by Alex Chan.
Printed and bound in Canada by Marquis Book Printing.

Unless otherwise credited, all images are courtesy of
the author, Leslie Main Johnson.

This book has been published with the help of a grant
from the Canadian Federation for the Humanities and
Social Sciences, through the Aid to Scholarly Publications
Programme, using funds provided by the Social Sciences and
Humanities Research Council of Canada.

Canadian **Federation** for the
Humanities and Social Sciences
Fédération canadienne
des sciences humaines

CONTENTS

FIGURES

TABLES

ACKNOWLEDGEMENTS

I would first like to thank my teachers, the Elders and others from whom I learned about the land, and my colleagues and collaborators at various phases of the research presented here. I also owe a deep debt to my various funders, the Social Science and Humanities Research Council of Canada, the Canadian Circumpolar Institute, the Athabasca Research Fund, the Jacobs Foundation, the Gitksan-Wet'suwet'en Education Society, the Kyah Wiget Education Society, the Gwich'in Renewable Resource Board, and the Canadian Institute of Health Research (Christopher Fletcher, PI, for the Sahtú research). I would like to acknowledge the diverse indigenous and local organizations I have worked with or for over the years: The Gitksan-Wet'suwet'en Traditional Medicine Project of the Gitksan-Wet'suwet'en Education Society, the Gitksan-Wet'suwet'en Tribal Council, the Kyah Wiget Education Society, the Kaska Tribal Council, the Liard First Nation, the Gwich'in Social and Cultural Institute, the Gwich'in Language Centre, the Gwich'in Renewable Resource Board, and various local organizations in Deline (the Deline band, the Sahtu Lands, and Resources Board).

My teachers and collaborators in the communities are too numerous list, but there are a few individuals I would like to mention who were very important in my journey. Among my community teachers, I would particularly like to acknowledge the late Olive Ryan (Gwans), Art Mathews Jr. (Dinim Gyet), the late Ray Morgan (Ksuu), the late Peter Muldoe (Gitluudahl), the late Pat Namox (Wah'tah'kwets), the late Lucy Namox (Goohlat), the late Elsie Tait, Alfred Joseph (Gisde we), Dan Michell, the late Madeline Alfred (Dzee), the late Alfred Mitchell, the late Sarah Tait (Wihalaite), Mary Teya, the late William Teya, Bertha Frances, Alestine Andre, Mida Donnessey, Alice Brodhagen, Leda Jules, and May Broadhagen. I would like to acknowledge the following colleagues and collaborators in the communities: Beverley Anderson, Darleen Vegh, Art Loring, Bernice Neyelle and Camilla Tutcho, Linda McDonald, Frances Carlick, Bobbie-Jo Greenland, Marie-Annick Elie, and Alestine Andre; and my colleagues Patrick Moore, Sharon Hargus, Ingrid Kritsch, Robert Wishart, Sheila Greer, Scott Trusler, Kenneth Rabnett, Allen Gottesfeld, Marni Amirault, and Christopher Fletcher for their help and insights. Mere Roberts, Maori biologist and colleague, provided insight into traditional knowledge of land in Aotearoa/New Zealand, which helped me to gain perspective on Indigenous Knowledge, and on what I knew from North America. I owe a deep debt of gratitude to two of my mentors, Eugene Anderson and Nancy Turner, for starting me on this journey and continuing to inspire and encourage me. Kat Anderson, the late Henry T. Lewis, Fikret Berkes, and Harvey Feit have also been sources of inspiration and insight. I want to express appreciation for the insightful comments of my two anonymous reviewers. Any errors which remain are my own responsibility. Lastly, I would like to thank my partner Glenn Eilers for his patience and support as I have struggled with the process of writing, and my daughter Rose for her patience and support during the earlier parts of my on-going research.

1

Trails and Visions

REFLECTIONS ON ETHNOECOLOGY, LANDSCAPE, AND KNOWING

The ways people understand and act upon land can shape cultures and ways of life, determine identity and polity, create environmental relationships, and determine economies, whether sustainable or ephemeral. Understandings of "land" also underlie the complicated dance of resource development, even the concept of "resource," as they are negotiated between local populations and larger socio-political and economic forces. This work undertakes an examination of understanding of the land, of ethnoecology and traditional knowledge of the land based on research with several indigenous peoples of northwestern Canada. The synthesis communicated here has developed over a period of years and in a variety of settings. My understanding of others' understandings too has been a journey, a traveller's path, a trail of story.

In some ways this investigation is rooted in indigeneity, in the concept that ancient or original connection of people and land engenders a unique relationship between them that at once creates social identity, and, as some have postulated, a deep and nuanced interaction with land which is, or should be, sustainable. In the post-Brundtland[1] world, sustainability is a concept that has been widely bandied about, imbued with political and ideological currency, but which is difficult to actualize or evaluate. Sustainability drives a number of trends in current practice, and underlies, together with post-colonial concepts of self-determination, attempts to forge ecologically sound and socially just development. This can be construed as building both economies and societies, as the forces of global market and society expand or intensify, drawing in peripheries in both North and South. As a Canadian and onetime resident of the region, my focus is on the insights to be gained through working with indigenous peoples and local communities of the North.

In northern Canada, ecological knowledge of indigenous residents has gained a substantial currency. Its use or consideration is now mandated by governments in the Yukon, Northwest Territories and Nunavut, and consultation processes have been written into legislation and enshrined in land claims settlements. Dealing in some wise with the knowledge of the land of northern residents, especially indigenous residents, has now become a necessary and somewhat fashionable step in the transformation of hinterland to economic dynamo, glossing over the distinction between frontier and homeland which was cogently pointed out in the 1970s by Thomas Berger (1988). Traditional ecological knowledge is nearly universally now referred to by the acronym TEK, or by one of its variants such as TRM (traditional resource management) or TEKW (traditional ecological knowledge and wisdom). Contemporary use of TEK tends to be in the public involvement tradition of resource management and land use planning, and typically solicits a restricted subset of input relating to a specific planning or management need. Consultation regarding wildlife and fisheries management and environmental impact assessment for proposed development are generally the fora in which specific "chunks" of TEK are solicited (also referred to as "TEKbites" in my parlance, or "TEK artifacts" in the apt analysis of Paul Nadasdy 1999, 2003). The overall frame of reference and indeed even the domain of inquiry are provided by the institutions and knowledge systems of the dominant society.

As a number of authors have articulated (Cruikshank 1998; Nadasdy 1999, 2003; Fienup-Riordan 1990; Brody 1988; Morrow and Hensel 1992; Stevenson 1998; Hornborg 1998), this approach may in fact do serious violence to the nature of traditional knowledge systems, and may seriously limit what can be learned from study of the understandings of traditional and local peoples.

I have in my investigations taken quite a different tack. In the course of my research, there has been considerable "un-learning" to be done, and a progressive widening of the frame of reference to avoid imposing my own categories in bounding my inquiry and in elucidating the nature of the connections that the people I work with make between phenomena and domains of knowledge and practice. I have spent time with people in a variety of communities, learning from, working with, and travelling with different people, observing and participating in land-based and community activities, and listening. I have cast my net broadly, seeking to understand how things are put together by people in a context outside the academy, within the practice of daily life, and how these understandings are learned and passed on. As I have not had the privilege of working in some pristine Eden-like society, isolated from change and outside impact, often what I have learned relates to past practices, or to practices which may be threatened by present and future resource development and social change. My emphasis is, perhaps, biased toward things of actual or potential relevance to contemporary people and communities. Part of the impetus for my work has been preservation and documentation, both for local communities and families, and arguably for the larger society, of knowledge and ways of life that may provide visions of alternatives or viable pathways for sustainable lifeways.

My research also necessarily deals with knowledge and knowing, epistemology and knowledges, and anthropology of science. This work is not a formal examination of epistemology or hermeneutics, nor a formal anthropology of science, but a consideration of what it means to "know" in different contexts, to understand how one knows. Keeping in mind the different ways that Western science and local peoples organize and experience knowledge is necessary to be able to explore local knowledge of land, and to consider its implications and entailments.

Perhaps this is a good place to consider the terms *land* and *landscape*, terms that I have chosen to employ in order to discuss people's relationships with and understandings of what we in mainstream Euro-North American society might call environment. The simple English term *land* designates much more than mere terrain or area on a map. It is not limited to meaning soil or the surface of the Earth. Instead "land" encompasses the totality of beings existing in the place that a people live. It is a homeland, and includes the earth itself and its landforms—the waters, the sky and weather, the living beings, both plant and animal, spirit entities, history, and the will of the Creator. Land in this sense cannot be measured in hectares or reduced to a value of dollars, though the land provides both livelihood and identity. Land constitutes place, rather than space (cf. Casey 1996). Land cannot be reduced to a grid or the static representation of a map. Land and people are neither separate nor separable, a concept well captured by the title of a popular work on Yukon indigenous peoples commissioned by the Council of Yukon Indians entitled *Part of the Lands, Part of the Waters* (McClellan et al. 1987). Land could be envisioned more as a medium than a (roughly) planar surface on which things happen, that is, more than a stage or backdrop for human activities. Colin Turnbull (reported in Tuan 1974) described BaMbuti perception of their forested homeland as "ambience" rather than "landscape," as the place in which they live and with which they maintain both social and spiritual relationships, an interesting rendering of the relationship to homeland where there is no remove, no separation, no distant views or prospects. In some ways, the homelands of the peoples with whom I have worked and from whom I have learned are more ambience than landscape, if by that we imply a distinction between lived spaces and the features of the land. Or perhaps better would be to describe "land" as a society, a network of relationships.

Trails rather than fields are the dominant land metaphor for people who travel through their homelands to make a living, who use a variety of resource sites located in different places throughout the cycle of the year, who hunt, encountering animals which sustain them in different places and at distinct times. Trails traverse even the spiritual landscape of time-space via the *kungax* (**cin k'ih**), or trails of song for Witsuwit'en of northwest British Columbia (Mills 1994), and Ridington (1990) eloquently describes the trail of dream leading to the hunter's encounter with an animal for the Dane-ẕaa of northeastern BC.

I began to think about ethnoecology some years ago when I was trying to represent habitat information for significant cultural plants in northwest British Columbia. I began to realize in conversations with elders and others about medicinal and food plants, that our systems of understanding the landscape differed in fundamental ways. As I struggled to interpret terms such as "gully," "swamp" and "halfway up the mountain" as predictive habitat types, or found myself confronted with a series of now obsolete local landmarks in elders' descriptions of key plant localities, I realized that local systems of representation of place kinds, or ecotopes, merited investigation. In the process of writing my doctoral dissertation on Gitksan traditional uses of plants, I included a short chapter on Gitksan place terms. Searching for comparative material, at that time it was difficult to find comparable studies in the literature. Between cultures, it appears that ways of discussing place kinds may be far more variable than ways of discussing plants and animals (Johnson and Hunn 2009).

The reasons for this may be many—among the simplest is that landforms themselves are less discrete than individuals of most biological species (Mark and Turk 2003; Mark, Turk and Stea 2009; Johnson and Hunn 2009). As discussed in Johnson and Hunn (2009), the scale of phenomena that may be relevant is also hard to bound. "Sandbar" is a logical candidate for an ecotope, but what about "sand"? My intuitive response is to include "sandbar" as an ecotope, a repeating landscape unit of definable spatial extent, but to exclude "sand" because it is a substrate and therefore lacks intrinsic spatial qualities. What about "moss"? At first glance, "moss" appears to be a term for a living kind, a plant life form, rather than a kind of place. However, for the Montagnais (Innu), the term meaning 'moss' is construed as a kind of "earth" (Clément 1990), while for Dene peoples "moss" may indicate the types of forest or muskeg stands which have thick layers of feather moss or sphagnum. These last are arguably ecotopes, landscape units typified by vegetative cover. These "moss" sites retain moisture, and the spongy texture makes them difficult to walk through, making them undesirable for trail routes or for camp sites in the summer season.

My research in indigenous knowledge of the land began with the premise that indigenous cultures in northwestern North America would encode their knowledge of ecosystems, habitats or environments in their languages, and that these recognized kinds of place might well reveal ecological understandings that differed from those of Western science and landscape management. I also felt that the way people understand land and landscape would likely vary depending on the landscape itself, and characteristics of their societies and ways of making a living, insights articulated in Thornton's volume *Being and Place Among the Tlingit* (2008). In order to get a sense of the variation between cultures and environments while limiting variation within these parameters, I chose a series of four research areas with different indigenous groups in northwestern Canada. Two areas were located in adjacent areas of the inner Coast Mountains in northwestern British Columbia, one along the Yukon-British Columbia border, and the last along the tundra-taiga ecotone in the Mackenzie Delta region. I have also worked with a fifth group in the taiga-tundra ecotone by Great Bear Lake. Four of the five peoples speak Athapaskan languages, and the fifth a Tsimshianic language. The communities and their homelands are introduced in the following chapters.

A variety of approaches have been made to investigating ecological relationships and ethnobiological knowledge by other investigators. However, I found few models for investigating kinds of place and the organization of ecological understanding of land as a domain of knowledge. My methodology then, of necessity, has been eclectic and somewhat pioneering in the effort to focus on the particular aspects of environmental understanding which initially interested me, and in the subsequent attempt to figure out what properly belongs in the "ethnoecology" box, and what methods are needed to learn about and explicate this understanding. In order to avoid biasing my results by the nature of my questions, my investigations have been framed to learn in an open-ended way. I have employed a mixture of participant observation, visual documentation, and an analysis of narratives in my ethnoecological research.

I found that ethnoecological knowledge is complex, and that it is often implicit more than explicit, in practice as much as encoded in language. It is linked with all other aspects of culture, as relationship to land is foundational for native North American peoples. I also found that there is not a tidy line demarcating knowledge of the land in an abstract sense, from knowledge of how to move on, or what to do on, the land. Neither is ethnoecological knowledge well demarcated in the sense of limiting itself to the physical and biological, but encompasses history and the sacred as well as what Western scientific traditions would understand as ecological. As the conception of the social network encompasses the human species, ethnoecology is necessarily social, and about appropriate behaviour as well.

My initial intent to focus on abstract categories and their interrelationships was confounded by the particularity of knowledge (leading to discussion of specific places rather than place kinds), its temporal fluidity (things do not stay put nor have firm boundaries, especially in the North), and, for Dene speaking peoples, the great importance of practice and learning through experience rather than by talking about things. The stories people do tell about land are multilayered, and do not lay out explicit ecological knowledge isolated from other aspects of life. As is common in storytelling traditions, the information—the meaning—in a narrative is up to the listener to decipher.

Indigenous ethnoecology includes people as a focal point of ecological relationships. Specific places are extremely significant, and knowledgeable people have a large inventory of specific places where they have travelled and harvested resources, and have a rich knowledge of stories of personal experience and events long ago that are tied to such places. The types of shifting and often poorly bounded kinds of place recognized by indigenous peoples, and areas of significance to them, are challenging to render in contemporary media such as GIS and may match poorly with the kinds of place understood by those trained in disciplines such as forestry or wildlife management.

I begin this volume with a consideration of key concepts, including ethnoecology, landscape and landscape ecology and a range of approaches, that people have taken in approaching the domain of cultural knowledge of land and landscapes. I then move into a consideration of Gitksan ethnoecology, and the linkage of landforms and overall orientation systems to social structure and the storied landscape, followed by a review of Witsuwit'en landscape ethnoecology. I continue my musings on people and landscape in northwest British Columbia by focusing on a key ecological type, the berry patch, and considering the apparently simple question, *What makes a berry patch?* I reflect on the ethnoecology of Dene (Athapaskan speakers) in northern Canada, beginning with chapters on Kaska and Gwich'in landscape knowledge, and concluding with consideration of commonalities and contrasts in Dene ethnoecology.

In Chapter 10, I reflect on named places. Finally, I consider the contrasts between indigenous landscape ethnoecology and the classification of habitats and landscapes in Western scientific thought, and the implications of these differences for how knowledge about landscape is presented and apprehended. In my concluding chapter I reflect on landscape ethnoecology and on its potential to inform social and ecological sciences, land management, and contemporary political debates.

2

Landscape Ethnoecology

NEXUS OF PEOPLE, LAND, AND LIFEWAYS

Patterning in landscape is complex. Understanding its nature, including anthropogenic patterning, and considering the implications of pattern for landscape and ecological process, is of both practical and theoretical importance. At another level of remove is the study and understanding of human cultural perception and understanding of landscape patterns, and the entailments and meanings imputed to these understandings of the land.

The comparative understanding of landscape terms, variously termed ethnophysiography (Mark and Turk 2003), ethnobiogeography (Hunn and Meilleur 1998), and landscape ethnoecology (Johnson 2000; Johnson and Hunn 2009), is an emerging area of research which articulates with other aspects of the study of traditional ecological knowledge, ethnoecology, the anthropology of landscape, and the study of space and place. I first briefly review the literature on anthropology of landscape, space and place, ethnoecology, and landscape in order to set the conceptual grounding for what follows.

Anthropology of landscape, space and place, and cultural landscape

Classic works in the anthropology of landscape in the broad sense have included the seminal works of Hirsch and O'Hanlon, and their contributors (1995) in the *Anthropology of Landscape*, and the papers in the volume *Senses of Place* edited by Feld and Basso (1996). These two volumes explore "landscape" as setting, image, soundscape, and object of local understanding in a range of cultural contexts, exploring place and meaning. Edward Casey's (1996) thought-provoking discussion of "space" and "place" from a philosophical perspective helped to set the parameters of the discussion of place in anthropological and philosophical thinking. The literature on "space and place" explores the differences between lived-in experiential "place," and a more objective sense of "space," teasing apart abstract space and the locales of people's lives. Although much of this literature deals with built environments, significant discussions of the experience of landscape and place embedded within larger regions is also present, and is pertinent to my explorations of meanings of "landscape." The review article of Lawrence and Low (1990) was an early exposition of issues of place and space in anthropological research, and their 2003 edited volume (Low and Lawrence-Zúñiga 2003) presents a synopsis of more recent writing in the field. Particularly relevant to conceptions of landscape are Rodman's piece on multilocality and multivocality, and Munn's chapter on excluded spaces in Australia. Rodman (2003:206) usefully differentiates two senses of "place" in anthropological thought:

1) Place is "an anthropological construct for 'setting' or the localization of concepts."
2) Place is "socially constructed spatialized experience."

Rodman (2003:206-207) articulates the tension between objective space and experiential place, quoting Entrikin (1991:203):

> This divide between the existential and naturalistic conceptions of place appears to be an unbridgeable one, and one that is only made wider in adopting a decentered [objective] view. The closest we can come to addressing both sides of this divide is from a point in between, a point that leads us into the vast realm of *narrative forms*. From this position we gain a view from both sides of the divide. We gain a sense both of being "in a place" and "at a *location*," of being in the center and being at a point on a centerless world. (emphasis added)

Rodman continues,

But places come into being through praxis, not just through narrative. One should also be wary of the assumption that the geographers' and inhabitants' discourses will be consistent and that all inhabitants (and all geographers) will share similar views. (Rodman 2003:207)

Munn's powerful piece introduces a number of significant concepts in anthropological approaches to space, place and landscape, including linkage to the morality and cosmology instantiated in the Land or country, and the conception of "relative spacetime," which has evident links to Ingold's (2000) concept of journeying. She differentiates *location* into *locale*, a place where things happen, and *locatedness*, which "refers primarily to mobile action rather than things" (Munn 2003:93). Munn describes "a moving spatial field" of the actor in contrast to fixed spatial localities or determined regions. The linkage to cosmology, morality and social order is especially evident as she describes linkage of the Law to the Land:

> I have noted that Aboriginal law is said to be in the ground, especially the rocks. "You see that hill over there? Blackfellow Law like that hill. It never changes . . . [It] is in the ground," said a Yarralin man to Deborah Rose. The "Law" is the hill, or is in the hill. The Law's *visible signs* are topographic "markings"—rocks, rock crevices and stains, soaks, trees, creek beds, clay pans, and so forth— remnants of the multiple, so-called totemic ancestors who made the land into distinguishable shapes. (Munn 2003:95; emphasis added)

More symbolic and archaeologically informed anthropological approaches to landscape are embodied in a trio of important works: Bender's edited volume *Landscape, Politics and Perspectives* (1993), Tilley's *Phenomenology of Landscape* (1994), and Ashmore and Knapps's *Archaeologies of Landscape* (1999). As one might anticipate, meaning of landscape, spatial arrangement of human settlements, paths and monuments, and a concern with built environments characterize these rich volumes.

Deriving from archaeological and heritage perspectives, the term *cultural landscape* is used by a range of authors in various ways, in their expositions of relationships between people and landscape. Most relevant to this work are Davidson-Hunt and Berkes (2003), Andrews and Zoe (1997) and Strang

(1997). "Cultural landscape" in their sense comprises the larger framework of meaning of *land*, including cosmology, history, the sacred, and the customary activities and places of activities of the people on the land, and is somewhat distinct from how the term cultural landscape is used in heritage conservation frameworks.

Ethnoecology and ethnoecologies

I characterize my approach to landscape and human relationships to land as "ethnoecological." What distinguishes ethnoecology from environmental or ecological anthropology? In my estimation, work is *ethno*ecological only insofar as it deals with local conceptions of environmental relationships, and local practices for managing, moving within or using elements of the local landscape. As with other ethnoscientific areas of inquiry, there is a productive tension between local and cosmopolitan scientific conceptions. Mexican biologist Victor Toledo (2002:513) quotes a range of authors' definitions of ethnoecology, beginning with A. Johnson in 1947, who characterized ethnoecology as "a distinctive approach to human ecology which draws its goals and methods from ethnoscience." Eugene Hunn in 1982 (p. 830) described ethnoecology as a "new field integrating ethnoscientific and ecological theory," and the late Darrell Posey wrote in 1986 that ethnoecology involved "indigenous perceptions of natural divisions in the biological world and plant-animal-human relationship within each division."

In order to distinguish my approach from the general ethnoecology, political ecology, and "space and place" literature, I have described my approach as landscape ethnoecology. Through landscape ethnoecology I highlight perception and understanding of the landscape, biota, and landforms, rather than focusing on specific resources or processes. I do not focus on landscape in the global system, in which significant political ramifications of power differentials are implicated in how the interactions of different peoples and systems of understanding and land use play out in particular contexts and in the present global arena, though this is of obvious importance.

Ethnoecology has meant many things in contemporary anthropology and related work, and typically encompasses a broader range of relationships between land and social and cultural institutions than is my intent to investigate in this work. Much of the literature is quite eclectic, and often process-oriented. Virginia Nazarea's 1999 volume *Ethnoecology: Situated Knowledge, Located Lives* is explicitly heterogeneous, and aims to capture some of the messy diversity of approaches and applications, focusing on *mezzo* scale theory as opposed to unifying or grand theory. Much of the literature on ethnoecology deals with topics such as agroecosystems, and issues of the commons and property regimes.

Seminal works by Victor Toledo (1992, 2002), Virginia Nazarea (1999), and Luisa Maffi (2001) lay out different conceptions of and theoretical perspectives on ethnoecology. In *On Biocultural Diversity, Linking Language, Knowledge and the Environment,* Gary Nabhan (2001:149) quotes an early definition of ethnoecology by ethnobotanists Bye and Zigmond published in 1976 that characterizes ethnoecology as "The area of study that attempts to illuminate in an *ecologically* revealing fashion man's [sic] interactions and relationships to his [sic] environment" (emphasis original). This minimal definition is rather circular, and does not get us into conceptual aspects of local understanding of environmental relationships. It also is not distinguishable from the broad sub-field of environmental anthropology. Nazarea's 1999 volume seeks to capture the rich ferment of current research on the nexus of people-place-environment, including knowledge, practice, and political ecology. In setting the background for the volume she quotes (page 7) pioneering ethnoecologist Hal Conklin, who wrote in a paper on shifting cultivation:

> *Ethnoecological factors refer to the ways in which environmental components and their interrelations are categorized and interpreted locally.* Failure to cope with this aspect of cultural ecology, to distinguish clearly between native environmental categories (and associated beliefs) and those used by the ethnologist, can lead to confusion, misinformation, and the repetition of useless cliches in discussing unfamiliar systems of land use. (Conklin 1961:6, emphasis added)

Later in her introduction, Nazarea writes:

> *Ethnoecology, as the investigation of systems of perception, cognition, and the use of the natural environment* can no longer ignore the historical and political underpinnings of the representational and directive aspects of culture, nor turn away from issues of distribution, access, and power that shape knowledge systems and the resulting practices. (1999:19; emphasis added)

Here she clearly lays out both the domain of ethnoecology, and then affirms that both historical and political factors must be considered in ethnoecological work.

More recently, I wrote "Ethnoecology is the broad domain of local understanding of the environment, of the land and the entities that dwell there, and of the relationships among them, including the relationships of people to other living things and the land" (Johnson 2008:146).

Toledo (1992, 2002) has explicitly theorized ethnoecology as a discipline. His approach has a focus on production, the active business of working the land to derive one's livelihood. Toledo has formulated a particular notion of ethnoecology that is composed "of the three inseparable dominions of landscape: nature, production, and culture" (Toledo 2002:514). In his theoretical formulation, he brings to bear notions of world view, or "cosmovision," and the cognized natural world (*kosmos*) with how people act in the landscape to procure their needs (*praxis*) and the body of indigenous knowledge, or TEK, which he calls the *corpus,* to explore how they form an integrated ethnoecological system in use (ibid.). Toledo's analytical frame is particularly relevant to the lifeways of small-scale cultivators and indigenous communities, such as the many peoples of rural and southern Mexico.

I share Toledo's interest in holistic perspectives that include cosmological and spiritual elements along with what people do, their practices, and their cognized and embodied knowledges. Currently my interest is more in researching and understanding this realm than in focusing strongly on the nuts and bolts of economic activities per se. In Toledo's (2002) schema of the types of human knowledge that comprise ethnoecology, he describes the landscape level of knowledge that is of primary interest in this volume as "ecographical" knowledge, though my own notion of landscape ethnoecology also includes elements of the "physical" realm, particularly substrates and waterbodies and their elements, as I discuss below.

Implicit in Toledo's formulation of the *corpus* is the importance of local languages in naming and shaping concepts and in carrying the cognized information of the ethnoecological realm. As has been elsewhere noted (cf. Maffi 2001; Krauss 1992), a high proportion of the world's languages are presently endangered, particularly those in high-diversity regions of North America such as British Columbia, and environmental knowledge is closely tied to language. Indigenous geographic and ecological understanding of landscape, or landscape ethnoecology, reveals similarities and differences between scientific and local understandings of "kinds of place" (geographic ontology) and their entailments or affordances (Gibson 1979 in Ingold 2000:169). The research presented here presents several North American indigenous landscape term systems, thereby contributing to the recorded environmental lexicons of several different endangered indigenous languages, and describes articulations of these systems of geographic nomenclature with other aspects of meaning of "landscape" within the framework of landscape ethnoecology.

Tim Ingold (1996a) offers a different approach to understanding of human relationships with homelands through the concept of "dwelling," which I take up in more detail later in this work. This process-oriented perspective on landscape and relationships deals with the domains of practice and meaning, and seems particularly apropos to the understanding of landscape held by non-cultivating people. Exploring the implications of local concepts of landscape, Ingold writes that in Pintupi understanding, landscape is

> not a given substrate awaiting the imprint of activities that may be conducted upon it, but is itself the congelation of past activity. . .
> Secondly, it is not so much a continuous surface as a *typologically ordered network of places, each marked by some physical feature, and the paths connecting them* (Ingold 1996a:139; emphasis added).

He continues later in the same paper, quoting his earlier work:

> "it is through *dwelling* in a landscape, through the incorporation of its features into a pattern of everyday activities, that it becomes home to hunters and gatherers." (Ingold 1991b:61)

Ingold then asserts that singing, storytelling and activities "of hunting and gathering" all are "ways of dwelling" (Ingold 1996:144).

"Place making" in the ethnoecological and ethnobiological sense includes how people think about and understand place(s) and landscape, both as cognized and through narrative, and what they do in place(s), including environmental management and manipulation, habitual practices, harvesting, and dwelling.

On landscape and land

Before we move further into questions of landscape ethnoecology, let us take a moment to consider the concept of landscape. What is landscape? A seemingly simple question, upon closer examination it becomes apparent that the term is used in a number of contrasting senses, which vary by discipline and over time. It behooves us, therefore, to reflect on the ways that this term is employed.

One perspective, derived from European notions of landscape painting and the scenic, sees landscape as a (framed) prospect, as it were, like the view from one's window (Gow 1995; Tuan 1974). The term *landscape* itself was derived from the Dutch *landschaft*. When this term crossed to England with the Dutch painters of the Tudor era, its meaning shifted from designating a tract of land, to a scenic painting of a view of a tract of land (Tuan 1974:133). Landscape, in this sense, is a visual backdrop, the scene of a stage. In this tradition, landscaping and landscape architecture render scenic surroundings around and within the built environment. In the common European and North American sense, *landscape* is largely equivalent to *scenery*, re-emphasizing the sense of land as a (generally aesthetic) backdrop to the foreground of human activity (Tuan 1974:133).

An interesting aspect to this framing of landscape as primarily visual is that dwellers of heavily forested environments may lack the ability to visually perceive anything beyond the "proximity" in the sense of Granö (1997), having no vantage point from which to view a "prospect" and so may, in that sense, lack a broad brush sense of place. For such peoples, both the trail, or pathway, and the acoustic environment may play a key role in organizing understanding and linkage of places in their homelands (e.g. Feld 1997, Gow 1995, Turnbull 1961 reported in Tuan 1974:79-81). Ingold (1993) also contains an extensive exploration of pathways and their significance in theorizing landscape. Landscape implies region, or contextual locational setting, as well as local or specific point sites.

A completely distinct understanding of landscape is found in geography, ecology, and natural science, where it comprises the suite of landforms and ecosystems existing on/in a landscape, a three-dimensional extent of territory. Landscape ecology is the interdisciplinary framing of the significance of spatial scale in ecological process. According to Monica Turner, a leading exponent of contemporary landscape ecology,

> "Landscape" commonly refers to the landforms of a region in the aggregate (Webster's New Collegiate Dictionary 1980) or to the land surface and its associated habitats at scales of hectares to many square kilometers. Most simply, a landscape can be considered a spatially heterogeneous area. Three landscape characteristics useful to consider are structure, function and change. "Structure" refers to

the spatial relationships between distinctive ecosystems . . . "Function" refers to the interactions between the spatial elements. . . . "Change" refers to alteration in the structure and function of the ecological mosaic through time. (Turner 1989:173)

In one of the defining papers of the field, Richard Forman wrote:

A landscape is a kilometers-wide area where a cluster of interacting stands or ecosystems is repeated in similar form; landscape ecology, thus, studies the structure, function and development of landscapes. The structural components, or landscape elements, are patches of several origins, corridors of four types, and a matrix. (Forman 1982)

How "landscape" is conceived and defined in a landscape ecological context depends on the nature of the research being undertaken, and the focal scale. Kevin McGarigal (2003) writes:

For example, from a wildlife perspective, we might define landscape as an area of land containing a mosaic of habitat patches, often within which a particular "focal" or "target" habitat patch is embedded. . . . Because habitat patches can only be defined relative to a particular organism's perception and scaling of the environment . . . landscape size would differ among organisms. However, landscapes generally occupy some spatial scale intermediate between an organism's normal home range and its regional distribution. In-other-words, because each organism scales the environment differently (i.e., a salamander and a hawk view their environment on different scales), there is no absolute size for a landscape; from an organism-centered perspective, the size of a landscape varies depending on what constitutes a mosaic of habitat or resource patches meaningful to that particular organism.
    This definition most likely contrasts with the more anthropocentric definition that a landscape corresponds to an area of land equal to or larger than, say, a large basin (e.g., several thousand hectares). (http://www.edc.uri.edu/nrs/classes/nrs223/readings/fragstatread.htm)

Landscape ethnoecology is ethnoecology focused on local understanding of local landscape. It is cultural understanding of landscape, including structure through time and space, predictability, disturbance, interactions with the landscape through management, and entailments of kinds of place, landscape elements, or ecotopes. It includes what one might call a human or anthropogenic "layer," to borrow an analogy from geographic information systems (GISs), which encompasses significant kinds of place such as places of habitation, orchards and fields, sites of story, and sacred places. It encompasses the network of relationships to the land and other entities that dwell there.

Synthesizing the ecologically based definitions of landscape above, the landscape level of environments or ecological systems includes a variety of habitat types, or patches, and a range of landforms. It is also characterized by scale (the size of the overall landscape under consideration) and grain (the uniformity or heterogeneity of the landscape, and the range of sizes of its components). For the purposes of landscape ethnoecology, which is explicitly anthropocentric, *landscape* may be more or less equivalent to the drainage basin. In anthropological usage, *landscape* may encompass the range of environmental types or patches within the "territory," "country" or "homeland" of a local group. As well as the range of environmental types or habitats, landscape in the ethnoecological sense also encompasses the broad aesthetic or cosmological sense of the local environment.

In this volume, "landscape" and "the Land"[1] can be read as synonyms. "The Land" is the way the homelands of indigenous north American peoples are spoken about in English, and is roughly equivalent to **nan** or **nánh'** in Dene languages such as Kaska or Gwich'in, or **dè** in Dogrib (Legat et al. 2001). "The Land" encompasses the relationship that originated in the distant past, of a people, those who dwell there, with a regional homeland. This concept encompasses the entire range of geographic, physiographic, and ecological features of the homeland, and all of the living beings, including the human population whose identity and way of life is strongly tied to the land. Sacred or spiritual components, which may include loci of power, are part of the concept of "the Land." Very similar conceptions of "country" are found in Australian Aboriginal cultures (e.g. Rose 2000, 2005; Strang 1997; Robinson and Munungguritj 2001; Morphy 1995; Layton 1995; Williams 1982; Merlan 1982; Turk 2008; numerous others).

This concept of Land perhaps has resonances in the "Back to the Land" movement of the 1960s and 1970s, in the sense of what the meaning of "the Land" is. The Land in this sense is also seen in opposition to the built environment, and is conceptualized as Nature. In the ethnoecologies of indigenous peoples there may also be somewhat of a sense of a distinction between core human/built environments such as "the village" and more peripheral environments such as "the bush," though this varies by culture and depends on the spatial patterning of their interactions with their homeland. (See the range of cases discussed in Dwyer 1996.)

Of environment and ethnoecologies

The word *environment*—meaning that which surrounds us, *medio ambiente*, a thing distinct from us—helps to encapsulate some of the differences between scientific perspectives and those of traditional local peoples. In many local ethnoecological perspectives, especially those of people who live in intimate contact with and make their homes in landscapes which lack permanent built environments and field systems, there is no sharp separation between the realm of people and an abstracted other called "nature" (e.g. Dwyer 1996; Ingold 1993). Rather, the landscape is a humanized homeland. This is certainly true in all of the communities in which I have investigated these topics (Johnson 2000; Johnson and Hargus 2007; Johnson 2009) and has been nicely articulated by many other voices for other places (e.g. McNeary 1976; Dwyer 1996; Nelson 1983; Davidson-Hunt and Berkes 2003; Roberts and Wills 1998; Nadasdy 2003; Cruikshank 1990a, 1990b, 1998, 2001, 2005; Turner 2005; Deur and Turner 2005; Rigsby 1982; Atleo 2004; Auld et al. 2005; and others), and in many statements and publications by local indigenous people and groups. It has now become almost cliché to articulate this holistic relationship between people and their homelands, but the relevance of local understandings remains important to acknowledge in the face of totalizing discourses which create global environments analytically and conceptually separate from people, in order to discuss environmental change and degradation on the one hand and resource potential and international resource development on the other. (See Tsing 2005 for a particularly cogent discussion of the affects of filtering out both local people and their landscape from the environment and natural resources of Kalimantan.[2]) Even in a somewhat more benign context, nation states are relatively limited in their readiness to respond to alternative conceptual frameworks of indigenous homelands. Julie Cruikshank comments for the Yukon:

> Oral traditions from northwestern North America consistently
> demonstrate the social nature of all relations between humans and
> nonhumans (animals, plants and landscape features such as glaciers),

a concept that fits awkwardly with Western science. Codified in government reports, information formulated as TEK tends to *reify and reinforce a Western dualism*—prying nature from culture—that local narratives challenge in the first place. Sentient landscapes shift their shape once they are engulfed by these frameworks and transformed into "land and resources." (2001:389, emphasis added)

It remains thus timely and important to investigate the landscape ethnoecology of local peoples, to record and share these perspectives as a counter to the globalizing and generalizing rhetoric, and to try to record the perspectives of peoples who have been arguably in a much more sustainable relationship with their homelands than has characterized the resource frontier or the large industrial nations. It is, of course, necessary to avoid vacuous environmental romanticism in the consideration of local ethnoecologies, as these caricatures reveal more about the inhabitants of industrial nations and the de-localized and dispossessed than they do about working relationships between people and the land. It is equally necessary to avoid reconfiguring local ecological understanding to mirror Western and scientific conceptions of environment, but rather to learn from peoples' understandings and practices, to present alternative understandings as fully and accurately as possible.

Reviewing the scattered but growing literature on landscape perception and systems of ethnogeography, many questions arise. A fundamental question that relates to notions of ecological setting and way of life is whether there are differences in landscape ecology between settled and mobile peoples, and between those who till the soil and those whose way of life involves hunting, fishing, and gathering the products of the land—recognizing, of course, that many gradations occur between these categories. A first order examination of the literature suggests that people who till the soil include soil characteristics in their ethnoecological classifications. Sillitoe (1996) gives an extensive exposition of Wola "ethnopedology" in the New Guinea highlands, while Atran's 1993 treatment of Itzá Maya agroforestry includes a number of soil categories, as does Anderson's Yucatec Maya chapter in Johnson and Hunn (2009) and Bandeira et al.'s treatment of Tzotzil landscape perception (2002). I have not found such categories in the landscape ethnoecologies of the Gitksan, the Witsuwit'en, or the Kaska, who are all Canadian indigenous groups whose main traditional economic focus is on fishing, hunting, and collection and management of certain favoured perennial plant foods, though the "habitats" described for Dogrib (Tłįchǫ) by Legat et al. (2001) do include characteristics of surficial deposits and soils in their defining traits.

Similarly, it is of interest whether people recognize and designate seral phases or successional communities. Several Mexican indigenous groups who practice swidden agriculture, including Mixe, Chinantec, Tzotzil and Sierra Nahua, are reported to recognize successional relationships and name seral phases (Martin 1993, 1995; Bandeira et al. 2002; Mora et al. 1985) as do the Wola of New Guinea (Sillitoe 1995, 1998). Anderson (2009), however, reports that the people of Chunhuhub (Yucatec Maya) recognize such phases but do not name them, bringing up a key issue also raised by Roy Ellen (2009) with regard to Nuaulu forest classification in Seram, Indonesia: how much of people's landscape and ethnoecological knowledge is lexicalized? I have also raised this question in terms of recognition of aspects of vegetation for the Gitksan. In my own research with Canadian First Nations, overt recognition of seral relationships, or naming of seral phases is weak or lacking, though the past action of avalanches or forest fires may be recognized. This does not imply people do not notice progressive change in vegetation after disturbances, but simply that they do not ordinarily name such phases. For example, they may well understand the ecological effects of fire on fungi and on berries, as well as on fish, game animals and aquatic ecosystems, without elaborating names for seral communities. (Plant communities themselves, including seral phases, are arguably abstractions; Gleason [1939] and Curtis [1959], among others, advocated a "continuum theory" of plant distribution and denied the objective reality of plant "communities.")

A key question regards the degree to which landscape ethnoecological systems, or ethnogeographies, comprise a single unified system, or whether they are a poorly ordered hodgepodge of partial, intersecting and overlapping classifications that are context-dependent. That is, do folk ecotopes fall into a single system, or might vegetation, river terms, other waterbodies, landforms, etc. perhaps represent different "filters" or "layers of information" in examining landscape (in the broad sense) or environment? These issues are debated by Hunn and Meilleur (2009) and Ellen (2009). In my own work, I have tended toward the perspective of overlapping and intersecting multiple classifications. An aspect of traditional knowledge in general, and landscape ecological knowledge in particular, that bears on these questions is, as Ellen suggests; how much of the knowledge is cognized and systematized, and how much is tacit knowledge-in-practice or experiential knowledge? Tim Ingold argues that a "dwelling" perspective involves substantial knowledge-in-practice and evolves through movement between places, downplaying the importance of cognitive mapping (Ingold 1996a, 2000). My own suspicion is that this may in fact vary between cultures and individuals, and perhaps between rural and urban or educated people as well.[3]

What is ecological and how are ecotopes recognized?

I have found it difficult to bound "ecological" terms, and have found that "kinds of place" that had ethnoecological importance were quite eclectic and included a mixture of vegetation, landforms, waterways and their features, and ambiguous categories like "swamp" or "quicksand." In my research I counted any place kind that seemed to have ecological relevance in local landscape understanding, using both language and practice as evidence. Vegetation terms in the areas where I have worked seem weakly developed, perhaps in part because vegetation is relatively depauperate in the areas I have worked, and perhaps also because in the long seasons of snow cover, vegetation, other than a few significant tree and shrub species, is not visible.

One important question is, how fundamental is the distinction between lands and waters? While this may be a higher-order branching point in the geographic knowledges of European peoples and their descendents, it is increasingly evident that for maritime peoples and for northern peoples, that water and ice features are included in their "landscape" ethnoecologies, a point made with particular force by Aporta (2000, 2009) with regard to the home "land" of the Iglulik Inuit, who still travel and hunt on both shore-fast and moving ice, and who have place names for recurring ice features as well as an elaborate vocabulary of place kinds for ice and associated water features. Indeed, there are traditional village sites that were on the sea ice adjacent to productive leads, or *polynyas*, which focused game and provided opportunities to hunt. Collignon (2006) discusses similar aspects of Inuin-nait geographic understanding in the Canadian Central Arctic. In a more southerly setting, Johannes (1981) has made similarly detailed observations of marine geographic and ecological knowledge for South Sea Islanders with regard to marine ecotopes and knowledge of current and wave features. These observations underscore the ethnocentric separation of land as subject to sovereignty and private property rights, and waters, which are open-access and therefore exclude sea claims and rights. This has been problematic for Torres Strait Islanders and Aboriginal Australians (Peterson and Rigsby 1998; Mulrennan and Scott 1996, 2005), the Makah of Washington State (Society of Ethnobiology conference field trip to Neah Bay 2003), and the Inuit, and also bears on questions of Canadian national sovereignty over seasonally or permanently frozen waterways in the Canadian Arctic Archipelago.

Another area of research interest is the degree to which there may be systematic variation in landscape ethnoecologies. Ways of life, depth of time in place, the nature of the land-/sea-/icescape itself, and features of language might all influence the ways that landscape elements are perceived and classified, and how the local people interact with their landscape. (See Collignon 2006 for a discussion of some of these issues.) It seems logical to me that those who till the soil, herd animals, hunt, or focus on marine or aquatic resources might all attend to different aspects of their respective environments, and elaborate knowledge about their components accordingly. It also seems logical that dwellers of tropical forests, which lack strong seasonality, might understand the land differently from those who live in highly seasonal environments such as the northern taiga or in Arctic landscapes. By the same token, dwellers in arid landscapes may be expected to perceive soil, vegetation and especially waterways and waterbodies differently from people who live in forested landscapes, dwellers of the plains from those who live in mountainous environments, and so on.

Mark and his co-authors (2003, 2009), based on research with desert dwellers, challenge the primacy of the division between lands and waters in another way; to peoples who dwell in places where surface waters are ephemeral, the bed of the watercourse, or the basin in which waters accumulate may be separated in local thought from the waters which sometimes occupy those sites. Northern peoples, along with dwellers of arid landscapes, appear to have very rich vocabularies describing features of the physical landscape and waters, and perhaps more depauperate vegetation terminology. Lehtola, describing Sami landscape knowledge in northern Fennoscandia writes:

> Leif Rantala counted the words describing landscape in one dictionary. There were 109 words depicting shapes of mountains and hills; 40 for bogs and marshes; and 60 for valleys, ravines and hollows. For example *vággi* is a "shortish, deepish valley"; *gorsa* is a "smallish, deep ravine"; *gurra* is a "ravine, gorge, narrow valley"; *roggi* a "pit"; *lákku* a "flat highland valley"; and *leakši* is an "ordinary marshy, widish valley on a treeless mountain. (2002:14)

I am not proposing environmental, economic or linguistic determinism, but I believe all of these factors influence the ways people perceive, cognize, articulate and interact with their environments or homelands. Indeed, the diverse ethnoecological systems reported in Johnson and Hunn (2009) suggest that these kinds of difference do in fact occur.

Notwithstanding diversity in naming and recognition of various features of lands and waters, certain patterns also recur. Vegetation, for example, is often described as 'place of x', such as 'place of corn' (Chinantec farmers in Mexico, Martin 1993), 'place of cottonwoods' (Akimel O'odham of the Sonoran desert in Arizona, Rea 1997) or 'place of pine' (***sbaayt sginist***), the Gitksan term for a pine stand (Chapter 3). Convex features such as the English concepts 'hill', 'ridge' and 'mountain' are recognized in all ethnogeographic systems I have been able to review, though as Mark and his co-authors (Mark and Turk, 2003; Mark et al. 2009) indicate, the division points between categories may differ between languages, a point also elaborated in Krohmer (2009) in her examination of Sahelian Fulani landscape knowledge, where substrate as well as elevation is important in local classification. Certain key environments defined by animal behaviour are pertinent to hunters, particularly mineral licks that attract game, which are widely recognized and named (Johnson 2009, this work; Shepard et al. 2004:147).

One factor that may be missed in an attempt to fix local landscape ecological knowledge, place kind inventories, and local ecological relationships is seasonality. In an equable low latitude environment, the nature of places and their human significance may not vary significantly through the year, while in seasonally arid lands (cf. Krohmer's 2009 exposition of Fulani ethnoecology) or in high latitude northern environments, the influence of season cannot be ignored (Johnson and Hunn 2009). While reading Peter Dwyer's description of human use and understanding of landscape in New Guinea (1996), I was struck that the relationship to land he described seemed very similar to the way landscape is understood in northwest North America, even to the potato gardens adopted by Gitksan, Witsuwit'en, and other groups in the nineteenth and twentieth centuries, which are similar to the New Guinea garden patches along waterways. The key difference between indigenous peoples in northwest BC and the tropical forest dwellers in New Guinea is the lack of seasonality as a prime organizer of activities and use of space.

Differences in kind between landscape understanding of local indigenous peoples and more recent migrants may be significant. A pioneering work which has investigated contrasting ways of viewing, articulating, and understanding the "same" landscape is *Uncommon Ground* by Veronica Strang (1997). She investigated Aboriginal and non-aboriginal grazier landscape understanding in northern Queensland, and found some systematic and important contrasts in how they saw their homeland. For Queensland graziers, in contrast to Aboriginal peoples, land categories are generic. Strang writes, "'types' of country—scrub, forest country, coastal plain, melonhole country, saltpan, wetlands, grassland-are thus described according to physical characteristics of soil and vegetation" (1997:182). This is very similar to my discussion of the contrast between Anglo-Canadian landscape categories, especially those of trained resource managers, and those of the Gitksan (Johnson 2000). In contrast to the graziers, Strang writes, "Aboriginal 'country' is primarily defined by its *story places*, mythological associations and the associated groups of people" (1997:182, emphasis added). This latter mode of understanding of country or territory has strong resonances with Gitksan perception of land, and also, at least as a storied landscape, with Dene peoples (cf. Andrews 1990; Andrews and Zoe 1997; Andrews et al. 1998; Cruikshank 1990b, 1997, 2005). Palmer (2006) has crafted a detailed account of Secwepemc narrative and landscape which underscores the importance of this relationship. Strang make some intriguing comments about the effect of language—here not of lexicon, but rather of mode of thought and expression—stating that aboriginal groups employ a "much fuller use of metaphor and analogue" (1997:182), and she speculates whether the very nuanced and particularized understanding of place may be facilitated both by the small size of the aboriginal community and the very deep time depth of local development.

Connecting place kinds with overarching structures of cultural meaning can be accomplished through story, as Strang and others have demonstrated in Australia and the Canadian North. Pierre Beaucage and his local associates (Taller de Tradiccion Oral del CEPEC and Pierre Beaucage 1996; Beaucage and Taller de Tradiccion Oral del CEPEC 1997) have analysed landscape knowledge in the Sierra Nahua in terms of three interlinked aspects: specific place names, place types, and two axes of symbolic and spiritual nature, with mountain as "good" and the river and valley as "bad." Certain portions of the landscape are recognized for beneficent, or malevolent, spiritual power. Beaucage and his associates also recognize and situate anthropogenic types such as communities and orchards. Martin suggests that there is an axis of wild-domesticated which is present in Chinantec ethnoecology as well (1993, Figure 4), with the mountain tops and higher elevations as wild, familiar more to men, and containing spiritually powerful places, while a mid elevation is the domesticated sphere of settlement and *milpas*, and a lower altitudinal zone is "semi-domesticated." The exposition of the Shoal Lake Anishinabe cultural landscape presented by Davidson-Hunt and Berkes (2003) also reveals structures of meaning; the community members felt that human and spiritual places had to be included to represent their homeland as they understood it.

The relationship between general ecological classes (folk ecotopes or "place kinds") and specific places is rich and revealing. Kari (1989) and Hunn and Meilleur (2009) have successfully used toponyms to establish "place kind generics" by analysing the included place elements in the names of specific places. It often seems in practice that people with deep knowledge of local environments refer to specific named places rather than designating ecotopes or more generic place kinds. When I asked Maori biologist Mere Roberts about general kinds of place for her people, she replied she was not certain if such concepts were developed in Maori; people tended to refer to places as specific, unique named places (pers. comm., 1997). I have found the same applies for Gitksan interlocutors. Meilleur (pers. comm. 2006) commented that he had to frame questions carefully in his ethnogeographic research in Savoie, France, to obtain generic rather than particular locations to obtain specific plants. It is clear that place names are important mnemonics in referencing ecological information (cf. Fowler 1999; Collignon 2006; Thornton 2008), and often are involved in other aspects of relationship to landscape, as when toponyms organize orientation information, or recall history (e.g. Tom 1987; Nyman and Leer 1993; Thornton 2008). Toponyms, and knowledge of named places often seems to evoke strong emotional attachment (Palmer 2006; Young-Leslie 2007). Some groups may be rather ad hoc in designation of places, perhaps indicating who is staying or has stayed at a particular site (e.g. Gwich'in place designation reported in Andre and Kritsch 1992; Kritsch and Andre 1994; Greer 1999), while for other groups there may be very specific "rules" in how places are named (Hunn 1996; Thornton 2008), and place names may be proprietary information that is revealed only to the proper owners of the land (Johnson 2000). For the Gitksan and Nisga'a, for example, toponyms are key aspects of corporate-owned territories, and are intimately entwined with oral histories of the land and a group's relationship to it. Thornton (2008) brings out connections of place to history, identity, social structure and resource knowledge for the Tlingit of southeast Alaska, describing both seasonal pathways and recalling past configurations of the landscape. Basso (1990a, 1990b, 1996a, 1996b) has eloquently explained how for the White Mountain Apache, the structure of place names includes components which explicitly locate the point of view of the observer in the name, and how place names are used to index stories with moral force, that are used to comment on, and to motivate, appropriate moral behaviour. Beatrice Collignon's work (2006) on Inuinnait place names and the memories associated with these places in the Canadian Arctic is also revealing in the deep connections of people and land-, sea-, and icescape. Early work of Cruikshank (1990b) strongly articulates the significance of place names in oral histories and the connections of story, named places, relationship to land, and moral and social values for Yukon Athapaskans and Tlingit. Named places of peoples discussed in this book are further explored in Chapter 10.

An area of persistent theoretical interest and practical significance is the degree of congruence between local landscape classifications, and the diverse classifications of Western sciences and managers. In my 2000 paper on Gitksan landscape ethnoecology this was a major theme, and is addressed also in Shepard et al. 2001, Shepard et al. 2004, and Mark and Turk 2003. In a sense, this is again a particular aspect of traditional, or local, ecological knowledge and its relationship to Western scientific knowledge.

The topic of local landscape knowledge and sustainability has garnered considerable interest (Posey and Balée 1989; Frecchione et al. 1989; Toledo 2002; Martin 1993; E. Anderson 1996; Turner 2005; M. K. Anderson 2005; numerous others). The relatively long duration of relationship with landscapes which remain intact or stable as evinced in local settings encourages the notion that local understandings may underpin, enable, or instantiate sustainable relationships with the natural world. Indeed, this is one motivation for recording and studying such systems of local understanding. An important caveat must be born in mind however: local landscape ethnoecology reflects local contexts and understandings, and cannot be unproblematically ported to other locales, or assimilated to international conservation agendas. Peter Dwyer cogently discusses some of these issues in his 1994 paper on conservation and traditional societies, drawing particularly on his New Guinea background. It is also true that the regional, national, and global contexts in which all local groups and their homelands exist cannot be neglected; as has been true in the past (e.g. Cronon 1983), these exert forces on local communities and landscapes which can constrain or completely transform them (cf. Tsing 2005; Scott 1998).[4] Subtler interactions play out in many places as local groups negotiate the articulation of their understandings and practices with those of state and regional entities under whose jurisdiction they lie.

Local ethnoecologies and ecotopes

The remainder of this book examines, in detail, local landscape knowledge and articulations of local landscape knowledge with mapping conventions and scientific conceptions of landscape, and concludes with a discussion of the significance of landscape ethnoecology. To provide some orientation to the rich and somewhat eclectic material contained in the various descriptions of landscape ethnoecological systems in the chapters that follow, I briefly review common themes in the ecotopes recognized by the Gitksan and Dene groups with whom I worked. First, broad topographic features such as ridges, mountains, slopes, peaks, passes and summits are recognized and named in all of the systems I examined. Similarly, rich terms for waterways such as 'river', 'slough', 'eddy', 'bank', 'canyon', 'waterfall', 'lake' and 'pond' are recognized and named. Complex areas such as 'swamp', or muskeg, are recognized and differentiated; these features offer a range of wetness, and of differing vegetation and water chemistry. Their classification and significance is variable, and revealing. Snow and ice terms are also recognized in all areas I have worked. These do have significance as kinds of place or ecotopes, especially for terms such as 'glacier' and various rich terminologies for kinds of ice, which encode aspects of travel safety. Similarly, multi-year snowfields are recognized, and may be rather loosely differentiated from glaciers, which are formally defined as ice that moves downslope with gravity. Vegetation, as indicated above, may be generally differentiated into treed areas—often designated by something that means 'among the trees'—and open non-treed areas. Treed areas may be further distinguished by the dominant species. Areas dominated by hard-to-traverse scrub or "brush" may also be specifically labelled. Treeless areas may be designated as meadows or places of grass, or may be classified by an absence of vegetation or by the character of winter snowpack. Trails, various types of camps and places of habitation, lookouts, and mineral licks are widely recognized. Finally, places of spiritual power may also be explicitly recognized as a class of places, as well as specific unique and perhaps named places.

I further explore the significance of various kinds of landscape entities, and issues of boundaries and flows in the chapters that follow.

3

Trail of Story

The Gitksan[1] relationship to land differs from that of most Western peoples. For the Gitksan, people are part of the land, in an inextricable and social relationship with it. The health of the land and of the people are intertwined, and there is a spiritual value to land and the relationship to other species. Gitksan ecology therefore has a holistic sense that includes spiritual aspects of land, morality, history, and health of both land and people.

Art Wilson (Sim'oogit 'Wii Muk'ilsxw from Ansbayaxw) told me a funny story from his childhood:

> When I was a little squirt I went out with Jonathan Johnson. He used to stop and talk to trees. He made me think before he answered my questions. At first I thought he was nuts. Then he chuckled and said, "I can tell you've been thinking. What do you want to ask me?" I asked why he talked to the trees. He said, "You have to respect everything. Everything has a spirit like you and me. If you use a tree you have to talk to it and explain why you need it," he said. "But that's not why I was talking to the trees. I was practicing flawless speech [for the Feasthall]."

It was a good teaching thing. He was always careful not to tell too much at once. (L.M. Johnson notes May 29, 1998)

Dinim Gyet,[2] a Gitksan Lax Gibuu Chief from Gitwingax, explained the interlinking of ownership, history and sacredness of land to me:

> You say you own this, your land, most of the place names are all
> in our language, hey, cause they say that the Creator gave it to us
> and he give us the names to go with it. Not by accident, but most
> of them, place names, are almost like totem poles to us. It might
> be an event that happened—in that certain area, so they just name
> the whole area. It's like a oral history. ...Place names are events that
> happen, that really happen to them. So that's why they really believe
> that their whole territory is sacred. You know, like I say, place name
> might have been a war or famine or whatever, and it's a constant
> reminder. All that the whole territory is like that. (L.M. Johnson
> transcript September 1996)

Figure 3.1 Gitksan territory map

The Gitksan ('people of the Skeena River') are Northwest Coast people who speak a Tsimshianic language. Their homeland is along the drainage of Ksan, the Skeena River, in the Coast Mountains, and the upstream portions of the Skeena River drainage (Figure 3.1). The Skeena flows through glaciated mountains with relatively steep slopes. The swift creeks and rivers are ascended by five species of salmon, and steelhead. Like most of British Columbia, the landscape is dominated by coniferous forest with alpine tundra on the mountaintops. The central portion of Gitksan Territory, where all of the historic village sites are located, is in the Interior Cedar hemlock zone (Houseknecht et al. 1986), where the broad valley bottoms and lower slopes are dominated by mixed forests and stands of hemlock and pine, with mountain hemlock or subalpine fir at timberline (Figure 3.2).

Figure 3.2 Gitksan land: Gitwingak from across the Skeena River This photo gives a sense of the historic approach to Gitksan communities, from the water with the row of totem poles visible. Photographed March 1991, by Allen S. Gottesfeld.

The Gitksan traditionally depended on salmon fishing, hunting, and gathering of plant foods, of which berries were the most important. Plants also provided important medicines. This subsistence economy persists today alongside the national and global economic systems. Gitksan society is organized into exogamous Clans (***Pdeek***), usually called Phratries in the anthropological literature. The Gitksan have four Clans; Gisk'aast (Fireweed), Ganeda or Lax Seel (Frog), Lax Gibuu (Wolf), and Lax Skiik (Eagle). Within these Clan groups, people belong to a series of *Wilp*, or Houses, which are matrilineal lineage groups from specific traditional villages and headed by a single Chief.[3] The Houses own bounded Territories, administered by the Head Chief and his or her sub-chiefs. The territories consist of tracts of land to which access is restricted for others not of the owning House. Delimiting of boundaries was and is important; tree carvings sometimes served that purpose (Blackstock 1996). Owned sites included extensive hunting territories or 'traplines' that might encompass a variety of other resource site types, and also specific sites or tracts of major rivers such as the Skeena for salmon fishing (Figure 3.3). These latter might occur in areas where the uplands away from the river were owned by another Chief.

Figure 3.3 A traditional fishing site on the Skeena River above the village of Ansbayawxs (Kispiox), along the Tenas Hill trail This site is adjacent to the remains of an elevated cache house and cabin or smokehouse, and was figured on a map of fishing sites on the Skeena River above Kispiox compiled in the early twentieth century. Photographed May 1995, by L.M. Johnson.

Named places form a kind of grid, which, like a relational database, links knowledge from many different domains; the sacred and moral, the historical, traditional ecological knowledge about subsistence, and about routes of travel and trade. Places also serve as landmarks and reference points in travelling over the land. Gitksan place names may evoke historical events, indicate resources or activities carried out in that place, be metaphoric or actual descriptions, or may indicate a spatial relationship.

Kinds of place

Kinds of place (ecotopes) recognized in the landscape ethnoecologies of the Gitksan and other indigenous peoples of northwest North America reflect topography, hydrology, vegetation, and animal habitats, and, I think, a geography of powerful or sacred places. A great deal of ecological knowledge is tied to these types of places, including potential areas of fish habitat and fishability, habitat of various game animals, ease or risks of travel through different types of vegetation or terrain, potential camp sites or dwelling places, and berry availability. Place kinds reflect the regional geography of each group, and also their ecological relations.

There are terms for many different types of landscape features in Gitksan (Figure 3.4). These vary in scale from very large (e.g. mountain) to very local (e.g. spring, muddy place, sand, rocky area). Kinds of places include terms that describe resource sites, topographic features, vegetation types, water terms, special river terms, snow and ice terms, and sites of history, occupation and trails. These features are described by generic terms, and some types may also be specified as named sites. Topographic sites, bodies of water, and sites of history, occupation and trails are particularly rich in named places. Some resource areas such as berry patches or goat (*Oreamnos americanus*) hunting areas may also be named, and owned, sites. General orientation is by drainage and topography. Basic orienting terms include *gew*, which has the sense of relatively open area near the river, that is, 'bottomland'; *gililix* 'upland', slopes away from the river; *gyeets'*, downstream area or region; and *gigeenix*, upstream area.

For purposes of presentation and analysis, I have broken landscape terms into several groups: terms for topographic features, water bodies and wet places, snow and ice, "slides" vegetation with forest, meadow, and berry patch types, terms pertaining to animal ecology, hunting areas and traplines, and spiritual places (see Table 3.1 at the end of this chapter). Topographic features include: mountain *sga'nist* (Figure 3.5), cliff *bii yaakhl*, scree slope

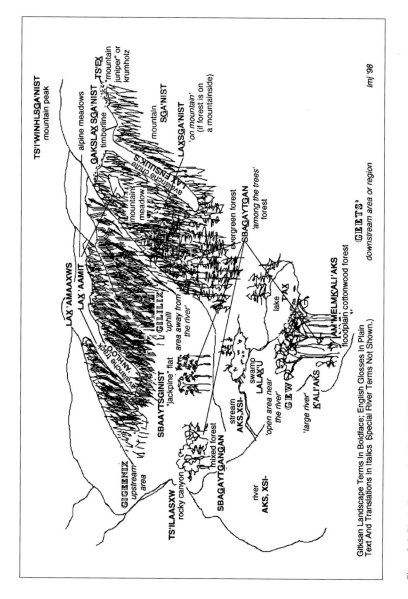

TS'IWINHLSGA'NIST
mountain peak

alpine meadows

GAKSLAX SGA'NIST TS'EX
timberline "mountain
juniper" or
krumholz

mountain
LAXSGA'NIST SGA'NIST
'on mountain'
(if forest is on
a mountainside)

LAX'ENSUUK'S
avalanche chute

LAX'AMAAXWS
LAX'AAMIT

mountain
meadow

ANHLOOX'
avalanche track

GILILIX
'uphill'
area away from
the river'

evergreen forest

SBAGAYTGAN
'among the trees'
forest

SBAAYTSGINIST
"jackpine" flat

GIIGENIX
upstream
area

TS'ILAASXW
rocky canyon

mixed forest

SBAGAYTGANGAN

stream
AKS, XSI-

swamp
LALAX'U
'open area near
the river'

GIIW

K'ALI'AKS
'large river'

lake
TAX

AM'MELMK'ALI'AKS
floodplain cottonwood forest

GEETS'
downstream area or region

river
AKS, XSI-

lmj '98

Gitksan Landscape Terms In Boldface; English Glosses In Plain
Text And Translations In Italics (Special River Terms Not Shown.)

Figure 3.4 Block diagram of an idealized Gitksan landscape

Figure 3.5 Seven Sisters with hill in foreground from Sedan Creek The tallest peak is called 'Wii Sg'anist, or 'Big Mountain'. Xsui Lax̱ Loobit, Boulder Creek, enters the Skeena in mid-frame, and the rounded hill before the snow capped peaks is the hill around which a Gisḵ'aast ancestor walked singing his mourning song, Limx̱ 'Ooy (Vincent Jackson, pers. comm.)

ksiip, hilly land *lax̱ ḵ'elt*, gully *ts'imts'uu'lixs*, valley *ts'imt'in*, peak *ts'i winhl sga'nist*, ridgeline *ḵ'elt*, island *laxlikst'aa*, and so on. Terms for bodies of water and wet places include river or stream *xsi-*, *aks*, while *ḵ'aliaks* is a term that describes large rivers such as the Skeena, lake *t'ax̱* (Figure 3.6), 'spring' *gwanks*, and *antl'ook*, a muddy place where moose go (also a salt lick). "Swamp," a wet or poorly drained area, could be seen as belonging here, although I group it with vegetation terms in this discussion. There are also various terms that describe types of river bank (cf. 'cutoff', a tall, steep, eroded river bank or bluff- *'wiinamḵ'* Figure 3.7), and creeks flowing into or out of lakes.

Another set of terms denotes types of snow and ice. I would argue that, in areas with long winters, snow and ice characters do describe kinds of places. Glaciers and snowfields *xsiunummaaxws*, and hanging cornices *speekx̱*, represent significant travel hazards in the mountains. A class of terms for kinds of "slides" includes snowslides: *yagahlo'o* when they are happening, or *en hlo'o* for a place that slides every year, and older avalanche tracks *lax̱ensuuḵs* (Figure 3.8), which slide with much lesser frequency. (The '*suuḵs*' are the logs that mantle the surface of such sites.) A rockslide would be called *hlo'om*

Figure 3.6 *Tax̱* a lake: Upper Watson Lake with Mt. Sir Robert in the background

sga'nist. Slide types grade into one another, because anyplace that experiences rockslides is also likely to experience snowslides in the winter season.

Reflecting the importance of the rivers for fish and travel, there are many terms that describe different parts of drainage systems and features of rivers. These include rock canyon *ts'ilaasxw*, bay *k'aldixgaks* or *wil luulamjax*, sandbar? *wisax* /*wisex*,[4] waterfall *ts'itxs*, whirlpool *ts'a'lixs*, dangerous, unnavigable whirlpool *antk'ulilbisxw*, back eddy *luuguuksbax*, back channel *ts'oohlixs*, slow side channel *t'aamiks*, rapids *laxk'elt aks* (lit. 'hilly or ridged water') (Figure 3.9), and confluence *wilnawaadihl aks* 'where the waters get to know each other' (Figure 3.10). A word with particular significance for navigation is *ts'iliks*, a place where the water goes over a rock that's just inches under the surface with no large visible standing wave. Reading the water is essential for safe travel and productive fishing (Figure 3.11).

Some landscape terms refer to vegetation types, notably swamp *lalax'oo*, forest *sbagaytgan* or *galdo'o*, small mountain hemlock *hlkuugan*, scrubby conifer growth *sba ts'ex* (which includes both low elevation juniper scrub and timberline krumholz), open areas or clearings *lax 'aamit* and *lax 'aamaaxs*, the thickets occurring in old avalanche tracks *luulaxsuuks*, berry patches *ansim'aay*, shrubby re-growth on berry patches *maaxsgan*, and 'burn' *lax an miihl*. Timberline (the upper edge of erect forest trees) is called *gakslax sga'nist*. Although forest is generally lumped as undifferentiated "bush", forest types can be differentiated by referring to a dominant species if need be. For example, in a discussion of the health-promoting properties of pine stands, I learned that a pine stand can be called *sbaayt sginist,* 'place where there are pines'.

Another set of terms encodes kinds of places significant in animal ecology such as goat hunting area *ensimetx*, goat trail *gena metx*, beaver dam *endelgan*, or a beaver lodge *goot* ('heart'). A site of refuge for hoary marmots (*Marmota calligata*) was described as *an liixw* 'where they hide', although I'm not sure if this was the name of a place, a kind of place, or just a description. Other terms pertaining to hunting denote hunting camp, trapline trail, hunting trail, and so on. Also belonging here as much as under topography is *en tl'ook* 'muddy place', in its sense as an animal mineral lick.

Considerable ecological knowledge may be uncovered in discussions of the land, whether or not kinds of places are linguistically coded. For example, people explained to me that spiny wood fern (*Dryopteris expansa*) rootstock, *ax*, a formerly important carbohydrate food, was associated with *giist* (*Alnus crispa*) and that one should look for it in a "ravine" (by which my consultant

'wiinamk<u>x</u>, nem<u>k</u>'ap

Figure 3.7 "High banks" are a type of feature named by both Gitksan and Athapaskan speakers, and constitute conspicuous features with implications for river travel. This high bank is adjacent to Dinim Gyet's fish camp by Wilson Creek, Xso Gwing̱oohl. The term in the Gigeenix or upriver dialect is given first, followed by the Gyeets or downriver dialect term for the same feature.

Figure 3.8 Avalanche track on Seven Sisters viewed from Coyote Creek moraine, July 1995 This slide area is good habitat for grizzly bears, according to Dinim Gyet.

Figure 3.9 Skeena River in flood: rough rapids where the river flows over a bedrock obstruction, described by Dinim Gyet as *lax ḵelt aks* 'hilly water'

Figure 3.10 Confluence of Kispiox and Skeena rivers from Gwin 'Oop fish camp: *wilnawaadihl aks* 'where the waters get to know each other'

gitxw *'swelling'* or
gitxwhlaks *'boil'*

lemksimks- *flat water*

Figure 3.11 Detailed river terms, of importance to those who navigate on rivers and net fish: "boil" and "flat water" identified on photographs from 4 Mile Canyon, Skeena River, by Dinim Gyet

meant the Gitksan term *lax'aamit*). People also listed specific traditional gathering areas for spiny wood fern rootstock. In another instance, Art Mathews also explained, while identifying a scouring rush species *Equisetum hiemale* as ***maawn*** in Gitksan, that spring salmon rest in the places along the river where the ***maawn*** grows. The sandy places in relatively sheltered spots where the rush grows are covered by water with moderate current during high water—the hydrologic conditions that favour the deposition of the sand substrate are also the right kinds of places for the salmon to rest.

A couple of place terms also exist which are not, in the usual sense, ecological or topographic. One term deals with a class of places of supernatural risk and power, called ***sbi laxnok***, and the other is the word for village or settlement, ***laxgaltsap***. ***Sbi laxnok*** are places of risk where the unwary and unprotected passerby can be 'pulled in' by the action of a malevolent spirit, sort of like a spiritual vortex or whirlpool. If the spirit of the person is not recovered, he or she will die. The locations of several such around the present village of Kispiox were mentioned by an Elder and Chief from that village. Other such localities are known, but are rarely spoken about.[5]

Villages are in some sense contrasted with 'out on the land', and are foci of the human and social environment. Such locations are not spiritually 'clean' (because of dog and human wastes, as well as the possible malevolent intentions of other human beings) and hence are unsuitable for, as an example, the gathering of medicinal plants. Gravesites may be another distinctive site type for the Gitksan, as they are for most human groups.

Discussion of kinds of place

Types of places are understood as animal habitat for significant species. Avalanche tracks, for example, were discussed as a hazard to travel in the mountains. Dinim Gyet also mentioned the association of grizzly bears *(Ursus arctos horribilis)* with the lush herbaceous and shrubby growth found in avalanche areas **luulaxsuuks** (Figure 3.8). The corollary of this association is avoidance of avalanche tracks late in the day—unless you are looking for grizzlies, in which case, you would go there at that time for that purpose.

Berry patches are an important kind of place for the Gitksan, and discussion of berry picking evokes mention of specific berry patches, and of maintenance of berry patches by burning (Johnson 1999). As I mentioned above, the Gitksan also have a special word for brush that has regrown on a berry patch. This term does not apply to seral growth after a forest fire or land clearing.

"Swamp" or "meadow" environments are also significant. Two economically important plant products were gathered in moss-dominated wetlands: sphagnum moss for babies' diapers and women's menstrual supplies, and "meadow" (bog) cranberries. Beavers *(Castor canadensis)*, cutthroat trout, or moose may also be associated with various types of swamp, depending on season, as may a type of grass or sedge formerly used for basketry. Swamps may also be obstacles to travel, offering difficulties for both summer and winter seasons.

Examination of Gitksan landscape terms reveals several things. First, neither vegetation typologies nor indications of soil types are particularly prominent. (Both are fundamental to Western plant ecology, and vegetation typologies are also in Western animal ecology.) What one might think of as more strictly geographic features are salient and constitute most of the terms reported. A careful analysis reveals that these terms are linked to considerable knowledge about kinds of places, their resource potentialities, and their relative ease or risk for human travellers.

Place names as indicators of perspective of Land

Place names serve as a reflection of the vision of landscape, and can reveal the kinds of places conceived by a given culture. There is an extensive literature on place names, or toponyms (including the papers of Basso 1990a, 1990b, 1996; Cruikshank 1990a, 1990b; Hunn 1996; Tom 1987; Kari 1989; others). As Cruikshank (1990a, 1990b), Thornton (2008), and Rosaldo (1980) have emphasized, history is written on the land, and is recounted and revisited by mentally travelling over the land, with place as the key to the past. Moral narratives too, are given force by their connection with the land: "in this place—it happened here." (cf. Basso 1990a, 1990b, 1997)

For the Gitksan the names and histories of their territories form the 'deed' to the property, demonstrating ownership in the feasthall, and are thus proprietary (Johnson 1997). Although the specific names are proprietary, general classes of Gitksan toponyms can be recognized. Names may commemorate or indicate the specific adventures of ancestors or of 'Wii Gyet, the "Big Man" who is the Gitksan trickster/creator. Names may also indicate resources present on the land, as Hunn (1996), Hunn with Selam and family (1990), Tom (1987), Kari (1989), Kari and Fall with Pete (1987), Fowler (1992) and others have documented for various other North American native groups. The Shegunia River, locally known as 'Salmon River', is such a name; the Gitksan name is Xsigunya'a (stream#point#spring salmon). Names may also describe a physical feature. The name of a small creek near Kitwanga, called Shandilla in English, is descriptive; it means the water coming down from a beaver dam, Ksa'endilgan (stream#from#beaver dam). Another such name is Gwax ts'a'lixs ("where there's always whirlpools"), a canyon and fishing site on the main Skeena River by the place called Ritchie. Names can describe actions appropriate to a place. Two examples from unpublished material provided by the Gitksan Treaty Office translate as "place where you make wedges," and "place where you set the fish trap" (Johnson 1997). Other names contain references to animals, such as Gwin watsx, 'otter point'. (Anonymous 1992).

Trail of stories, the Gitksan perspective of the Land

Gitksan elders talk of specific resources and places, mixing personal history with oral narratives, *adaawk* (histories) and *antimahlasxw* (stories or folklore), often with reference to their own travels of the past. Each place has its names, stories, and histories, and serves as a reminder and tangible evidence of the verity of the events recounted by Chiefs and elders, as suggested by the statement of Dinim Gyet at the beginning of this chapter.

The Gitksan conception of the land involves a cyclical reciprocity and social relationship with other entities on the land. One Gitksan friend told me a short story. She was talking with a white woman, looking at Stekyood-enwhl, a prominent local mountain. The woman asked Sadie, "Do you really believe everything has a spirit? Even that mountain?" and Sadie answered yes, she did. She said that the mountain talks to her. She said you can tell the weather by the clouds on the peak, a certain kind of clouds that hang on the peak. Then she talked about the river. "You can tell what is going to happen if you listen to the river. If you go down there and listen and it's really silent, the river is not going to rise and you can leave your net in. If you hear a whooshing sound when you listen, the river's going to come up, and you pull your net." Mike Morrell, a fisheries biologist who worked with the Gitksan, questioned Sadie about it when she said, "You listen to the river." He asked, "What does the river say to you?" Sadie found that a foolish question (S. Howard interview notes October 1997).

Gitksan understanding of land encompasses a mesh of various generic topographic, vegetation, and substrate types (including snow and ice), situated in the context of an overarching perspective of land as owned territories and sites. One can envision the understanding of territory as a series of 'overlay maps' that unite diverse knowledge of the land from the perspective of travelling over the land, with named sites serving as the reference points that focus recall. History, spirituality, resource harvesting, and travel through the seasons are all united by a web of trails that traverse or connect named sites. I envision these trails as "trails of story" as well as physical trails, that take one on a journey through territory, where named places serve as markers for resource sites, areas of travel hazard, reminders of history, loci of danger or supernatural potency, and of ancestral experience, which teach moral behaviour as well as serving to locate territory boundaries.

Dinim Gyet (Art Mathews) reminisced with me about his own territory, and how he had learned its stories as a child. He said:

> Yeah, well,—you could picture it as you're saying it, if you've been there? Like a lot of our territory, they describe, and it's just words until you go there and you appreciate what you see, why the names are given—to a certain spot.

… at a very young age, and they tell you all these. And then—when Granny's telling us a story, she goes over, and now that I think back, I think [s]he deliberately stops and then—"Oh, I forgot the name of that place." And then somebody volunteers, "Granny, hey . . ." so. And I think that's just her way of seeing if we remember and there's *all* the remembering of all she was telling us. I think that's a little test, when I think back, she just goes a little ways, and then she stops—"Well what do we call that?" . . .

Then somebody voluntarily says "Granny, it's . . ." "Oh, yeah, OK, OK" and then she gives you a hug. "You remember that," and then she goes on. While she describes things. So she pauses in between. Almost like Jeopardy."

I asked: So, then when would you go out? I assume you were like four or five years old when your Granny was telling you stories?

Art answered: Oh, yeah, right through, even when you've been already there they still- Cause they don't write it and they want to make *sure* that it's burnt in your mind. …

Yeah they just keep—and then, like I say, when you *go* there, it really captures your whole imagination of, you're just sitting there listening, and wondering what it is when you *get* there. You really, let's say, appreciate *why* certain place is called…

and there's a little place where they cross—like this and it's an ***en tl'ook'*** and where it's deliberately, I mean, it's year after year after year there's a slide area. So when they come through there in March, they have their own markers across. They're old dry, I've seen we have some, we called ***gwulaxhon***, where they're old burn, and they're really dry and they're strong, you can't knock them down. …

Yeah. And there's certain place in our terri[tory]—it's like this and they just, right at the foot of the mountain, and they go, I mean right at the cliff, and they cross it. And they got markers and we call ***en sgazel ts'el*** and I used to wonder, why would the trees have faces, eyes?

Until I really went with Dad and—that's the snow melts during the day, these little eyes where they carve the faces, of these trees, ***sga ts'el gan***, and once they stick out, they go across. Cause of the—avalanche danger…

Art describes many types of places on his territory; groundhog and goat hunting areas, with names and associated stories of how they were hunted, an array of named berry patches which used to be maintained by burning, areas where sacred medicine plants were gathered, hazardous avalanche tracks, the peak where the ancestor's raft grounded after the Flood. The recollection of the ancestors prompted him to talk of where they had lived before the Flood, and named sites and resource areas on that associated Territory. One of those sites commemorates an old caribou (*Rangifer tarandus*) snaring site, and also an ancient murder.

For the Gitksan, trails are traversed first by listening to teachings by Elders, and continue to be travelled in story as well as by actual travel on the land. The stories of the land and its named places are thus deeply enmeshed in traditional training of the young, and continue to serve adults as mnemonics and repositories of history, moral behaviour, and traditional ecological knowledge as they guide the uniquely Gitksan perception of their land.

In contrast to Gitksan perspectives, Western ecology is generalized rather than rooted in particular place. Human history, culture, geography, and biology are seen as separate, although they all occur on the same landscape. The sacred is not incorporated into ecology, with the possible exception of the "Deep Ecology" movement. Kinds of places in the ecological sense, or ecotopes, are typically defined by a combination of vegetation and soil characters, which are rooted in our own agricultural culture. Scientific ecology tends to differentiate more among plant communities of potential economic use. For example, biogeoclimatic zonation of alpine tundra in BC is far less differentiated than is zonation of forest or grassland types. Early travellers to northwestern BC such as George Dawson in the 1870s described the vegetation and ecology of the landscape in terms of agricultural potential.

Indigenous understanding of landscape as revealed by the Gitksan is, in contrast, multilayered and based on the specific, rooted in particular places, deep knowledge, and personal experience. Ecological knowledge can also be based on 'intuition' or 'dreaming', perhaps based in recovered knowledge from ancestors through reincarnation. Kinds of places significant in local ethnoecology include a mixture of topography, hydrology, vegetation, animal/fish habitats, substrates, sites of human use or travel, sites of history, and sacred or powerful places. Ease or hazards of travel and resource potentiality are integral to kind of place. The deep and reciprocal relationship with land is fundamental to social structure, and is seen as fundamental to identity and culture. It encompasses history and territory and cosmology and morality, as well as the business of living on the land.

Table 3.1

Gitksan Landscape Terms
Topographic Terms

Gitksan terms	Approximate English Equivalents	Translation
laxk'elt	hilly land	
k'elt E, *k'ilt* W	top of hill, hill crest, ridge line, summit	
sga'nist	mountain	
ts'i'winhl sga'nist	mountain peak, summit	
gililix	upland	
ts'ilasxw	rock canyon (as in Kitselas, people of the rock canyon)	
biiyaakhl	sheer cliffs	
hahumxsim lo'op	rock wall, sheer cliff (as the headwall of a glacier)	'wall of stone'
ts'imts'ilaasxw	a newer way to say cliff	'in the canyon'
kslo'op	rock face	
sdaats'isda	big square boulders on the side of mountains, blocks which have fallen from a cliff	
ksiip	'black shale that slides' talus accumulation under cliffs; also unstable scree or inside of moraine	
xsiip	sand	
laxxsiip	sand area, beach	
tsaldem lo'op	where there's lots of thin shale piled up	'thin rock'
lo'op	rock, stone, small rock hill	
ts'imts'uu'lixs	'gully', ravine	'in the gully'
ts'imt'in	'valley'; basin	'in the valley'
usim ges	a narrow place on the mountain	

(Table 3.1, continued)

Water Terms, Including River Terms

aks; xsi-, [xsan, xsu-]	river, stream	a form of the term for water
baam'aks	running water, stream	
golim'aks	running waters or streams	
k'ali'aks	large river	a form of the term for the upstream direction
wilnaawadihl'aks	confluence, where rivers come together	'where the waters get to know each other'
t'aamiks	pond; slow side channel	
ts'oohlixs	back channel, deep embayment, doesn't have current	
luuguuksbax, luuguuksbax' aks	a real back eddy, with current, where you set net	
laxk'elt aks	standing waves, rapids	
gitxw, gitwhlaks	a boil	'swelling'
lemksimks	flat water, a quiet place	
ts'itxs	waterfall	
k'aldixgaks	bay	
wil luulamjax	bay	
ts'a'lixs	whirlpool	
antk'ulilbisxw	impassable whirlpool as at Kitselas Canyon; 'maelstrom'	
laxlikst'aa	island	
wisax /wisex	sandbar	
ts'iliks	where the water barely covers a rock, but there is no wave	
'niilok	when sticks and leaves snag on a rock that's just at surface	
gwildim aks	high, dry river bank	
namk E	steep bank of a river	
nemkap W	steep river bank, steep eroded river bank	
'wiinamk' E	cutoff, steeper river bank, cf. bluff	
pteliks	rising water, keeps coming up, or "swelling"	
disleks	high water, flood stage	
t'ax; t'am-	lake	
sagalaan t'ax	where a creek flows in from the back of the lake	
xsi t'ax	a creek that flows out of a lake	
gwanks E; *gwenks* W	a spring (not a swamp)	
antl'ook' E *en tlook* [W]	where moose go, a muddy place; salt lick, black mud	'place of mud?'
tl'ook'	mud	

(Table 3.1, continued)

Snow and Ice Terms

sbeek̲	cornice	
bumksim maaxws	powdery snow like sugar	
bumks	powder, powder [snow]	
yeesims	powder snow that blows all around; even snowshoes don't hold you up	
'moos	sticky wet snow	'it sticks'
'muuxws	snowdrifts, powdery blowing snow, any kind of blowing snow	
s'yunim maaxws	snowfields, snow on glacier	
s'yun	glacier	
hlo'omks	wet snow in early spring; cohesionless 'slide snow'	from the verb to slide
'wiluks	wet snow that doesn't stick together (from calendar)	"the sun hits your trail in snow and it gets wider"
g'ipx̲	"frozen over"; river ice that a person can walk on	
pdaalast	water on ice	(either in cold weather or in March)
lulitx	candling ice "the sun hits the ice in March and it becomes like icicles"	

Slide Terms

hlo'o	"slides"	'it slides'
enhlo' [W] *anhlo'o* [E]	avalanche track, place where it slides every year	'place-slides?'
hlo'om sga'nist	rockslide or landslide	'slide-mountain'
'yagahlo'o	snowslide, avalanche	
hlo'om gan	"blowdown"? or a landslide involving trees?	'timber avalanche'
lax̲ensuuk̲s	landslide or snowslide scar; has slide alder	

(Table 3.1, continued)

Vegetation Types: Meadow, Swamp

laxʼaamit	'meadow' (snowbed areas and other treeless places)	'place that's good, that has no trees'; 'prairie'
laxʼamaaxws	'meadow' (alpine and other treeless flats)	'prairie'
laalaxʼu	swamp, wet meadow, muskeg	

Vegetation Types: Forest and Scrub

sbaaytgan	forest	
sbagaytgan	forest	'among the trees'
sbagaytgangan	mixed forest	
sbagayt-am'mel	cottonwood forest [may be a neologism]	'among the trees, cottonwoods'
sbaayt sginist	pine grove, pine stand	'place where there's pines'
sbaa ts'ex	scrubby coniferous growth (juniper), krumholz (timberline)	juniper place'
sbagadegantx	forest	'out in the bush, in the forest'
laxsgaʼnist	forest area if it is up a mountain	
am 'melmgaliaks	floodplain cottonwood, cottonwood-along-the-river	
luulaxsuuks	dense scrub regrowth in old slide area	

Vegetation: Burns and Berry Patches

ts'i'naast	burnt over patch (for berries or deer browse); clearing	
laxʼanmihl	burnt over area	'place that is burnt or charred?'
lumks tsee gantx	"all the timber coming up again" after the burn	
ansimaaʼy	'berry grounds'	
maaxsgan	too much brush or undergrowth on the berry patch	
genimsimaaʼy E	berry patch trail	
ginimsamaaʼy W	berry patch trail	

(Table 3.1, continued)

Hunting and Trapping Area Words, Trails and Campsites

ensimetx	traditional hunting areas [for goats]	
gena metx	goat trail	
ginimxsga'nist	goat hunting trail	
genimsiilinasxw	hunting trail	
genim jap	trap trail	
genx	trail	
ksdaamoos	hand or foothold on cliff	
endilgan	beaver dam	
goot	beaver lodge, from the shape when the pond is dry	'heart'
ensinhun W *ansinhun* E	place away from the village where you do fish	
anjok E, *enjok* W	campsite, dwelling place (eg berry camp, fish camp)	
antl'ook' E *en tl'ook* [W]	a muddy place, used by animals as a mineral lick	

Spiritual Places

sbilaxnok	a place of spiritual power and danger

Sources of Information

Art Mathews, Dinim Gyet; Peter Muldoe, Gitluudahl; Beverley Anderson; Tommy Tait; Sara Tait, Wihalite; David Green; Kathy Holland; Commission Evidence/Court Case information; Bruce Rigsby; Sadie Howard; Gitksan Interpreters' Gitxsan Glossary; Gitxsan Dictionary; Edgar Good; Mary Johnson, Antgulilbisxw

4

Traveller's Path

Just upstream from the place once known at Skeena Forks, in the drainage of the river called the Bulkley by the newcomers and Widzin Kwikh[1] by its inhabitants live the Witsuwet'en (people of Widzín Kwikh), neighbours of the Gitksan to the south and east. Their present village of Tse Cäkh[2] or Hagwilget was ceded to them in the 1820s by the local Gitksan to allow them access to fishing sites when a landslide in Hagwilget Canyon blocked the river temporarily, and prevented the movement of salmon to the ancient summer fishing place at the canyon now called Moricetown Canyon, the site of the village of Kyah Wiget (Morice 1978 [1904]:8). The Witsuwit'en homeland includes the drainage of Widzín Kwikh or the Bulkley River, and the adjacent headwaters of the Fraser River system (Figure 4.1). The Witsuwit'en live in an environment and cultural setting broadly transitional between the Northwest Coast and the sub-boreal interior of British Columbia and speak an Athapaskan language, though their culture has many similarities with the neighbouring Gitksan and other people of the Northwest Coast, as well as many elements in common with other Dene.

Northern Athapaskan speakers (Dene) have in general been nomadic hunters and fishers, such as the Kaska Dena and Gwich'in I will discuss in

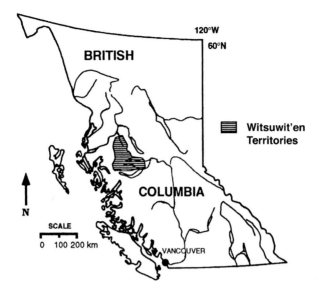

Figure 4.1 Map of Witsuwit'en territory

Chapters 6–8. The Witsuwit'en have depended more heavily on harvest and catching of salmon than many other Athapaskans, made possible by their residence on rivers of the Pacific drainage with rich salmon resources. After dispersed hunting in the winter season, they traditionally spent the summer season settled in villages adjacent to the major salmon fishing areas. The Witsuwit'en share many features of Northwest Coast life, including division into named exogamous Clans (called Phratries by anthropologists), and have a ranked society with Chiefs, commoners and (formerly) slaves. Their Houses (***Yikh***) and Clans own hunting grounds, and fishing sites which are formally owned and passed down along descent lines. Witsuwit'en social organization and ecology are discussed in more detail Mills 1994, and Daly 2005, and much rich material is also presented in *Hang onto These Words, Johnny David's Delgamuukw Evidence* (Mills 2005).

The Witsuwit'en homeland ranges from mountainous to plateau country, with some large lakes in the southern portion, and is traversed by the broad valley of the Bulkley River in the northern portion (Figure 4.2). Most of the landscape is within the Sub-Boreal Spruce biogeoclimatic zone, charac-terized by stands of aspen, and forests dominated by spruce and pine, with Engelmann spruce-subalpine fir forest at timberline, except in the northern

Figure 4.2 Bulkley Valley landscape showing mountains *dzilh*, a grassy meadow *tl'o k'it*, a small lake called Ts'en co Tanedilh, lit. 'swans land in the water' (Toboggan Lake in English), and the mountains called Ts'idek'iy (Hudson Bay Mountain behind Smithers). Mixed forest grows along the far shore and conifer forest mantles the mountain slopes. Slide area tracks are also visible. Pat Namox commented about the snowfield *lhk'aygyuts'iy* in the cirque to the right of the cleft with the glacier, "them snow drift, 20 feet deep that's the one you see in July."

portion, where the inner edge of the Interior Cedar-Hemlock Zone is found in the Bulkley Valley. The exposition of Witsuwit'en landscape knowledge presented in this chapter is the result of my ongoing ethnobotanical and ethnoecological research in northwest British Columbia, and of a long collaboration with linguist Sharon Hargus of the University of Washington, the expert on the Witsuwit'en language, who independently elicited landscape terms and narratives, as well as carrying out linguistic analysis of terms (Johnson and Hargus 2007).

I explored Witsuwit'en understanding of local landforms, vegetation and habitats by conducting interviews in peoples' homes and going on field trips to different local areas. I used voice recording where feasible to record narratives accurately and allow linguistic transcription of Witsuwit'en terms. I also made written notes, and took photographs and video to record terms and provide a visual record of different kinds of place in the local environment.

I used visual methods for both as a prompt for terms and stories, and to document places and ecotopes, and recorded associated English narratives to achieve a fuller understanding of the meaning of different kinds of place. I also recorded narratives to document geographic vocabulary and to learn what the entailments or affordances are of these kinds of place. The research on which this chapter is based was carried out principally in 1997-1998 and 2005; my previous work with Witsuwit'en speakers and elders focused on ethnobotanical and healing knowledge. Translation and orthography of terms was checked with Sharon Hargus, who also conducted independent research into Witsuwit'en geographic terms; she has worked with documentation and revitalization of the Witsuwit'en language since 1988.

In my initial research design, I desired to compare the perception and understanding of landscape of groups whose languages and landscapes differed, to help to understand how their recognition and naming of landscape features and the meanings these places and kinds of place had might differ. I hypothesized that place kinds or ecotopes recognized by a group of people would reflect the regional geography of local groups, and also their ecological relations, encoding information about resource types and knowledge of the land necessary for successful travel. In the previous chapter I discussed landscape classification and meaning for the Gitksan, a group of Tsimshianic speakers whose homeland is just north and west of the Witsuwit'en lands.

Places also serve as landmarks, and reference points in travelling over the land, an activity almost synonymous with the traditional northern Athapaskan way of life, and are therefore important in ethnoecology. Athapaskan toponyms reveal how a place looks from the vantage of the traveller and what its characteristics are. (The placement of the observer in the landscape, conspicuous in Athapaskan place names [cf. Basso 1990], is facilitated by the extremely rich set of directional or locational adverbs and nouns in Athapaskan languages, which are incorporated into descriptive words and narratives [Kari 1989; Hagwilget Band 1995]). Named places link knowledge from many different domains, the sacred and moral, the historical, traditional ecological knowledge about subsistence, and about routes of travel and trade. Athapaskan peoples also have a set of names for larger physiographic regions (Andrews and Zoe 1997; Kari 1989; Kari and Fall 1987).

Named places also serve to identify social groups for Athapaskan speakers, particularly terms related to the local hydrology or physiographic regions; for example, groups are often named for rivers or for large fish bearing lakes, which may be foci of summer gathering of groups widely dispersed in the rest of the year. This is certainly prominent for the Witsuwit'en (Bulkley River People) and their various neighbouring Babine and Carrier groups. Kari (1989) has reported that Athapaskan groups in Alaska may be named for physiographic regions. In contrast to Alaskan and northern Dene, Witsuwit'en place names are proprietary and serve to validate the relationship of Houses (**Yikh**), and Clans to bounded Territories where members are entitled to harvest resources. Only features of regional significance or associated with major trails seem to be "public" place names for the Witsuwit'en.

It is now apparent that substantial variation can occur in which features of landscape are named, and how they are subdivided, across environments, cultures and languages (Johnson and Hunn 2009). In this chapter I present a Witsuwit'en lexicon of landscape terms and discuss the system for describing landscape, its relationship to other Dene landscape classifications, and to scientific systems of landscape classification (see Figures 4.3 and 4.4 for examples of the range of landscape terms). I focus on general "kinds of place" or ecotopes, rather than presenting a detailed exposition of specific places in the Witsuwit'en landscape, in part because of the significance of named sites as owned properties of Chief and Clans.

Toponym studies and linguistic studies of spatial terms provide a useful context for consideration of Witsuwit'en ethnogeography. The toponym studies by Kari (1989), Kari and Fall (1987), working with Dena'ina, another Athapaskan language, and Hunn (1996) working with Sahaptin in the Columbia River drainage, are particularly relevant to landscape ethnoecology. Starting from a corpus of toponyms, Kari and Fall, and Kari elaborate a set of 'place kind generics', which reveals underlying concepts of significant kinds of place. Kari's work on hydronymic districts, and his cross linguistic analysis of stems referring to water, streams and rivers, and lakes is quite useful (Kari 1996). Tom (1986) provides a rich illustrated record of Southern Tutchone toponyms, while studies of Andrews and co-authors provide a sense of the link between locale, place names, and relationships to the living landscape and its mythic past in the Northwest Territories (Andrews 1990, Andrews et al. 1998), which are relevant to understanding of Witsuwit'en ethnogeography. A variety of dictionary efforts and land claim research also include both toponyms and their meanings (e.g. Andre and Kritsch 1992, Kritsch and Andre 1994 and Greer 1999 for Gwich'in; Kaska Elders 1997, for Kaska; and Hargus 1999 for Witsuwit'en). Linguistic studies that focus on spatial terms in Athapaskan languages, and their literal and metaphoric significance in the storied landscape include Tlen (2006) on Southern Tutchone directionals, and Moore (2000) on Kaska directionals.

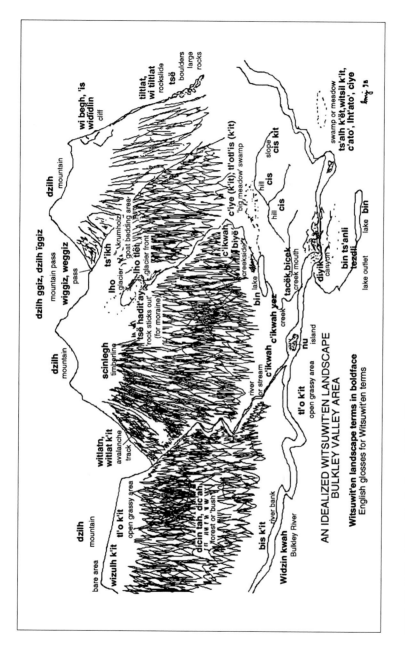

Figure 4.3 Idealized Witsuwit'en landscape, Bulkley Valley area

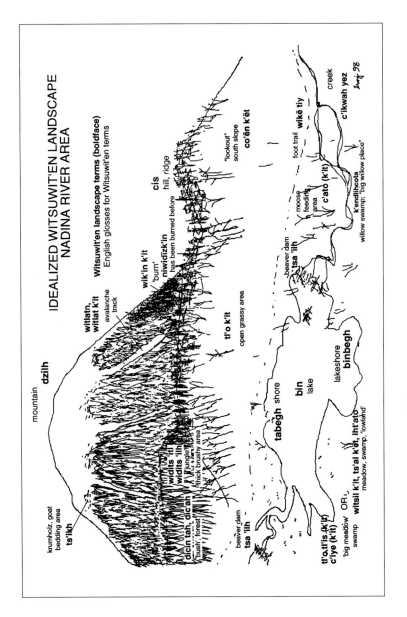

IDEALIZED WITSUWIT'EN LANDSCAPE NADINA RIVER AREA

Witsuwit'en landscape terms (boldface)
English glosses for Witsuwit'en terms

mountain
dzilh

krumholz, goat bedding area
ts'lkh

witlatn, witlat k'it
avalanche track

wik'in k'it
'burn'
niwidizk'in
has been burned before

cis
hill, ridge

"lookout"
south slope
co'ën k'ët

tl'o k'it
open grassy area

dicin tah, dic'an
"bush", forest

widits 'it
widits 'ilh
'jungle', thick brushy area

beaver dam
tsa 'ilh

tabegh shore

bin
lake

lakeshore
binbegh

beaver dam
tsa 'ilh

moose feeding area

foot trail **wikë tly**

c'ato (k'it)

k'endilhcota
willow swamp; "big willow place"

creek
c'ikwah yez

'big meadow' OR
c'iye (k'it)

tl'q,tl'is (k'it)
swamp
witsil k'it, ts'al k'ët, lht'ato
meadow, swamp, "lowland"

Figure 4.4 Idealized Witsuwit'en Landscape, Nadina area

Witsuwit'en landscape terms

In this chapter I present terms for physiographic features and their parts, vegetation terms, and other habitat terms. Though the landscape forms a unified fabric of spatial relationship and is all of a piece (e.g. Figure 4.5), for purposes of discussion it is useful to group terms analytically. As with Gitksan landscape terms, I have broadly divided these into terms for flowing water; other water bodies; snow and ice; physiographic features and land surface types; timberline, open areas and burns; berry patches, meadows and wetlands (Figure 4.6); and terms related to hunting and animal habitats. (see Table 4.1 at the end of this chapter). These groupings are partially dictated by convenience, and partly by the way that terms pertaining to certain broad environments seem to group together. Terms for flowing water, and features of rivers such as banks form a natural grouping that reflects the high importance of the main rivers for transportation, in shaping ecological communities, and for fishing (Figures 4.7 and 4.9). Lakes (Figure 4.8) and ponds are similarly important as are springs, forming another grouping of water related terms. Terminology for ice and snow is also well developed, reflecting the high importance of ice and snow features for winter survival and travel, and for traversing mountains with permanent glaciers and snow-fields. The Witsuwit'en homeland is mountainous, so terms for mountains, hills and cliffs also seem to form another natural group. Perhaps artificially, I have separated timberline and alpine terms from the mountain terms, but some justification for this is given by the fact that terms for open areas can refer both to alpine environments above timberline and to clearings or open areas at low elevation. Burned over areas are also included in this grouping. The broad category of forest and scrub is generally indicated by terms which translate as 'in the bush' or which specify the dominant species as *tighiz co tah* (among) aspen woods. Finally there is a significant domain of landscape terms that relate to animals and animal habitats, an important part of environmental knowledge for hunting peoples. Sacred places are another category; these are generally named places on territories, or gravesites, and are usually not openly discussed.

Witsuwit'en terms are transcribed in the local orthography. For correspondences with standard phonetic symbols see Hargus (2007).

Narratives of landscape

Listening to Witsuwet'en narratives about the land, one has a sense of the re-creation of specific journeys through specific places. Elders recalled their

Figure 4.5 View up Peter Alec Creek toward Nëdin'a, Nadina Mountain, May 1989 This view and the following photo were the places I had in mind when I drew by idealized block diagram. Photograph by Allen S. Gottesfeld.

Figure 4.6 Marsh along Peter Alec Creek, May 1988 Wetland terminology is highly elaborated in Witsuwit'en, depending on the focus of attention and the characteristics of the site. Photograph by Allen S. Gottesfeld.

Figure 4.7 Fishing at Moricetown Canyon on Widzin Kwikh, the Bulkley River A 'canyon' is *diyik* in Witsuwit'en. At the centre of the photo is a fishing station for gaffing spring salmon. Photographed July 1980 by Allen S. Gottesfeld.

Figure 4.8 Sdic'odinkhlh Bin, Blue Lake, from the lakeshore *(bin begh)* Blue Lake is an example of a place with many layers of significance in the landscape. Blue Lake figures in a narrative of Estes, the Witsuwit'en Trickster/Creator, and I was told that first time visitors to Blue Lake were supposed to put ashes on their face before they arrived (Herb George, pers. comm.). The Blue Lake area is also an area where the traditional root food *diyii'n* was harvested (Elsie Tait, L.M. Johnson interview notes), and was a harvesting area for mountain goat, black huckleberry, and traditional medicines. It was heavily used by residents of Hagwilget as it was one of the closest productive resource areas on Witsuwit'en territory. Blue Lake is on the massif called Sdic'odin, known in English as Rocher de Boule. Photo by Allen S. Gottesfeld.

Figure 4.9 Hagwilget Canyon, *diyik*- at fall low water (term provided by the late Pat Namox (Wah'tah'kwets) and Lucy Namox (Goohlat). Photo taken from the modern suspension bridge over the canyon. In the 1950s, Federal Fisheries orchestrated the blowing up of "the rock" under the bridge, which eliminated the traditional salmon fishery that was the reason for the siting of Hagwilget or Tsë Cakh 'under the rock' in that location. Recently, the Witsuwit'en have taken the government to court to try to restore their fishery by emplacing an artificial rock. As of this writing, the outcome is pending.

own early experiences of hunting, trapping, and berry picking, their training, the wisdom of their Elders. The land is experienced in the specific; these experiences may then be generalized as a guide for other similar circumstances. Narratives mixed discussions of winter travel or travel techniques in the mountains, preventative self-discipline, and techniques for avoidance of many specific risks. 'That's *danger!*" as the late Pat Namox said a number of times, discussing items as diverse as the need to show respect for grizzly bears or proper ax technique when clearing a winter trail of boughs and branches bent over by heavy snowfall.

The Witsuwet'en perspective of the land seems to be one of learning to look after one's self, travelling over the land to make one's living, and of learning one's own place. A major topic of discussion was learning to travel the land safely and avoid dangerous places and situations. Safe winter and spring travel in the mountains of Witsuwet'en country requires recognition of, and extreme care in crossing, avalanche tracks, which extend to the bottom of many higher elevation valleys and cannot be avoided. As Pat Namox recounted:

> Pat: You know, uh, when that thing it's uh, well, in the first snow, the same thing again. Too much snow at one time, big hill like that, they start to slide again. And that's the one they call ***witl'atk'it***. And they knows the area where it is, there, you have to watch.
> Leslie: Yeah, you can see on the land.
> Pat: Yeah. Yeah. Well, there's uh, I don't know, them old people they knows about that avalanche, at, uh, wintertime. You know, you go across that dangerous place that it, there's a avalanche there, but they said you have to, uh, get them boughs from the tree like this. Lots of them, and you in a hurry to go across through that avalanche area, with the snowshoes. You have to take one little—and you threw like this.
> Leslie: OK, you throw the boughs in front of you and then you step on it?
> Pat: Yeah. And you step on that one there, with snowshoes across there. They'll never go down.
> (Pat Namox interview transcript August 25, 1997)

Mountain goat hunting without rifles requires a superb knowledge of the habits of the animals and ability to traverse steep slopes without slipping over cliffs. Other types of hazardous terrain discussed included the risks of crossing glaciers, of stepping on slopes of cohesionless sand or fine gravel on mountains, and of avoiding frostbite crossing swampy areas on snowshoes.

For the Witsuwet'en, place also has another dimension. Because of the Territory system, they are attentive to the characteristics of the land as indications of their history and for demarcating boundaries (see Thornton 2008 for a detailed discussion of this aspect of geographic knowledge for the Tlingit in southeast Alaska). One Elder commented, as he described his experiences as a Land Claims researcher, that in the old days nobody would have been asking about and learning the kinds of things he was documenting for the Court Case[3]; as knowledge of one's territory is not public, it is inappropriate to seek to learn about, and to discuss, somebody else's Place.

Place also has a spiritual and mythic dimension, as attested for other Athapaskan peoples (cf. Andrews 1990; Andrews and Zoe 1997; Andrews *et al.* 1998; Basso 1990a, b; Brody 1988; Ridington 1990). Some kinds of place may have more meaning in these terms than in strictly ecological ones, though I believe this would most often be on the level of specific named sites or features. As for other indigenous people, burial sites are, for example, sacred places. Other kinds of place also have spiritual implications: while discussing the word for 'glacier', one Elder began to speak of the glacier on the mountain locally called Hudson Bay Mountain (Ts'idek'iy). Her grandfather told her that if it disappeared, it would herald the end of the world. It has diminished in recent years as climatic warming has brought about diminution of montane glaciers throughout the region, perhaps a portentous observation.

As with other Athapaskan languages, the structure of Witsuwit'en encourages reference to parts of the landscape in relationship—relationship of features to each other, and to the speaker. Considering the landscape sketches I used for elicitation (Figures 4.3 and 4.4), elders and language experts provided terms that indicated motion, flow, relationship of creeks to slopes, and whether they flow into or out of lakes. Certain terms indicating the position of a feature on the landscape *k'it* 'on' or in relationship to the speaker *tah* 'among' (placing the speaker in the described landscape) occur repeatedly in Witsuwit'en construction of landscape descriptive terms.

Witsuwit'en, in common with other Athapaskan languages, has a rich lexicon describing terrain, of quintessential importance to travelling people. Sizes of features from entire mountains or rivers to banks, peaks, or cliffs, to rock, sand, quicksand and mud are named. Vegetation types, wetlands, and habitats of animals can be described with nuance, and the entailments of terms, such as the plant or animal species which favor certain habitats are often described. Locations where plants may be picked or animals likely encountered are known. Landscape processes, and their visible indicators such as burns, rockslides and avalanches are recognized and named. Associations of various features with plants and animals that are significant in Witsuwit'en traditional life are known and can be elucidated.

Orienting terms indicating upslope/downslope and facing upstream/facing downstream are also well developed, as well as other terms indicating spatial relationships [across, under, etc.] (The Hagwilget Band 1995, Hargus 1999). Sophisticated constructions indicating relationships of features to each other and to speakers or observers are ubiquitous.

Thinking about places and kinds of place often puts speakers in mind of specific places on the territories on which they were raised, or which may be accessed from locations such as Moricetown, and people may tell stories or recall memories from their past, a phenomenon recorded by others for non-Athapaskan languages (Palmer 2006, Thornton, n.d.).

It may be that not all knowledge about kinds of place is neatly coded with particular words. I asked Alfred Joseph if there was a term for south-facing slopes that are open and grass covered (Figure 4.6), and melt early in the spring; these are good habitat for deer and moose in the southeastern portion of Witsuwit'en territory. His musing answer suggested he understood easily what kind of place I was referring to, and had a specific example in mind, but was uncertain if there was a generic word for it:

> A: Well, like 6 mile hill?
> L: Yeah, probably.
> A: Yeah, it's nice, south slope, well, they always, they, I don't know, it just sounds like the time. Could be too, like in the spring time when the deer start feedin' there. That's when they talk about it. They say *k'ëbiggeslal*,[4] maybe *k'ëbi* is the south slope. I didn't think about that. That's what they always say, when the animals appear on the south slope in the springtime…
> That's when they go after the deer, they say *k'ëbikeslal. keslal* is the animals crawl- or migrate to this area. There's a whole bunch of them.

Later on in the interview, Alfred speculated about a possible parallel to a place where goats can be found:

A: And uh, when they, uh, when the mountain goat bed down for the night, they call that *as* [*'is*][5] *tanëlal*. So, *as* [*'is*] is a cliff …That's where the *as* [*'is*] *tanëla* and *k'ëbïkehla* is about the same thing, eh? ***Kë'bïkehla*** is - deer go on the side.

On another occasion I was discussing grassy south-facing slopes with a different Elder, the late Pat Namox.

It's like a little hill and grass 1 side, and that's where that animal goes and get in in springtime. Bear, grizzly bear or deer. Everything coming out in the bush. Hillside, first grass coming out first everytime. Lookout *co'enk'it* eye is ***onen*** or *o'en*. You see or you look, that's what it is *co'enk'it*. Well, you have to go down below and you see the animal up there. You have to go around and place that animal there and what place you coming out on the top before you go- you have to go away from the wind and gauge the wind. You'll see and you'll get that. That's professional Indian hunters.

Some of they they try to get it. They go up. Even no wind, they smell you and the run away.

Down Frances Lake area there lots of place like that. There's one in my father's hunting ground, *co'enk'it*.

No Supervalu, nothing. Supervalu is right in the woods. Animal, fish, all different kinds of berries they can use. They have to learn right from the start, like. They learn from their uncle or grandmother or grandfather. They train them. now they gonna work through the bush. It's very important for young people then.

[untranscribed story about an orphan omitted]

That's really true. They live on the country. They know how to hunt everything that they live on, even that sap [pine sap or 'cambium'].[6] They make a cornflakes and dry it up, sun dry for winter time. Take it out and soak it. Get it right now. They know what kind of timber, what kind of tree, new young short jackpine, with the bark so shiny. Juice coming in there. So sweet and it's good for you too. You'd been Indian you'd be 150 years old! [Laugh].

Now our life is so short—chemicals.

Their hair was white and then it turned blonde. They lose all their teeth, and new teeth coming in. They live to 150 years old. They crush drymeat to powder on a rock and put in water and

that's what old people eat, and they live a long time.
(tape transcript 980528A recorded May 28, 1998)

Pat's narrative combines a specific analysis of place kind, its name, etymology, and significance with comments on the overall importance of knowledge of the land to health and Witsuwit'en life.

Comparisons with other Dene languages

Witsuwit'en shares with other Athapaskan languages the way it encodes spatial relationships, surfaces and topographic positions in the construction of place terms and in ways of speaking about places. As with other Athapaskan languages, drainages, upstream/downstream, and upslope/downslope, are important ways of thinking about the land. The relationship between generic place kinds and the names of specific places is rich, and places are often named descriptively ['head of the lake'] or ['water flowing in among the cattails'] in ways that give a strong sense of the place. Witsuwit'en place kinds carry entailments that give information about animal and plant habitats, and perhaps a sense of kinds of place in the annual cycle of movement and harvest on the territory.

In Athapaskan languages, place kind terms are used alone, and in compound descriptions to refer to specific named places. Kari (1989) and Kari and Fall (1987) have explored what they term "place kind generics" for Athapaskan languages, as well as documenting in detail Dena'ina and Ahtna toponyms. The rich relational sense of place names and the way they encode Athapaskan relationship to land has been eloquently described by Keith Basso for White Mountain Apache (Basso 1990 a., b.; Basso 1996).

A number of Witsuwit'en geographic terms are cognate with terms in other Athapaskan languages, and appear to indicate similar or identical concepts, a topic that will be discussed in greater detail in Chapter 6. Many similarities occur between terms in Witsuwit'en and Kaska and Sekani (Johnson unpublished manuscript and Kaska Tribal Council 1997). More broadly shared appear to be constructions including -_____ *[co] tah* ['among (big)'] as in *ts'o co tah* 'among big spruce trees' (Witsuwit'en) and *gat chō tah* 'among big white spruce trees ' (Kaska) for vegetation types. Constructions including *k'it* or other terms for 'on' also seem be widespread and appear to apply both to physiographic features (such as *cis k'it* 'hillslope' Witsuwit'en term, *bus̲k'ut* 'river bank' Carrier term [Antoine et al 1974] and *héskage* 'alpine', lit. 'on mountain' Kaska term [Kaska Elders 1997]) and wetlands and meadows (***witsil k'it, tl'o k'it***, Witsuwit'en terms, "Klokut" [***Tl'o k'it***] Vuntut Gwitchin place name).

As hunting is of paramount importance in Dene traditional economies, Athapaskan languages have a rich domain of terms pertaining to animals, habitats and hunting. Some key examples include terms for lookout, trail (differentiated by the animal who made it, or as a human foot trail), and, of great importance to hunters, mineral licks ("lick" or "muddy place"). In addition, physiographic and vegetation features which are preferred habitat of various animals are described by hunters, such as areas where mountain goats bed (for Witsuwit'en), mountain sheep take refuge (for Kaska; see Chapter 6), or "sloughs" or "swamps" where moose feed in the summer (both Witsuwit'en and Kaska).

Sophisticated "partonomy" (cf. Brown 1976) or terms for parts of rivers and drainage systems is characteristic of Athapaskan languages in general, and is significant for both Witsuwit'en and other Athapaskan speakers of Canada and Alaska (cf. Kari 1999, Kari and Fell 1987, Kaska Elders 1997). The complex and detailed river terms such as 'eddy', 'rapids', 'canyon', 'slough', 'confluence' and associated features such as 'high bank' are highly important for both travel along rivers (on ice or by boat) and for fish habitat and fishability. In Witsuwit'en country, river fishing for salmon with traps and weirs, gaffs and more recently gill nets has been important, and requires sophisticated knowledge of river features to locate fish and to navigate safely. In other Dene regions, and in the more southern and interior parts of Witsuwit'en territory, lake and river fisheries for trout, whitefish and other fish such as loche (lingcod) are significant.

Reflections on Witsuwit'en place kinds and the landscape

The presentation of Witsuwit'en landscape understanding in this chapter is still partial and preliminary. What is included, and what is not, are influenced by a number of factors: gender—mine and that of those with whom I have worked; location—where was the information recorded? in the kitchen? by the river? and so on; and methods of elicitation—use of photographs or line drawings, explanation in the midst of narrative, asking on site on the land. How and by whom information was recorded are significant influences on the types of information and level of detail provided. Gender is an obvious influence, in that the contexts for sharing of hunting related terminology are substantially fewer for female researchers speaking with male Elders and language experts. It has been observed by language researchers that it is much more difficult to recall vocabulary in the absence of a context, while a rich narrative naturally arises in the course of shared activities on the land. The need to spend more time on the land with fluent speakers engaging in land related activities and visiting significant locations, and my lack of fluency in Witsuwit'en, restrict detail and nuance in what I have recorded. In particular, terms for kinds of place in the mountains, hunting related terms, and specific river terms are substantially underrepresented in the material I have amassed because none of my work occurred in the specific contexts of fishing or hunting.

Despite these limitations, it is clear that the Witsuwit'en possess a rich and sophisticated vocabulary of landscape terms that reflects detailed understanding of the features of the Witsuwit'en homeland, and linkage of geographic terms to ecological knowledge, oral histories and cosmology. Witsuwit'en ethnogeography places people in the landscape, and speaks of things in dynamic spatial relationships. Physiography, hydrologic features, vegetation and wildlife habitats and animal behavior are all present in Witsuwit'en geographic terminology, which is linked both to specific place names and to narratives of personal experience and of tradition.

The corpus of ecotope or place kind terms recognized in the Witsuwit'en, as with other Athapaskan speakers of Northwest North America, reflects topography, hydrology, vegetation, and animal habitats. A great deal of ecological knowledge is tied to these types of places, such as risks in winter or spring travel in the mountains or over ice, risks of river or lake travel or potential areas of fish habitat and fishability, habitat of various game animals, ease of travel through different types of vegetation or terrain, berry availability, and spiritual risk or potency. "Trail" is itself a specific kind of place, as well as metaphor for human history and cosmology, and places people, travelling, in the landscape.

The *trail* appears to be a preeminent Athapaskan metaphor or organizing principle. Ridington (1990) eloquently expresses the pre-eminence of the *trail* as an organizing principle of experience and understanding for the Beaver (or Dunne Za, now spelled Dane-z̲aa):

> The Beaver (Dunne Za) people viewed human experience as a
> life-sustaining network of relationships between all components of a
> sentient world. They experienced their world as a mosaic of passages
> and interactions between animate beings in motion against the
> backdrop of a terrain that was itself continually in process through

the cyclical transformations of changing seasons. *They looked upon the trails of people and animals as a record of these interactions.* Each trail, they believed, continued backward and forward beyond the point at which it could no longer be followed physically. the trails that lay ahead, as well as those that lay behind, could be followed by people in their dreams. The trail of every adult could be followed in the mind back to the point of visionary encounter with a medicine animal, just as the trail of a successful hunter could be followed ahead to his point of encounter with the spirit of an animal. Each actual point of meeting between person and animal was believed to be the manifestation of antecedent meetings in the medium of dream or vision. (emphasis added)

The Witsuwit'en '*kungax*' (*cin k'ih*) are "trails of song" (Mills 1994:122) linking past, present and future-*situated in place* (Mills 1994; Hugh Brody, address to Gitksan –Wet'suwet'en Tribal Council Convention 1986). The *cin k'ih* can be represented by a historical narrative, or can be shown by enactment in the feast hall of the crest of the House Chief, and make publicly manifest the connection of people and Territory. Witsuwit'en stories which relate the early shaping of the world, the stories of Estes, too are linked to places in this world, at least in that they are said to have happened near modern recognized places such as the village of Moricetown (Kyah Wiget and nearby locations), François Lake, or along the Skeena River.

In the narratives of Athapaskan speakers, and other residents of the region such as the Gitksan, types of places are understood as animal habitat for significant species. For example, the late Pat Namox gave an extended discussion of goat habitat (including bedding areas in krumholz and access trails) and goat huntability when discussing travel in the mountains. He also took care to describe minimizing of risky encounters with grizzly bears in open alpine meadows, such as avoidance of leaping over large stones with a dip on the far side-where you might jump on or over a resting bear.

Berry patches are an important kind of place for the Witsuwit'en, and discussion of berry picking brings up discussions of specific berry patches, and of maintenance of berry patches by burning. The topic of berry patches will be taken up in detail in Chapter 5. "Swamp" or "meadow" environments are also important, because two economically important plant products were gathered there: sphagnum moss for babies' diapers (and women's menstrual supplies) and "meadow" (bog) cranberries. Specific localities for gathering moss and cranberries are reported by women when discussing diaper moss.

Table 4.1
Witsuwit'en Geographic Terms

Witsuwit'en term	English gloss

Flowing Water Terms

c'ikwah	'river, stream'
c'ikwah yez	'creek'
tacëk	'mouth (of river, creek)'
bin k'ënli	'creek flowing into a lake'
bin ts'anli, tëzdli	'creek flowing out of a lake'
bis k'it	'bank (of river, etc.)'
diyik	'canyon'

Other Water Terms

bin	'lake'
tabegh	'shore'
nu	'island'
tadiz'ay	'pond, backwater, puddle'
hanli	'spring'
tak'iz k'ët	'spring'
talhtis	'deep water'
tëwhilh	'deep water'
dzen	'muddy water'

Ice and Snow and Related Terms

lho	'glacier
lho tl'ët	'glacier foot' (lit. 'glacier front')
lhim	'ice (chunk)'
tin	'ice (flat)'
yis	'snow'
lhk'ëc'ots'iyh	'snowdrift'
witlat, tiltlat, witiltlat	'slide, avalanche'
witlatn, witlat k'it	'avalanche track'

Mountains, Hills, Cliffs and Caves

cis	'hill, ridge'
dzilh	'mountain'
weggiz, wiggiz	'pass'
dzilh k'it	'summit' (lit. 'on mountain')
dzilh iggiz, dzilh ggiz	'mountain pass'
wenin	'sidehill'
'is	'cliff'
wibegh	'cliff'
wididlin	'cliff'
tsë bï hon'a	'cave'
c'i'an	'den, hole, cave'

(Table 4.1, continued)

Rocks and Sand

tsë	'rock, boulder'
tsë hadït'ay	'moraine' (lit. 'rock sticks out')
say	'sand, fine gravel'
say k'it	'sand bar'
say titgut	'quicksand'

Timberline, Open Areas, Burns

ts'ikh	'dwarf trees at timberline, krumholz'
scinlegh	'timberline'
wize begh	'timberline'
wik'in k'it	'burned area'
widïnk'in' k'it	'burned area'
niwdïzk'an	'burned area'

Vegetation–Berry Grounds, Meadows and Swamp

nit'ay k'it	'berry picking ground'
wizulh k'it	'open area, also above timberline; bare ground with nothing on it'
tl'o k'it	'meadow, open grassy area' (e.g. a lawn, a grazed slope, alpine meadow)
tl'otl'is (k'it)	'meadow, marsh' (where large grass grows)
c'iye (k'it)	'swamp' (where moss grows?)
ts'al k'ët	'swamp' (lit. diaper place)
witsil k'it	'damp place'
c'ato', lht'ato'	'swamp'

Vegetation– Forest and Scrub

dic'ah,	'(in the) bush'
dicin tah	'(in the) bush', 'among the trees/ sticks'
widits'itl	'brush, brushy area'
ts'o co tah	'big spruce country, spruce forest area'
t'ighis co tah	'big poplar country, poplar woods'

Terms Related to Animals

lhiyil c'itiy	'goat trail'
ts'ikh	'dwarf trees at timberline, krumholz (goat bed at edge of cliff)'
tsa 'ilh	'beaver dam'
c'ikën	'(beaver) lodge'
c'itok'ët	'moose watering hole'
co'ën k'it	'lookout' (e.g. open south facing slope)
lhëtl'is c'ididlet	'mud lick'

5

Of Berry Patches

The array of place kinds or ecotopes, habitats, or vegetation communities recognized by a culture as having special value or utility in a specific landscape cannot be assumed, but must be established through empirical investigation. Nor can their correlation with the habitats or environmental features recognized by Western sciences be neatly predicted. It stands to reason that peoples with differing ways of life and relationships to the landscape of their homeland may recognize and name the features of their landscape in distinctive ways. In the previous two chapters, I discuss the array of landscape terms used by the Gitksan and Witsuwit'en. Here I want to focus on a particular ecotope that is widely shared among British Columbia First Peoples, from the vantage of Gitksan ethnoecology and that of their close neighbours, the Witsuwit'en—the berry patch. In northwest British Columbia, the berry patch is a highly salient and significant ecotope. Most often a berry patch is a recognized and productive, perhaps named, site where large amounts of black huckleberry (*Vaccinium membranaceum*) can be harvested.

The historic importance of berries as a carbohydrate source, storage and trade item, and valued good to be consumed at feasts (potlatches) calls attention to this distinctive cultural ecotope and the question of how berry patches are recognized, created, and maintained. Given the widespread dominance of forest, especially dense coniferous forests, shrub-dominated ecosystems are not normally persistent but require burning to retard forest succession (N. Turner 1999; Johnson 1999; other studies in Boyd 1999). Black huckleberry is culturally the most salient berry in the region, a status underscored by its Gitksan name *sim maa'y,* which means 'real or true berry', and black huckleberry patches were formerly important foci of the seasonal round, and important owned properties of corporate House or Clan groups for the Gitksan and Witsuwit'en (Trusler and Johnson 2008; Johnson 1998, 1999; Daly 2005). Several other berry species were harvested and consumed in relatively large quantities, though I have learned less about their ethnoecology, harvest and management. The two most significant of these are saskatoons (*Amelanchier alnifolia*) and lowbush blueberries (*Vaccinium caespitosum*).

Although significant edible plant species may be widely distributed within a region, the highly productive sites necessary for effective harvesting are not uniformly distributed across the landscape. Instead, these sites tend to be patchy (cf. Hawkes et al. 1982; Turner et al. 1992; Johnson 1999). As Nancy Turner and Douglas Deur and others have demonstrated in British Columbia (Deur and Turner 2005; Turner 1999; Johnson 1999; Darby 2005; Thornton 1999) important plant resources such as berry patches and root gardens are frequently managed to enhance productivity. It appears that for the highly prized and productive black huckleberry, indigenous people actively managed it throughout its extensive range (Trusler 2002; Mack 2001; Mack and McClure 2002; Turner 1999), making it an important and at least partially anthropogenic ecotope. But how do people decide what are appropriate sites to manage for berries? Are there biophysical parameters that are recognized by local groups such as the Gitksan and Witsuwit'en? What characteristics must a site have to be an actual or potential berry patch? (For the actual case, large numbers of fruit-bearing bushes are an obvious clue; a potential or former berry patch is much more elusive to locate.)

An understanding of berry patches in northwest British Columbia must begin with a sense of the cultural importance of berry patches, and of the landscape context in which they occur.

The historic and cultural importance of berries

Berries, and particularly black huckleberries, were the most important carbohydrate food in northwestern British Columbia before the introduction of rice, flour, and potatoes by Europeans. Aside from berries and other fruits, only tree cambiums, fern rhizomes, and rice-root lily bulbs were available sources of carbohydrate that could be harvested in some quantity, and that could provide some carbohydrate in the winter diet to complement the protein from dried fish and what could be obtained in the hunt (Gottesfeld 1995; Johnson 1997). Black huckleberries are extremely productive on good sites.[1] They are relatively high in carbohydrates and provide vitamin C and other vitamins (Kuhnlein and Turner 1991; Gottesfeld 1995). Few other significant sources of carbohydrate were available which could be gathered in quantity and stored for the winter. Huckleberries were harvested and preserved in large quantities by both Gitksan and Witsuwit'en, historically from large high-elevation berry camps accessed by well-constructed trails, as well as more opportunistically. Before the introduction of canning and freezing, huckleberries were processed by cooking and drying into large berry cakes, in which form they could be stored for the winter or traded, and which were much lighter to transport than the fresh berries. This process is described in *Gathering What the Great Nature Provided* (People of Ksan 1980) and in Johnson 1997. Other berries were sometimes dried separately like raisins (saskatoons), preserved in boxes or bladders with grease (lowbush blueberries and cranberries), or added to the berry cakes (Gottesfeld 1991; Johnson 1997; People of Ksan 1980; Smith 1997). Berries were and are an important gift for distribution during potlatches, and black huckleberries retain a symbolic role in the Witsuwit'en potlatch, where distribution of them is still accompanied by singing of berry songs by the recipient chiefs. In contemporary understanding, giving large quantities of berries is a demonstration of generosity on the part of the ascending chief, and demonstrates the cohesiveness of the social group and its link to the land. Dried berry cakes also were highly prized by coastal peoples and were one of the most important trade goods which the Gitksan and Witsuwit'en transported over the Grease Trails to the coast to trade for oolachan grease and other coastal delicacies such as dried seaweed and herring eggs (People of Ksan 1980).

As I described in the previous chapters, for the Gitksan and the Witsuwit'en of the Bulkley Valley, the landscape is divided into territories and smaller resource properties such as fishing sites, which are owned by corporate groups. Allocation of resources is mediated by hereditary chiefs, and access to resources follows kinship and marriage ties. For the Gitksan, the House (*Wilp*) is the most important territorial level, while for the Witsuwit'en the Clan is also significant. Figure 5.1 provides an overview of the location of traditional berry sites in relation to the main twentieth-century Gitksan and Witsuwit'en villages.[2]

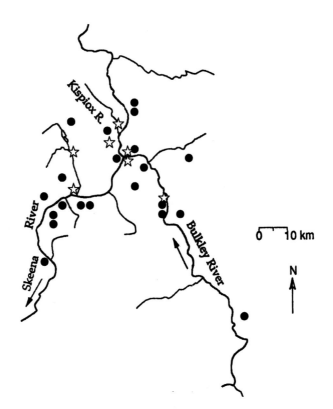

Figure 5.1 Location of traditional berry sites in relation to the main twentieth century Gitksan and Witsuwit'en villages Berry patches are represented by filled circles, and village locations by stars.

Management of berry patches

The importance of black huckleberries in the traditional economy and the high value placed on the fruit meant that berry patches were an extremely important kind of place or ecotope, and were important properties of House/ Clan groups. In the absence of management for early successional stages by periodic burning, huckleberry patches become unproductive over time (Johnson 1999; Turner 1999; Trusler 2002).

Burning was undertaken in the spring or in early fall, when the huckleberry patches could be safely burned without starting a conflagration (Johnson 1999). Timing of burning varies between sites and with species, and would be integrated into the seasonal round of the local people. Black huckleberry sites, particularly those at higher elevation, were often burned in the fall, while lowbush blueberry sites and low-elevation huckleberry sites would be burned in spring, or just before a rain.

A burn that was too hot would destroy the duff layer and the huckleberry rhizomes, while too mild a burn would not remove competing vegetation nor effectively stimulate vigorous new stem growth. Roles and responsibilities associated with huckleberry management were aspects of territory management shaped by the reciprocity between different clans, especially those of husbands and wives. Berry patch burns were suppressed by the BC Forest Service in the 1930s and 1940s, and have not been successfully reintroduced in the region, despite interest by both First Nations and the Forest Service (Johnson 1999).

Scott Trusler (Trusler 2002; Trusler and Johnson 2008) attempted to estimate the quantity of black huckleberries required before alteration of the local traditional economy by colonists and traders. Based on historical population estimates (from Ray 1985 and Mills 1994, in Trusler 2002:53) and estimates of historic consumption figures per capita (discussed in Trusler 2002:52), Trusler believes that total combined harvests for the Gitksan and Wet'suwet'en were in excess of 400,000 US gallons (approximately 1.6 million litres) per year, including berries harvested for domestic consumption, feasts, and trade. His estimate is based on a number of assumptions regarding the extrapolation of population figures from archival sources discussed by Ray (1985) and Mills (1994), as well as a series of assumptions, also based on historical figures, about the observed magnitude of berry harvests in the nineteenth and early twentieth centuries. Trusler stresses that the values arrived at must therefore be regarded as indicative of the magnitude of aboriginal harvest, but cannot be considered definitive.[3] Average black huckleberry yield figures based on research by Don Minore of the US Forest Service were 827 L/hectare; thus a harvest of the inferred magnitude would have required nearly 2,000 hectares of productive huckleberry area per year for the Gitksan and Witsuwit'en (Trusler 2002).

The need for large quantities of huckleberries for the feasthall provided an important impetus for management of the berry resource in the past. The current lack of huckleberry management has made it difficult for First Nations to access sufficient quantities of berries for customary purposes and poses a challenge to the traditional use of huckleberries for ceremonial purposes in the feasthall. Furthermore, the lack of management at the House territory level creates an additional barrier to cultural use of this species when House groups are not able to locate harvestable quantities of berries within their House territories and must seek access to berries on the territories of other House groups.

The ecology of berry patches

Black huckleberries are a medium height shrub that forms patches, spreading by underground rhizomes. They tolerate a wide range of environments in northwest British Columbia, but thrive in sunny sites with somewhat acidic soil. Though they are long-lived, they are not tall, and are easily overtopped by willows, aspens, young coniferous trees and the like. Once overtopped, they persist for very long times, but are stunted, spindly, and fruit sparsely or not at all. The experience of someone who walks or hikes extensively in northwest British Columbia will reveal that productive berry patches are not widely and evenly dispersed across the landscape. In contemporary northwest British Columbia, productive and accessible berry patches are often found in timber cuts, which are of course managed to replace growing coniferous trees as quickly as possible, resulting in shifting and ephemeral berry resources. Huckleberries can be found throughout the Interior Cedar-Hemlock Bio-geoclimatic Zone from elevations near the valley bottoms to near timberline. The British Columbia Ministry of Forests funded some research into berry productivity and autecology in an effort to better understand which sites might be best suited to huckleberries (Burton 1998; Wintergreen Consultants 2001a, 2001b). Scott Trusler and I both sought to explore Gitksan and Witsuwit'en understanding of the ecology of berry patches, reasoning that the peoples who had harvested and depended upon black huckleberry and other culturally important fruit species might have a depth and subtlety of knowledge unlikely to be arrived at by relative newcomers through a few limited studies.

Ethnoecology of berry patches

While doing research on Gitksan and Witsuwit'en ethnobotany, I recorded information about aboriginal burning, and on the harvest and processing of berries (Johnson 1997, 1999). During that research, a number of specific berry patches were mentioned, several specific berry patch locations were referred to by name, and narratives of berry patch burns and late summer traditional berry camps were shared. When I returned to the region in the late 1990s to focus on landscape ethnoecology, I asked again about berry patch locations and names to elucidate local understanding of a key cultural ecotope. At about the same time, Scott Trusler was doing field research on Gitksan and Witsuwit'en berry ecology and was working closely with the Office of the Witsuwit'en, the local Witsuwit'en hereditary chiefs' office. Trusler's approach was complementary to mine, and involved a series of visits to known historic berry patches to characterize their ecology, and look for evidence of cultural features and past management. (See Trusler 2002 for a full exposition of Trusler's methods and findings.)

Berry patches I first heard about were on the slopes of the mountains, from mid-slope to near timberline. Older Gitksan men and women recalled travelling to berry patches along well-kept trails, accompanying older family members to well-known places on dedicated berry picking trips. There are words in Gitxsanimax̱/Gitksenimkx̱ for "berry camp" and "berry trail" (see Table 3.1). Elders recalled prolonged trips to high-elevation berry camps in the company of a large group of people, as in the late Olive Ryan's (Gwaans) account of her Grandmother Sigidimnaḵ Ha'naamuux̱ (Fanny Johnson) leading the people of Andimaul across the new railroad bridge at Skeena Crossing and up to her berry patch **Kslawt** in the early years of the twentieth century when Olive was a girl. People camped in the subalpine berry patch for a couple of weeks, picking and caching their berries before cooking them down to jam in large cedar bentwood boxes, and then drying them on berry racks (**skeex̱sin**) to make the large rolled berry cakes. This berry patch is on the mountain massif now called Rocher de Boule just behind South Hazelton. When Olive was a grown woman, she used to ascend the mountains across the Skeena River from the village of Gitwingax̱ to pick berries. By this time berries were preserved by canning, and large parties no longer spent a week or two in a single berry camp, but went on short one- or two-night trips, carrying down the fresh berries to be processed in the village. There were still maintained trails to these patches, which also had names (see below).

Two other elders, the parents of the present Sim'oogit Dinim Gyet of Gitwingaḵ also told me about berry patches on the mountain across from where I lived. Art Mathews Senior (Sim'oogit Tsii Wa) and his wife Kathleen recalled how the berry patches had been burned in the fall when the men were ascending to the alpine zone to hunt mountain goats, and explained to me how that service was related to the House structure and reciprocity. (See Johnson 1997 and 1999 for more detail.) Art had himself participated in a berry patch burn on this mountain when he was a young man. When I returned to this research in the mid 1990s, Art Jr., Dinim Gyet talked to me about the locations of the named berry patches on his territory, the trail net, and the relationship of these sites to other properties of the House territory, including the goat hunting camp, the groundhog (marmot) hunting area, places to gather medicines, the summer fish camp, and the boundary with the adjacent Frog (**_Ganeda_**) territory. These sites were also all mid- to high-elevation sites.

Visiting in Moricetown and speaking with the late Pat Namox (Wah'tah'kwets) and his wife Lucy (Goohlat) talked to me about huckleberry patches, at lower elevation on the low rolling hills behind Moricetown, and on the timing of burning, also in fall but carefully timed to be just before a rain. Pat explained:

> Before it was going to rain they would burn the hill behind Moricetown, down to Dowdie. The old people knew when it was going to rain. They *hear* it. Not for shower. Maybe 2 days in advance. My uncle knew. That's when they burn up the hill. The rain put the fire out. Burn up just one side. [They would burn for] all kinds of berries. (L.M. Johnson interview notes August 8, 1991)

Lowbush blueberry sites I had heard about were at low elevation, and were perhaps managed by spring burning. Those near Hazelton had been eliminated by the conversion of the landscape to farms and pastures, and by the cessation of management; several trips to the Upper Skeena above Euro-Canadian settlement in fall 2005 and 2006 revealed how rich the lowbush blueberry resource must have been on the wide low flats by the rivers.

Although I had learned about a number of formerly harvested and managed black huckleberry patches and a smaller number of areas in which lowbush blueberry had been harvested, and recorded peoples' recollections about their management by burning, I had done no "ground truthing". I had only once, years before I began to record information about traditional berry patches, walked through a traditional black huckleberry berry patch, and I had made only casual observations of the site, beyond the fact that berry bushes were sparse, and little fruit was in evidence. I had never attempted to climb the thickly forested mountain slopes or find remnants of old trails to see what those sites were like some fifty to eighty years after the cessation of active management. I had in fact never pondered what made a site suitable for berries in the first place, nor how one might recognize such a site.

Characterizing black huckleberry patch sites

After working with the hereditary Chiefs, the Strategic Watershed Analysis Team (a Gitksan resource management consulting group), and the Office of the Wet'suwet'en, Trusler had learned about a number of historically used black huckleberry patches in the Bulkley and Skeena River drainages. Trusler made site visits to several of these, and finally selected six areas for more detailed ecological and fire history analysis (Trusler 2002; Trusler and Johnson 2008). Three sites were in Witsuwit'en territory near Moricetown, and three sites were in Gitksan territory near Hazelton and Kispiox. Study site elevations ranged from valley bottom to timberline, and both slope and aspect were variable (Trusler and Johnson 2008, Table 1). In addition to slope and aspect, the current vegetation and soil characteristics, fire history, and cultural heritage features, of all six berry patches were described and compared (Trusler 2002). The diversity of these sites in terms of ecological parameters was striking. Some sites were substantially different from the "ideal" huckleberry site type that had been determined through autecological research on *Vaccinium membranaceum* (Burton 1998). Yet all had been important traditional black huckleberry sites. It became apparent that low-elevation sites such as Bek'et Digii Ts'ooyiin, a site in the Bulkley Valley near Moricetown, have cool north or east aspects, making them relatively moist and cool sites for their valley bottom location, while high-elevation sites such as La̲x Ansa Matsa were found to have relatively warm aspects, giving them a longer growing season than other high-elevation sites. Selection of berry patch sites, then, appeared to be quite sophisticated, showing an understanding of what the huckleberry plants need to thrive, rather than using simple heuristics like aspect, slope position and elevation.

The six studied berry patches showed the following pattern: the two low-elevation sites had cool aspects, and had undergone succession to mature deciduous or coniferous growth. These sites ranged from about 400-600 m. The mid-elevation sites had predominantly warm aspects and ranged from about 600-1000 m, while high-elevation sites ranged from about 1000 m to 1300 m, and favoured warm aspects. Slopes tended to be steep on mid-elevation sites, and succession to dense coniferous growth or a mixture of coniferous and deciduous forest was typical. High-elevation sites were more rolling, and were characterized by an open scrub/conifer mosaic, commensurate with much shorter growing seasons and slower succession at higher elevations.

Other known berry patches

Although equally detailed information for other known berry patch sites in Gitksan and Witsuwit'en territories is lacking, the general range of characteristics seen in these six study sites seems to be consistent with the available information for other known historic berry patches. Several of these sites were surveyed by Trusler in a cursory manner as part of his initial field reconnaissance. Others were described in ethnographic interviews. High-elevation sites with warm aspects include Kslaawt, Anxsi 'Maa'y Litisxw, and Fiddler Creek. Grouse Mountain near Houston in the Bulkley Valley is a high-elevation rolling plateau site. En Tookw is a low-elevation site, and two other sites on Dinim Gyet's territory west of Gitwingak represent mid-elevation sites. Trusler found that two other low-elevation sites near Moricetown in the Bulkley Valley (Ooniin'aay and Decen Det'ekw)[4] were very similar to Bek'it Digii Ts'ooyin.

Huckleberry Harvest in the Seasonal Round

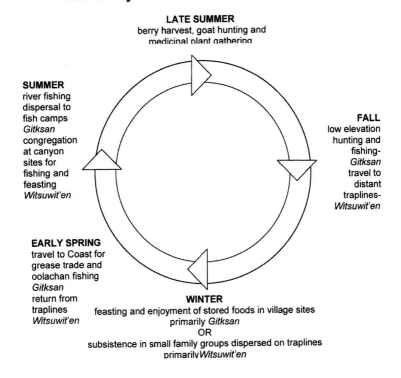

LATE SUMMER
berry harvest, goat hunting and medicinal plant gathering

SUMMER
river fishing dispersal to fish camps
Gitksan
congregation at canyon sites for fishing and feasting
Witsuwit'en

FALL
low elevation hunting and fishing-
Gitksan
travel to distant traplines-
Witsuwit'en

EARLY SPRING
travel to Coast for grease trade and oolachan fishing
Gitksan
return from traplines
Witsuwit'en

WINTER
feasting and enjoyment of stored foods in village sites primarily *Gitksan*
OR
subsistence in small family groups dispersed on traplines primarily *Witsuwit'en*

Figure 5.2 Seasonal round of the Gitksan and Witsuwit'en

In order to understand the criteria for selecting a berry patch site we need to think both of spatial aspects of berry harvest and seasonal timing. Some of the Elders' stories about berry patches situate their use in the context of the range of seasonal activities, and the places that these occur. The huckleberry harvest, as it occurs in mid to late summer, overlaps both summer salmon fishing and processing along the main rivers, and the late summer harvest of alpine resources, especially groundhogs and mountain goats. The grease trade with the people of the Coast occurred in late winter, between the winter feast season and the onset of summer fishing. The diagram in Figure 5.2 shows the Gitksan annual cycle with feasting in the winter, and the contrasting Witsuwit'en pattern with feasting in the summer when people came together to harvest the salmon at Moricetown or Hagwilget, a pattern similar to northern Athapaskans, who frequently gathered at fish lakes in the summer season. After the fishing and feast season, Witsuwit'en then dispersed to their winter hunting and trapping areas, which could be up to 200 km from the fishing sites at Hagwilget, known in Witsuwit'en as Tsë Cakh, 'under the rock', or Moricetown, which was traditionally called Kyah Wiget.[5]

In contrast, Gitksan fisheries are scattered at a number of locations along the Skeena mainstem and its tributaries that belong to different House groups. In the past, large log traps in canyons with rapid currents were combined with more upstream weirs and basket traps. Since the early twentieth century War of the Barricades (Galois 1993-1994; Daly 2005), the Gitksan have fished at a number of eddy sites with gillnets and at Kisgega'as with dipnets. The key difference is that the Gitksan summer fishery was dispersed, and people congregated again in the villages in the fall and winter.

Once the fish are caught, they must be processed immediately, because they spoil quickly in the warm weather of summer. In both Gitksan and Witsuwit'en ideology, waste of fish is a serious violation of respect, and will result in failure of future fish runs (Gottesfeld 1994c). Preserving this rich and temporally restricted harvest for winter is the major focus of the midsummer for both groups. Traditional fish processing is labour-intensive and the fish needs constant attention until it is fully dried and can be stored away.

Low- to mid-elevation huckleberry patches such as Bek'et Digii Ts'ooyiin, Decen Det'ekw, Ooniin'ay and Sool Nii were sites that could be reached by a day's journey from Moricetown, to take advantage of the first berries while completing the harvesting and processing of the spring salmon and sockeye runs at Moricetown. Access to these sites would allow fresh berries to be served at Witsuwit'en summer potlatches. These sites were located within the Laksilyu territory of Utakghit.

Cultural contexts specific to berry patches

In this section I present information on the relationship of selected berry patches and other resource sites in greater detail. The first six sites were Trusler's ecological study sites (Trusler 2002).

Bek'et Degii Ts'ooyiin. The name means 'we pick huckleberry on it' (Dan Michell, pers. comm. 2005); *"degii"* [*digi*][6] is the Witsuwit'en word for black huckleberry (Johnson-Gottesfeld and Hargus 1998). This low-elevation site was historically one of the most important sites for the people of Moricetown/Kyah Wiget. It is accessible by road along the Bulkley Valley, and was located on an important historic trail linking Kyah Wiget with the Gitksan village of Gitsegukla. Two other significant lower-elevation huckleberry patches were also along this trail (Trusler 2002:74). Bek'et Degii Ts'ooyin was the first site within the local territory to have ripe fruit, owing to its low elevation. Apparently this site was used until about the 1960s, when forest succession depressed berry productivity.

Sool Nii (Reiseter Ridge). The Sool Nii site is located on a southwest facing slope along the Telkwa Highroad, which follows the route of a major regional trail along the East side of the Bulkley River. This berry patch is about 10 km south of Kyah Wiget, and shows a range of elevations and contemporary vegetation, ranging from areas presently dominated by aspen below 750 m, with seral pine on the upper slopes. The lower areas yielded primarily saskatoons (*Amelanchier alnifolia*) while the upper area was a productive huckleberry site. Ethnographic data indicates this whole area was a very important berry gathering area for the Witsuwit'en (Trusler 2002:82, 90), though usage declined after forced removal for the Wet'suwet'en from their historic winter village at Glentanna (Trusler 2002:96).

Harold Price. This site was discovered primarily by cultural evidence on site, as there is no ethnographic evidence of picking in the area for the past 90 years. The site is on a montane slope now largely dominated by western hemlock in the upper Harold Price Creek (Ses Kwe[7]) drainage. On the slope in the successional hemlock stand evidence of an abandoned berry camp was found, including the remnants of berry racks stacked against a tree, and sighting of another camp was reported in the 1980s that had cedar bentwood berry boxes and assembled berry racks (Trusler 2002:110). The Harold Price

(Ses Kwe) site is located among a number of other culturally significant sites, including a coho salmon fishing site 8 km upstream, a winter camp, and a winter whitefish site, and is adjacent to a clearly marked trail near the south end of the berry area. A winter village was also reported approximately 15 km from the coho fishing site. Although no oral histories of recent use have been recorded, archaeological and ecological evidence, together with proximity to a major historic trail route linking Babine Lake with the Skeena River system, suggest a formerly quite important site. Scars indicating collection of hemlock cambium, another important traditional carbohydrate food (Gottesfeld 1995; People of Ksan 1980), also indicate heavy use of the area approximately 100 years ago (Trusler 2002:111).

Stakaiyt and Lax Ansa Maatsa. These sites are found on the territories of Gutginuxw (*Delgamuukw vs. the Queen*, exhibit 609) and are across the Skeena River from the Gitksan village of Kispiox, near Pinenut Creek on Sidina ("Caribou") Mountain. They are montane, relatively high-elevation sites with warm aspects (Stakaiyt sites) or are relatively flat-lying (Lax Ansa Maatsa). They have been important berry patches for quite a long time. Traditional trails traverse the area that are connected to the major trail extending up the east bank of the Skeena River to Kisgega'as, a very important fishing site and settlement at the confluence of the Skeena and Babine Rivers. Numerous fishing sites are found along both sides of the Skeena River in this area (Johnson 1998). Extensive ethnographic and interview data (Trusler 2002; Gottesfeld 1994b) attest to historic use and management of the area. Berry camps and message trees are found along these trails near historic berry patches (Trusler 2002:128-129; Johnson personal observation, 1985). Evidence of collection of cedar bark, used in lashing berry racks and making mats and baskets, is also found in the area (Trusler 2002:130). Hunting grounds for mountain goat and, historically, woodland caribou (*Rangifer tarandus caribou*) are found in the alpine areas of the mountain above the berry sites. Other nearby berry sites and a major village site were also found slightly to the north of these sites (Sampson and Abel Brown, cited in Trusler 2002:139).

Other berry patches

Blue Lake (Stic'odinkhlh Bin). Blue Lake is a higher-elevation gathering area near Hazelton. This site is about a day's travel from the other main Witsuwit'en village, Hagwilget (Tsë Cakh). Later in the season, higher-elevation areas yielding a variety of resources could be reached by carefully constructed trails. Black huckleberries, mountain goats, fall medicines, and the rhizomes of spiny wood fern, another important carbohydrate food which could be stored for winter, were present in the Blue Lake area, and elders from Hagwilget have shared stories about harvesting trips in late summer to the Blue Lake area (The Hagwilget [Tse-Kya] People 1995; L.M. Johnson interview notes).

The late Maryann Austin (also known as Maryann Alec) said:

> They used to go in the summertime, in the last of August to pick berries. Young people they hunt goats all around Blue Lakes, around the ridges. No creek flow out of the lake. I saw that when they walked across the valley from the berry camp to retrieve the goat that was shot.[8] They kill goat. They throw it down. We skin it all. Pack all that meat up to camp. Five. Hang meat on stick over fire. Squeeze berries. Cook potatoes and rice. Invite a lot of people to eat. Serve first, eat after. That was four or five years ago now, I guess. We used to use pack horse to go up there. Two hours we get up there [from Hagwilget]. (L.M. Johnson interview notes February 6, 1990)

More recently, huckleberries have been harvested from a clear cut about halfway up the mountain along the access trail.

Dinim Gyet's territory. The Wilson Creek Wolf Clan (La̱x Gibuu) territory west of Kitwanga has a number of berry patches and other resource sites, as mentioned briefly above. Dinim Gyet (Art Mathews Jr.), a Gitksan La̱x Gibuu chief from Gitwinga̱k, has explained the locations of some key resource sites on his territory (Johnson 2000), and his father and mother described management of berry patches by burning in this area (Johnson 1999). Figure 5.3 shows part of the mountain called Enjegwas. In the centre of the photo is a berry patch, Win Luu Mesxw, which is connected by trail to other sites, berry patches, and lower down, the fishing site at Wilson Creek on the Skeena River. Above it was a traditional groundhog (hoary marmot) site, and a territory boundary at Ensidelaks is marked, part of the social structure of resource harvesting and localities. Downslope beyond the lower left corner of the photo is the main fish camp for this territory, and other high-elevation resource sites such as a goat-hunting area were reached by another trail system from the fish camp at Wilson Creek. Wilson Creek is

Figure 5.3 A portion of Dinim Gyet's territory showing resource sites, trail location, and territory boundary near Wilson Creek, Xso Gwingoohl; note berry patch Win Luu Mesx in centre of photo, near a rock bluff

one of the highly productive fishing areas along the Skeena River. Dinim Gyet has a smokehouse and cabin there, and conducts commercial beach seining for sockeye in the fishing areas nearby. The smokehouse site is also the place where Art's father was born in 1913, showing the continuing relationships to territory maintained by marriage over the generations. As Gitksan are matrilineal and Clan exogamous, Art Senior was not Chief of the territory on which he was born; he was a Frog (Ganeda, Sim'oogit Tsii Wa)—his mother's crest, not a Wolf. As "father's side" (*wilksiwitxw*) he participated in burning one of the berry patches on his wife's territory when he was a young man. Tsii wa described this experience in 1990:

> Just the berries, that's why they burned.
> Where they are getting goats up on the mountain, close to where they get their meat [they burn]. Not on the flat. When they start to hunt in September, close to where they get the meat.
> They told the Forestry, "There's no timber way up the mountain. We burn the bushes, that's all. Burn them and look after them."
> When we left from our camp we didn't put the fire out. We left it. When we go up the mountain the fire is coming after us.
> (L.M. Johnson interview notes December 11, 1990)

This brief description sets the season, emphasizes stewardship as the reason for burning, indicates responses to the interference of the Forestry officials, and shows the spatial and seasonal linkage to other resources on the mountain area described by Dinim Gyet several years later.

Shandilla area. About 10 km upstream of Wilson Creek in the immediate area of the village of Kitwanga, there are another series of trails and traditional berry patches in the area generally referred to as "Shandilla" (Xsa Andilgan[9], 'Beaver Dam Creek'). Gitksan land-use researcher Art Loring and the late Ray Morgan helped to mark trail and berry patch locations on the 1:50,000 topographic maps (Figure 5.4). Narrative accounts of berry harvesting in the Shandilla area were recorded from the late Olive Ryan and Gertie Watson (L.M. Johnson field notes). Management by burning was also described for these sites, along with post-management forest succession. Although at relatively high elevation, these sites were harvested in the mid twentieth century by overnight trips from Kitwanga, and the fruit brought back to the village for processing. This allowed access to berries while fishing occurred at sites along the Skeena mainstem near the village. It is likely that these trails also

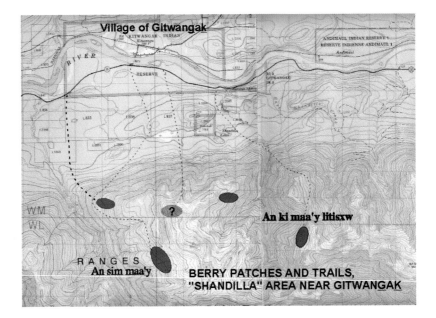

Figure 5.4 Map of Shandilla area

access various alpine resources such as mountain goat, and perhaps in the past woodland caribou. Two sites were named An Sim Ma'ay ("Real Huckleberry on It," an#sim#/m'aay 'on it'# 'true or real'# 'berry') and An Ki Ma'ay Litisxw ("Blue Grouse's Berry on It"). Comparison of photographs taken in ca. 1899 and in 2001 (Figures 5.5a and b) reveals the extensive forest succession on the slopes of the Shandilla area. Olive alluded to forest succession when I asked about the sites. "Big tree now," she told me in the mid 1990s. Her son James had gone up to see the site at An Ki Maa'y Litisxw and found mature forest.

It is likely that maintenance of productive early-successional sites at high elevation through burning may have affected other resources than the berries. Perhaps grouse abundance was increased by greater fruit production, for example. "Blue Grouse's Berry on It" may commemorate this relationship. Mountain goats too may respond to the browse offered by huckleberry bushes, creating a sort of synergy between different resources that may all be enhanced by human management, and accessed from the same trails. Narratives by elders talk about mixed trips, where men may go goat hunting and/ or burn the berry patch, while women may be picking at a higher-elevation productive berry patch. (L.M. Johnson field notes).

Kslaawt. This is the large berry patch area accessed from the missionary village of Andimaul in the early years of this century. Kslaawt ("Underneath") belonged to Sigidimnak Ha'namuux. As the late Olive Ryan described, the area was used by many people, and the berry picking lasted several weeks. A fuller account of berry picking on this site is given in Johnson 1997. The site was apparently a relatively high-elevation site up Juniper Creek in the Rocher de Boule massif. The area would also have offered medicinal plants and mountain goats.

Succession on berry patches

Trusler's fieldwork revealed what had happened to the formerly productive berry sites in the seventy-odd years since cessation of active management. Low-elevation sites such as Bek'et Digii Ts'ooyiin and Decen Det'ekw have succeeded to deciduous woodland or conifer (pine) stands which have little remaining *Vaccinium* cover, and no fruit production. The area of Bek'et Digii Ts'ooyiin was apparently last used for huckleberry picking in the 1950s (Sam Wilson of Moricetown, pers. comm. to Trusler). The name Decen Det'ekw ('burnt stick') recalls the importance of berry patch burning.

Figure 5.5a Comparison of ca. 1899 and 2001 photos of Shandilla area from Gitwinga<u>k</u>: view of Shandilla area, circa 1899 Image number PN12106, Royal British Columbia Museum.

Figure 5.5b View of Shandilla area, 2001 Note complete forest cover below timberline on slopes of higher mountain in the recent photo.

On the Harold Price/upper Ses Kwe site, the mid-elevation area has succeeded to a dense productive western hemlock forest. Remnant huckleberry on the site is diminutive, and does not flower or fruit. Although now completely forested, Trusler found that there was no evidence of a pre-existing forest stand, such as down logs or snags, to corroborate its former open state. A dense productive conifer stand has also developed at the mid-elevation portion of the Stakaiyt site. This is probably the situation for An Ki Maa'y Litisxw near Gitwingak as well, judging from Olive Ryan's description.

In general, high-elevation sites have largely remained more open, forming a conifer-shrub mosaic. In the absence of burning, fire-tolerant *Vaccinium membranaceum* is being overtopped by more fire-sensitive species such as fool's huckleberry (*Menziesia ferruginea*, an Ericaceous shrub that does not produce berries), and sometimes highbush blueberry (*Vaccinium ovalifolium*), whose more watery and acidic fruits are not preferred by Gitksan and Witsuwet'en berry pickers. The upper portion of Stakaiyt on Caribou Mountain, Lax Ansa Maatsa, and sites at Grouse Mountain and Fiddler Creek exemplify this successional pathway. The slower pace of succession and conifer establishment, and the shorter growing season on the upper montane and subalpine slopes result in persistent open-structured plant communities where *V. membranaceum* can persist but loses productivity over time.

Because it is rhizomatous, *Vaccinium membranaceum* can persist for decades under low light conditions. However, such clones may be so weakened by the time the canopy is removed that they are not competitive with early seral herbs and scrub vegetation, and the huckleberry patch may not regenerate. Plants growing in higher light conditions grow vigorously, though they do not always fruit productively. They do survive light burning well, producing vigourous sprouts from the rhizomes when the above-ground stems are killed (Minore 1972).

Ethnoecology

There is linguistic evidence for the significance of berry patch ecology and management in local ethnoecology. The only term recorded denoting ecological succession that I recorded from Gitksan speakers in my landscape research was the term **maaxsgan**, which was translated for me as "too much brush on the berry patch". This suggests that tracking successional status on berry patches and responding to brushiness were important. The berry patch itself is called **ansimaa'y** in Gitxsanimax. In Wet'suwet'en, the berry patch is **nit'ay k'ët**. No Witsuwit'en language term for 'brush on the berry patch' has yet been recorded, though I have recorded terms for "a brushy place you can't walk through, jungle" and for "a burned place" (Johnson and Hargus 2007; this text, Chapter 4).

The broad issue of how berry patches or potential berry patches are conceived of, or recognized as, kinds of place or ecotopes is an important ethnoecological question. I have sought to elucidate Gitksan and Witsuwit'en knowledge of environment and habitat through linguistic research focusing on place kind terminology (Johnson 1997, 2000; this text, Chapters 3 and 4) following on earlier work by Eugene Hunn (Hunn with James Selam and family 1990; Hunn and Meilleur 1992, 1998). Examining the influence of the biophysical environment itself (if we concede this to be separable from human societies) and the nature of the economy and social system of different cultural groups on their characterization of their environment, sheds light on the diverse ways human beings conceive of their lived worlds. Such understandings have implications for considering the relationships of local human groups to their homelands, and the co-management of resources in these areas, an important contemporary issue in many parts of the world.

This extended examination of one Gitksan and Witsuwit'en ecotope—the berry patch—demonstrates that not all ecotopes can be characterized solely by biophysical characteristics; some kinds, such as berry patches, also require consideration of human geography and culture. Proximity to village sites, fishing sites and/or alpine resources, and major trails or other access routes are all involved in the selection of sites for management as berry patches. It is also impossible to consider traditional berry patches without acknowledging the traditional social and political structure—the House/Clan territory system—as the context for use and management of berry patches.

The fact that a wide array of sites potentially support black huckleberry, while only some of these will in fact receive human management, is reminiscent of the kinds of decisions other indigenous groups make about manipulating vegetation or promoting growth of specific species for human use. In this it is similar to the approach to vegetation management described by Alcorn (1981), where she found that the type of manipulation of species by Huastec farmers depended on the context in which the species occurred, its usefulness and other potential sources of the same species or resource.

Another aspect of managing diverse sites for black huckleberry may be related to minimizing risk. If late frost destroys the flowers of a high-elevation patch, for example, possibly the fruit will still be good in a warmer lower elevation site. Or in a year of prolonged summer drought, possibly the cool, moist high-elevation sites will still be productive even if low-elevations sites fail to fruit. Gitksan and Witsuwit'en use of a range of sites that have differing responses to climatic variation buffers climate and weather events, and serves as a resilience mechanism (cf. Colding et al. 2003).

"Berry patch" is a concept that is easily recognized in the ethnoecology of other northwestern indigenous peoples. (See Thornton 1999, 2007; Deur and Turner 2005 and authors therein, among others.) McDonald (2005:245-246) presents intriguing evidence for management of montane berry resources, including *V. membranaceum* and other *Vaccinium* species by the Kitsumkalum people, an interior Tsimshian group just west of the Gitksan on the lower Skeena River. The significance of constructed infrastructure in facilitating access and management of these sought-after high-elevation berries is particularly highlighted in McDonald's account, as are the consequences of disruptions to access and maintenance activities. Black huckleberry patches were maintained by burning and by rotation of use areas in other parts of its range, in ways that seem very similar to the way that Gitksan and Witsuwit'en historically managed their berry patches (N. Turner 1999; Gottesfeld 1994b; Ross 1999). In particular, the description of early twentieth-century burning of high-elevation berry grounds in the Gifford Pinchot National Forest in southern Washington state (Mack 2001; Mack and McClure 2002), and the ethnographic data on the use and management of high-elevation berry sites by Sto:lo (Lepofsky et al. 2005) are very similar to what Trusler and I have reconstructed for the Gitksan and Witsuwit'en (Trusler and Johnson 2008). Nancy Turner (1999) has also documented widespread management of black huckleberry by burning in British Columbia. In some ways, the concept of the "berry patch" ecotope has resonances with orchards and root gardens, as ecological types defined and managed by people, integrated into their economies, and produced or maintained by their agency.

Another aspect of berry patches that bears consideration is their status as owned properties. Richardson (1982) discussed the relationship of various resources in the northern Northwest Coast area, which by extension reaches up the rivers into Gitksan and Witsuwit'en territories. Richardson contends, following earlier discussion of Dyson-Hudson and Smith in 1978, that

> A territorial system is most likely under conditions of high density and predictability of critical resources . . . If a resource is so abundant that its availability or rate of capture is not in any way limiting

to a population, then there is no benefit to be gained by its defence and territoriality is not expected to occur. (Dyson-Hudson and Smith 1978:25)

Richardson comments that where resources are very widely distributed and abundant, they are unlikely to be subjected to access limitations. However, resources that are spatially and temporally limited may be worth controlling access, and enhancing through management.[10] He writes:

The resources most frequently subject to access restrictions on the Northwest Coast were predictable and abundant, but also *geographically restricted* to limited areas or *patches*. This third variable of resource patchiness was not explicitly included in the economic defensibility model, but seems essential to explaining resource control patterns on the Northwest Coast. (Richardson 1982:95, emphasis added)

Later in the same article he writes:

The geographical and *temporal* restrictions of resources put a premium on management of both resources and labor. In this situation the tightly organized unilineal kinship groups should perhaps be expected . . . The factor of patchiness would also be important in an analysis of resource exploitation emphasizing organization of labor and change in seasonal settlement. (Richardson 1982:108, emphasis added)

While I find the optimal foraging language and deterministic analysis a bit uncomfortable, the realities of resource distribution and the need for mobilization of social resources to enable their effective use are clear. In a social and economic perspective, then, ownership of berry patches, and regulation of the timing and frequency of harvest and management activities, is an effective strategy to conserve these resources and contribute to the stability of the economy of House groups. Similar types of resource patch ownership and management is reported by authors in Deur and Turner 2005 for a range of resources—root patches, berry patches, crabapple trees—and ownership and access limitation for shellfish resources is also reported (Moss 1993).[11]

In conclusion, one cannot characterize traditional berry patches in the Hazelton area solely in terms of biophysical characteristics. In Northwest BC, the ecological amplitude of *Vaccinium membranaceum* is wide, but it is not persistent as a productive vegetation type in the absence of a fire regime with a relatively short return interval, which here can only be produced by human management. The human management regime helps to create convergent ecological characteristics in diverse sites to create optimal conditions for black huckleberry growth. Maintenance of (relative) predictability in quality and quantity of resource was important for the viability of the aboriginal economy, as black huckleberry harvest was a major focus of the traditional harvesting cycle. A key characteristic of the known managed Gitksan and Witsuwit'en berry patches Trusler and I have examined is their proximity to village sites, fishing sites, and significant access trails to the alpine zone. The siting of berry patches, therefore, reflects human geography, spatial, seasonal and social patterning of movement and resource harvest, and the effort of human managers from the appropriate social groups to look after and maintain their berry patches.

The ecological characterization of traditional berry patch localities revealed a wide range of site characteristics such as elevation and aspect, and post-management successional pathways. The actual siting of the berry patches appears to be strongly related to the traditional seasonal round—berry patches were areas that could fit into the annual cycle of harvesting activities. As I have discussed, the Gitksan and Witsuwit'en are both groups with a highly developed territory system that shapes access to land areas according to Clan and House groupings within the community, which requires that each House or Clan group have a reasonable range of resource areas for the most important resources such as salmon and huckleberries.

6

Lookouts, Moose Licks, and Fish Lakes

CONSIDERING KASKA UNDERSTANDING OF THE LAND

In this chapter I shift attention from the productive inner Coast Mountains and plateau country of northwestern British Columbia, to the boreal forests of northernmost British Columbia and the southwest Yukon, and the Athapaskan speaking peoples who live there. These people are known as Kaska, or Kaska Dena, a term that originally applied to peoples living around what is now called Dease Lake in the Cassiar Mountains of British Columbia (a name apparently derived from the same root as the name of the people). The picture of Kaska ethnoecology I present here is garnered from experiences travelling on and talking about land with Kaska people in the southeast Yukon Territory (Figure 6.1), especially in the area of Watson Lake. My research combines analysis of Kaska and English terminology, and narrative and practice, with use of visual methods. By using this "shotgun" approach, I have sought complementary evidence from different aspects of Kaska life in order to gain multifaceted appreciation of Kaska understanding of and interaction with the Land.

As a prelude to more fully describing Kaska understanding of the land, I describe past Kaska relationship to the land. Until recently, the Kaska

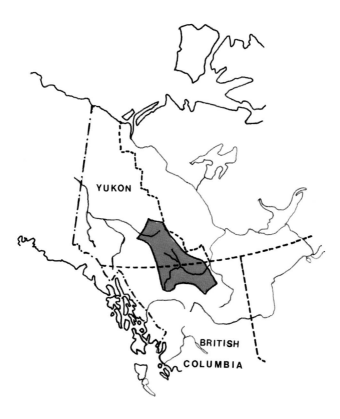

Figure 6.1 Generalized map of Kaska territory

moved around a great deal through the seasons and from year to year, fishing, trapping, hunting, and picking berries in season. At least during the historic period, families tended to have particular hunting and trapping areas that they used over prolonged periods of time, fallowing them as needed (cf. Weinstein 1992). Like other northern Dene people, before the advent of white traders the Kaska came together in the summers at lakes with fish runs, to catch whitefish and to socialize, and dispersed into small family groups for much of the year. Some time after World War I, Kaska shifted to congregating at trading posts in summer, and this is what anthropologist John Honigmann experienced when he did fieldwork in Lower Post, British Columbia in the mid 1940s (Honigmann 1949; Weinstein 1992).

Flexibility in use of areas likely was mediated by kin relations, allowing movement between different family areas for winter hunting and trapping, in response to the abundance of animals or for personal preferences. Many aspects of Kaska life have changed since the construction of the Alaska Highway, the establishment of the town of Watson Lake, and the construction of housing for Band members at Watson Lake, Upper Liard, and Lower Post. Contemporary Kaska people are generally year-round residents of the modern communities rather than spending much of the year on the trapline or in camps on the land. However, they are often out on the land for short trips, especially in the summer season, and many have traplines and line cabins at considerable distances from their nominal permanent residences.

Before the construction of the Alaska highway in the 1940s, the main access into the Kaska territory was up the Mackenzie-Liard-Dease River systems, along which ran river boats, and up the Pelly River (a tributary of the Yukon) to Finlayson Lake, and from there down the Frances. Early contact centred on Fort Halkett, on the Liard River not far above the Grand Canyon at the confluence of the Smith River (Karamanski 1983). Robert Campbell established short-lived posts on Frances Lake and at Pelly Banks in the mid nineteenth century. A trading post was re-established in the late nineteenth century and remained a feature of Frances Lake until the mid twentieth century. In the 1870s there was a gold rush in the Cassiar District near Dease Lake in northern BC, pre-figuring the 1898 Klondike gold rush (Dawson 1987). Associated with the Cassiar gold rush, a trading post was established at McDames on the Dease River across the border in northern BC, south and west of the present town of Watson Lake, then moved in the late nineteenth century to the mouth of the Dease near the present community of Lower Post (Daliyo). Though the main impacts of the Klondike gold rush were felt outside of Kaska territory, prospectors on their way to and from the Klondike goldfields traversed Kaska territory. Oblate missionaries arrived in this century to convert and minister to the people, and established a residential school at Lower Post on the Liard River (Allard 1929; Moore 2002). In the early twentieth century a number of trading posts operated at locales such as Dease Lake, McDames, Ross River, Pelly Banks, and so on (Weinstein 1992; McDonnell 1975).

Rivers and trails

Trails connected places on this landscape, converging on centres such as McDames, Lower Post, and Frances Lake, travelling along the rivers, connecting key sites such as fish lakes and overlooks, and providing access to traplines. In the memory of living elders, and in the stories they learned from their relatives, camps and routes of travel organize perception of land. Today the Alaska Highway, the Campbell Highway, and two or three other roads or truck trails serve a similar mnemonic function. Rivers and lakes too are key places on the land, and also may order travel. Similar organization of geographic knowledge is reported by James Kari for northern Athapaskan speakers in Alaska and adjacent Canada (Kari and Fall 1987; Kari 1989).

The Liard and Frances Rivers provide access to large areas of hunting territory. Critical habitats such as sloughs, which focus game animals at certain seasons and are also the habitat of valued medicinal plants, are also found along rivers, and can be accessed either from the rivers or from trails running along the valleys. Frances Lake (Tū Chō Mene) has long been a focus of Kaska Dena activity. A large lake consisting of two arms that converge to form a single lower lake, the east arm has a caribou crossing site and a narrows that does not freeze in winter. This site allowed fishing during the winter season, and ancient settlements are focused in these areas of the lake (Gotthardt 1993).

The trail net from Big Eddy to McDames and to Lower Post figures in the mental geography of my teacher Elder Mida Donnessey from her childhood. Trails extending up the Rancheria River (Tsį́h Tué) and from there to Blue River (a tributary of the Dease) also shape her sense of the land. Big Eddy is a good fishing site near the confluence of the Rancheria and Liard Rivers, and is a former village site. The site can be recognized from a long distance by the sharp horseshoe bend in the river and the high banks. The route of the truck trail from the present village of Upper Liard to the Rancheria River runs roughly along the route of the old trail, prompting reminiscences of what the trail route was like and how it passed through stands of tall forest (***dechen chō'***). On one occasion we sat overlooking Liard Canyon, and Mida talked about the route from that spot to the site of the present town of Watson Lake, where there was then a camping place for overnighting on the return journey. The open wet meadow (near what is now a tourist campground) represented an opportunity to look for moose on the journey.

Liard Canyon below Watson Lake, Cranberry Rapids near Fireside, and the Grand Canyon of the Liard all figure largely as hazards to boat navigation, and cost many lives during the period of river boat travel (Karamanski 1983; Campbell 1958). There are other canyon sections on the Frances River, a tributary of the upper Liard linking Frances Lake to the Liard and

Mackenzie. Sitting at the old McDames site, now abandoned, the late elder Bob Watson talked about travelling by boat from McDames to Lower Post when he was a boy, and Mida recalled the cross-country trail link from McDames to Big Eddy.

The "layered" land—stories and places of power

The Kaska view of land is holistic and integral. As one moves along trails, travelling to specific places and harvesting from the land, another aspect of the land which is experienced is that field of power instantiated in place, in the land itself and in the living beings and powerful entities who dwell on the land, linking the moral with the quotidian. McDames, as well as being the site of the Sylvester's Landing trading post, was the site of a disaster in the past where "half a mountain" fell away and buried ancestors, perhaps for failing to observe moiety exogamy by marrying Crow with Crow, Wolf with Wolf. More recently, McDames is said to have been precipitously abandoned as a result of a flu epidemic. Another possibility raised was that giant worms in the nearby Horseranch Range, said to cause rain and bad weather, might have prompted the move from McDames to Lower Post (L.M. Johnson field notes).

Figure 6.2 Liard Canyon between Watson Lake and Lower Post

People tell tales of times long ago, in which local places are tied to stories involving powerful beings. Watson Lake itself, Łuwe Chō, named for its formerly abundant whitefish runs, is known as the site of a past encounter with a supernatural monster. A killer elephant,[1] which some have interpreted as possibly a mammoth, was tricked onto thin ice on this lake by a resourceful boy. The elephant went through and drowned, thus saving the remaining people from its ravages. As others have noted, passing by places may elicit localized stories (Palmer 2006). The first time I heard the Elephant Story, Elder Mida Donnessey and I were driving by the lake on a trip up the Campbell Highway to collect moss and medicines. As we drove on, Mida then continued with the story of another elephant, whose lair was in the upper Hyland River, which was also killed by humans. On another occasion we walked near the Liard Canyon below Watson Lake (Figure 6.2). Yellowlegs put his legs across the canyon, I was told. He helped two sisters escape a pursuing wolverine (Moore 1999).[2] A mountain in the Cassiar region in BC has bones of a large creature on top. One can never forget that the landscape is an empowered landscape, and a landscape that holds history.

Ethnoecology—the view from here

Travelling with Dene teachers, one learns about significant kinds of place as well as specific places of significance, and general rules of proper behaviour. Determining the linkage of terms describing different kinds of land with places on the land, and learning why places are significant in Kaska ecology, is challenging for the outsider and requires a blend of participant observation in the "bush," recording of narratives and indigenous terms, and documentation of what the referents of the terms are through visual methods—still photography and videography. In contrast to my earlier research with Gitksan and Witsuwit'en, I found travel on the land and visual recording of kinds of place was the appropriate strategy in the Kaska context, where knowledgeable Elders still may travel widely on the land but be less comfortable with, or less skilled at interpreting, out-of-context representations on paper.

Kaska are keen observers of animals and the rhythms of animals' lives—the rut, where they feed at what times of year, where and when they travel. Licks are an important class of Kaska place. Moose licks, which are muddy areas that the moose come to for the mineral content, draw other animals as well. Such places are reliable spots to encounter animals. They can be changed by things such as nearby road construction, but may continue to be active licks even after a road is built nearby. People mentioned the licks and former lick sites whenever we were in their vicinity. The Kaska noun dictionary (Kaska Elders 1997) corroborates the importance of "lick" as a kind of place, and gives terms for caribou lick, moose lick, sheep (*Ovis* sp.) lick, and so on. Some places are named for the presence of a lick, such as Elés Tué' or 'Lick Creek', now known as Money Creek after the trapper and miner Anton Money who settled there in the early twentieth century (Money 1975). I was told of the localities of several active licks, and one that was formerly effective but is now apparently spoiled by the Campbell Highway. In 2003, I photographed two lick areas, and drove by a third, which was described to me but not visible. I was also told of the location of a sheep lick at the edge of the highway near Good Hope Lake, but apparently Kaska rarely hunt sheep or mountain goats at the present time, so animals are not disturbed there. The visual profiles of the various areas that were described as "licks" were quite dissimilar, as the defining characteristics are the presence of mineral rich mud or earth, rather than any specific vegetation or landform.

Swamps (***tûtsel***) were mentioned various times, and also sloughs (***ts'ele, tili***) as places to which game comes (Johnson 2005, 2009). The pairing of a "lookout" with a slough, or swamp meadow, is an especially effective situation (Figures 6.3, 6.4 and 6.5). An old foot trail to the Rancheria River traverses such a site, and there is a camp conveniently located by the lookout.

Figure 6.3 Lookout: old trail with blazes

Figure 6.4 Lookout: hunting camp—camp along the foot trail with a view of the lake below

Figure 6.5 Lookout: view from the camp—lake with fringing swamp meadow *tütsel* and beaver lodge

Another slough that Mida mentioned for game can be seen from a lookout along the Meister Road. The spot is also known for its berries on top of the steep bank. We made note of the abundance of white cranberry flowers in June, and came back in late August to harvest the abundant cranberries. Persuading me to go with her in the truck, it was "just red" she said. It turned out that she used to climb up to that site from down below to look for berries, long before the truck trail was made, when she came to the slough to camp with her Aunt in her childhood.

When I was in the Watson Lake area in late August of both 2001 and 2002, the main occupations of the women that I spent time with were hide processing and berry picking. Hunting and fishing were also happening. By early September, everyone was talking about moose and caribou. People like to go up into mountains looking for game; families travel out together to find "something," looking for caribou, berries and certain medicines. When Mida and I sat on top of a mountain called in Kaska Tse Dek'ese 'Blue Rock Mountain'. It is now the site of a sporadically active jade mine, so is sometimes also called "Jade Mine Mountain." Mida called my attention to the caribou trails visible on the opposite slope. The grassy alpine patch we were sitting on also had caribou trackways and old scats, though we saw no caribou the day we were there. She remembered camping there with her children when they were small. Because of the mining activity in the area, a rough truck trail has gone up "Jade Mine Mountain" for several decades, making hunting access easier. The same kind of travelling occurs in other areas where there is truck access to areas near where caribou are expected, up the network of truck trails constructed for mineral access since the mid twentieth century. Tootsie (Tudzie) Mountain is another alpine area to which people travel, and Mida explained the habitat differences between "rock mountain" (Figure 6.6) and "grass-topped mountain" (Figure 6.7) pointing out how "rock mountains" are good escape habitat for sheep, while "grass-topped mountains" provide forage for many animals, including sheep and caribou. Older foot trails to the alpine zone also exist, and are accessed from the Frances River and other travel routes.

Spring time is a good time to pick medicines—e.g. June just after leaves come out when sap is running—especially the barks. It is also a time to avoid solo travel in the "bush," because the bears are "running" (rutting). I was scolded for walking alone in the bush at that time of year with neither gun nor dog. In the fall, you have to watch out for moose when they are in rut; a careless scraping sound may bring a hopeful, hopped up, and dangerous bull

Figure 6.6 "Rock mountain" *tsē dzę́h*

Figure 6.7 "Grass mountain" (grass-topped mountain) *hés*

running to you, ready to charge a rival. Bark medicines are hard to gather in fall, but it is a time to lay in a supply of some other plants such as Labrador tea and green black spruce cones, and to make sure that an abundance of cranberries is picked and put away.

Traplines order people's sense of who is where. People can and do move around, and establish ties to new areas, especially through marriage. But narratives of Elders such as Mida Donnessey and Alice Brodhagen give a sense of where people were in the past, and the knowledge of these two Elders seems to be tied especially to family areas. Although formal registered traplines were an innovation of the territorial government in the early twentieth century, Weinstein (1992) corroborates the traditional importance of family hunting and trapping areas in the Ross River area, and indicates that this approach to hunting areas is a widespread Dene pattern.

Language also reveals ethnoecological knowledge, a topic explored in greater detail in Johnson (2009). Terms such as 'high bank' (Figure 6.8), 'rockslide', 'swamp', 'eddy' and 'fish lake' give a strong sense of the Kaska landscape. People talk about disturbance events—fire, floods, snowslides, landslides—and describe ecological entailments of fire and the personal risks of snowslides (L.M. Johnson field notes).

Figure 6.8 High bank *tl'étāgī* bluff along Dease River below French Creek

Like other Dene, Kaska people are resourceful and constantly aware of opportunities. Respect pervades their attitude toward the land and other beings. The land, the animals, and plants are aware, and some are very powerful. People gain access to meat and healing from medicines by a kind of negotiation with powerful Others. Everything must be treated with respect, and one must never be boastful. Offerings should be left when gathering medicines. Powerful animals must be spoken about circumspectly, especially when they are present and you are in the bush. "Bushmen," often called "kidnappers" by local elders (Nagone), are in a way emblematic of untamed Others (Basso 1976). Stories of the Bushmen were used to encourage girls to stay close to camp when Elders Mida and Clara Donnessey were growing up. Elders such as Alice Brodhagen and Mida Donnessey tell stories about the origins of various animals, which bear on both edibility and proper behaviour.

People have a sense of plant habitats and vegetation as well. Bear root (*Hedysarum alpinum)* and caribou weed (*Artemesia tilesii)* grow beside rivers or along creeks. Balsam (*Abies balsamea* ssp. *lasiocarpa*) and mountain ash (*Sorbus* sp.) are found in the mountains, not in the "moss." Tamarack and Labrador tea are prevalent in the moss or muskeg. Stands of tall "big trees" (**dechen chō**) including both white spruce (**gat**, *Picea glauca*) and black spruce (**ts'ibé'**, *P. mariana*) are found along the Liard River in various places along the trail back down to Lower Post. These contrast strongly with the more stunted, black spruce and tamarack (**tadūze**, *Larix laricina*) on organic soils. From the overlook above Tom Creek, Mida commented about "brushland" (**naw'a**) by which she meant the expanse of unbroken conifer stands below us. She recalled the abundance of berries after a burn in the Tom Creek area, and was surprised by how much the site had changed through forest succession since she had last spent time there. People differentiate meadows, or grassy areas, the timberline dwarf birch-tundra mosaic, areas with emergent aquatics, and so on. They also recognize old burn areas with phrases such as "fire come through," and understand the dynamics of channel change and slough formation along main rivers as well as changes in wetlands due to the activities of beavers and to their cessation.

From another perspective, land and the activities that go with land, are also seen as the key to identity, in opposition to watching TV and drinking and getting in trouble in town. People hold meetings such as General Assemblies on the land, and have healing camps, language workshops, and youth camps on the land when possible. The land offers a sense of self-reliance and insurance to those who have the skills; it can be relied upon if you know how to take care of yourself, no matter what the government does or does not do, whether or not there are jobs or transfer payments.

Framing my understanding of Kaska ethnoecology

My understanding of Kaska ethnoecology is necessarily limited by the fact that I have only worked with Kaska in the short green season, from late spring to early fall, so the discussion presented here has been biased toward the non-winter world. As an ethnobotanist and a woman, and since the elders I have worked closely with are also women and are known for their knowledge of medicines, much of what I have learned is focused on plants. If I were a hunter or fisher, different domains of knowledge of land and waters and the significance of their features would be revealed through practice, verbal explanation and narrative.

I found that I could not draw a landscape block diagram on the basis of my experience with Kaska Dena, in contrast to those presented in Chapters 3 and 4. I had the sense that it was in part because key aspects of human interaction with land could not be fixed in space, drawn definitively and labelled. Partly this may be a consequence of Athapaskan languages and their polysynthetic-agglutinative nature, and the significance of relational terms. The Kaska language is rich with deictics or directional words, which are used to describe motion and spatial relationship in talking about both the land and social relations (Moore 2000, 2002).

Partly this may be a consequence of the nature of the topography and boreal forest landscape; it is harder to encapsulate a view including all the significant ecotopes in one diagram, for big country with more subdued topography and a range of local landscapes. Another significant factor is that vegetation types do not seem to be delimited as a significant way to see the landscape, though they can be described (Johnson 2007, 2009). Perhaps most significant is that a block diagram is of necessity static, while the Dene way to experience land is fluid and dynamic, and depends on what aspects of land, history, and personal experience are being referred to.

Interestingly, Iain Davidson-Hunt and his co-authors found that they had to consider Shoal Lake Anishinaabe landscape from the framework of "cultural landscape," and the landscape diagrams they drew did not make sense to the community until they included the human layer as integral with the biophysical (Davidson-Hunt and Berkes 2003, 2009; Davidson-Hunt 2003).

Talking with and travelling with my Kaska teachers, the story of the land that emerges is rich: a medley of sloughs and overlooks, old trails, camps and places of power, places of past stories, moose licks and fish lakes, edible and medicinal plants, and berry patches. Ethnoecology is complex, as it links many aspects of a people's life. Like other northern Dene peoples, the Kaska view of land is not based primarily in vegetation types; variations in vegetation seem less significant than topographic features. Kaska knowledge of land is organized around season and place, and united by a net of trails and rivers, memory, and an active eye. In the past, Kaska moved widely over the land to harvest meat, fish, furs and berries. Like other northern places, seasonality is extreme and winters long, placing a premium on adaptability. With the exception of wood, plants are largely a concern of the summer season, and while important, in terms of cultural salience they are overshadowed by relationships to animals.

At present, Kaska relationships to land have of necessity altered, through settlement into villages and towns, integration into the money economy, and the increasing pressure on their homeland by outsiders as global forces intensify their interest in the Kaska homeland as a source of raw materials (emeralds, mixed sulfide ores, oil and gas, even timber), for transportation corridors (for example, for natural gas from the shores of the Beaufort Sea via the Alaska Highway route), as "scenery" and wildlands, and for recreation. Contemporary Kaska, like other northern indigenous peoples, are confronting challenging decisions about their future relationship to the land and how their communities will sustain themselves. To what degree can a balance between traditional values in the sentient land—the land as source of identity and self-reliance, physical and spiritual well-being, history and knowledge, food and home—be reconciled with the conversion of Land and nature to natural resources, which must be articulated with the limitless appetites of global markets and global concepts of property?

7

Envisioning Ethnoecology

MOVEMENT THROUGH PLACE AND SEASON

This chapter is based on my fieldwork with Gwich'in who live in the Mackenzie Delta region of the Northwest Territories, near northern timberline (Figure 7.1). This is a region of taiga and big rivers, peatlands, lakes, low rounded mountains and permafrost (Figure 7.2). Consistent with Dene notions of learning, much of my research has consisted of shared experience on the land, in different places and in different seasons.

The highly seasonal landscapes of the North require constant adaptability of the people who live there; creative improvisation and the ability to make the best of the opportunities at hand are essential. Life is like a dance over the land as it changes through the seasons: all of the plants and animals that live there have their cycles, and interact with others in a vast complex net through space and time, through place and season. Knowledge of the land in the North is an engaged ethnoecology—the understanding of landscape involves an active human community in interaction with other species who are active agents, and an awareness of how everything is spatially and temporally in motion, including people. Survival in the North is based on the skill and subtlety with which one can assess risks, dangers, and possibilities, and proactively respond.

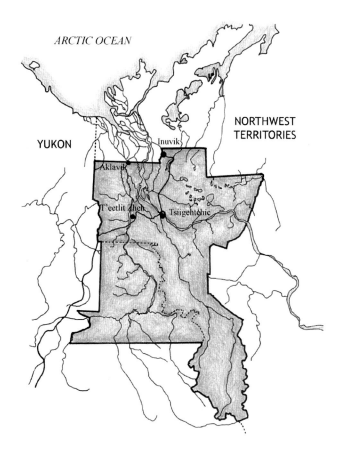

Figure 7.1 Map of Gwich'in Settlement Region in the Mackenzie and Peel River drainages, Northwest Territories and northern Yukon

For northern Dene peoples, as for many Native North Americans, the land is still seen as the root of identity, culture, and health, despite the changes in daily life brought about by wage employment and year-round permanent residence in village settlements or in towns.

When I began ethnoecological research in the North, I initially thought in terms of a seasonless landscape model, with repeating units—landforms, substrate types, vegetation communities, places where particular types of resources are found. My model was based on terrestrial ecology and vegetation studies. I quickly learned that in the North, season was paramount. I also began to get a sense of a net of pathways, rivers and trails, and nodes of

Figure 7.2 View of Peel River and low Arctic landscape looking downstream from Shiltee Rock (Shildii)

memory. My conception of ethnoecology had to be broadened to include movement, in the form of the wind, the weather, and the flow of the rivers.

The land is constantly changing, and requires the humans who make it home to be constantly responsive, continually reevaluating plans and possibilities and adjusting action to match. Alice Vittrekwa said, "Our old people used to tell us not to make plans. Because you never know if it's going to work out."

This sense of motion, transformation, and relationship is encoded in Athapaskan languages with their rich set of relational prepositions and verbal structures, as earlier detailed by Basso (1996) with reference to the Western Apache in New Mexico, by Moore (2000, 2002) for Kaska, and Kari (2008) for Ahtna. Coming from a noun-centred Indo-European linguistic tradition, I tend to conceive of the world as a series of things with discrete names. If I want to view things from a perspective of interaction, I can, but my language allows me to conceive of temporally frozen immutable objects, without consideration of change, relationship or context. When I asked my friend Bertha, Elder and Gwich'in language teacher, what you would call those hills across the river in Gwich'in, she hesitated. Where I anticipated "hills," "upland," or some term such as "pediment," she answered, "I could call it 'under the hills' *nan t'ee* or 'under the mountains' *ttha t'ee*." One of the main channels of the Mackenzie Delta, called Husky Channel in English, is called Ttha t'e di' ("river under the mountains") in Gwich'in. Specifying relationships among places is required in Athapaskan languages.

For Gwich'in, even place terms such as "Road River" or "Tree River" designate a complex of places in an area linked by a web of seasonal activities; the fish camp, the winter camp, spring and fall camps within an area (Figure 7.3). Indeed relational terms in Athapaskan languages carry connotations of "area of" as well as referring to points (Kari 2008). Rivers are routes of travel into and between areas. I came to think of the rivers as highways, where travel is by boat in the summer and in the winter by snow machine and sled, or sometimes by truck where an ice road has been graded. The main rivers are the arteries of the transportation net. From these, trail form networks up valleys and ridges, into the high country where one may encounter caribou.

My Gwich'in teachers have also taken me on journeys that reflect their understanding of the land. I spent time with William[1] and Mary Teya from Fort McPherson is their summer fish camp on the Peel River in 1999, during the Midway Lake festival in 1999 and 2000, and in their winter camp at Road River in February 2000. I also spent time in the fish camp of Noel

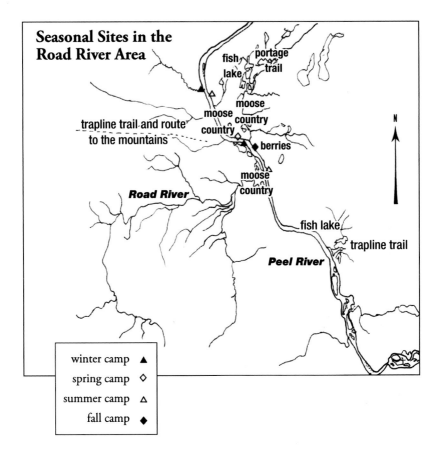

Figure 7.3 Cluster of sites in the Road River area (northern Yukon) along several intersecting travel paths: the river, trapline trails, and portage trail along Three Cabin Creek

and Alice Andre on the Mackenzie River in August 1999, and travelled with Alestine Andre to her family's traditional fishing site at Tree River on the Mackenzie in August 2000.

When I was with William and Mary, I spent a good deal of time observing and helping, allowing Mary or William to determine both activities and verbal content. A great deal of the learning was practical: how to set net, how to cut dry fish and dry meat, how to set tent. We went for yellow berries on the highway, and drove up to James Creek (Figure 7.4) for water. Mountain water is good. James Creek is also a place where Mary's Aunties like to camp in the late summer and fall, picking berries for a month or so. The cranberries

Figure 7.4 James Creek area in the Richardson Mountains, July 2000

Figure 7.5 The summer fish camp and winter trapping camp at Road River, July 1999

Figure 7.6 The winter trapping camp at Road River, February 2000

and blueberries are good there. The mountains around James Creek are a place one may encounter early-migrating caribou in August or September, and much of the attention of people from Fort McPherson is focused on this place when caribou are anticipated. Sometimes Mary talked about the misadventures of Crow (Deetrin) the trickster/transformer. Sometimes she told tales about her youth and how her parents and grandparents had lived. Mary's family maintained a seasonal complex of sites by Road River, about 50 miles by river south of Fort McPherson. In the summer, we made a day trip by boat to the area, and Mary talked about the land there. Travelling with William and Mary and their grandson, I learned about the Peel River as trail, the portages (winter dog team cutoff trails), and the hazards of the different seasons in different places. I heard about whose camps were in which places, where moose had been seen, and where you could hunt. I learned where the different trails to get to the caribou ran up into the foothills and mountains. As we approached the winter cabin site or the summer fish camp, tales of family history emerged, about moose shot, bears seen, or porcupines (*Erithizon dorsatum*) clubbed (Figures 7.4, 7.5 and 7.6). We saw where Mary's grandparents had had their winter and summer camps, their spring camp and their fall camp. On the way up and back, Mary commented about Shiltee Rock, a sacred site above the Peel River that commemorates an event of long ago, when a girl violated her puberty seclusion, and looked at her father and brothers returning from a long trip—and they turned to stone. Mary casually mentioned the place the family had been camped when the girl had looked on her relatives, as we went by in the boat on our way back down the river.

When I came back in the winter, we travelled the same trail by snow machine. I learned first-hand about travel hazards such as overflow (Figure 7.7), and about the wind. At the Road River camp there was a homemade wind meter that showed the direction and strength of the wind. When a chinook or west wind blows, lenticular clouds form (Figure 7.8). The west wind is warm. Usually it is followed by a north wind, which is cold and bad for travelling. We stayed in the winter camp, and I learned about winter skills such as setting rabbit snares, cutting dry wood, and maintaining the camp. Double ice on the river prevented us from being able to fish. William hunted for moose—not an easy thing for a lone hunter. There were moose around, but they became aware of William and he was not able to shoot one. They made a noise at him. Finally he was heading downriver to take a load of things to a halfway camp, when he saw something. He quickly returned with the dogs

Figure 7.7 Overflow on river ice, a challenge of winter travel Travelling to the Road River winter camp in February 2000, we encountered overflow under deep snow, forcing us to turn back to Ttrondii to wait for colder weather.

Figure 7.8 West wind with typical lenticular clouds at Road River, February 2000

and tied them up, then went back with the snow machine. After a while he returned, exultant. He had been able to shoot cow and calf at the edge of the willows along the river. They had not been aware of his presence, and he was able to drop both. The next three days were devoted to processing the meat, which turned the inside of the cabin into a place to hang dry meat. Although caribou were not around, and the snow was too deep to bother with marten trapping, the journey had been successful. We had obtained a good supply of meat.

The following summer I returned to the Mackenzie. Alestine Andre, Gwich'in ethnobiologist and linguist who is about my age and was then Director of the Gwich'in Social and Cultural Institute, took me to her family's fish camp on the Mackenzie about 40 miles east of Tsiigehtchic.[2] Working with Alestine was interesting, because she is articulate and conversant with Western knowledge and perspectives as well as with those of her people. At times Alestine would turn to me and put into words some of the things she thought I should think about. At one point Alestine said, "Our relationship to the land is not something I can talk about. I have to show you . . . you are experiencing our relationship to the land." On another occasion she stressed the importance of being constantly aware of your environment, of looking up river, down river, across, and all around, and to be aware of what animals might be there. She also stressed the importance of paying attention to the wind, to the rise and fall of the water, to the sounds of the birds, and to the dogs. Discussing this chapter, Alestine painted the classic image of the Indian standing on a hill, shading his eyes, looking all around. This image is a good metaphor or symbol of the Dene relationship to the land: to be constantly aware of everything, attuned, she said. The people know where the animals are. Alestine commented about lookout places, "In our country, people situate camp along the river, where you can look up river and down, and be constantly aware." Her camp at Diighe 'tr'aajil is just such a place. Mary commented too about the fish camp at Road River that you could look down the whole stretch: nothing came up the river without people seeing it a long way off. Travellers were spotted as soon as they rounded the point, and were welcomed, fed, and given warm tea when they arrived.

People watch and listen to the birds and animals. When loons call, they are wishing for a wind. When the geese fly high, that tells something about the coming weather. And, as Alestine said jokingly, when they land right in front of you, that means dinner. For Gwich'in too, observing all animals in the environment and attending to signs of their presence is important. Mary and her grandson spotted a swimming moose by the twitch of its ears, virtually the only part of it not submerged in the river. After a long while I saw it too. When it came out of the water and stood up on shore, William and Mary decided not to shoot it, because it was a cow and might have a young calf. Noel and Gabe Andre (Alestine's oldest brother and her uncle) spotted a swimming bear in the current at Tree River in summer of 2000 while we were having tea; I would have thought it a floating drift log.

The landscape and all the beings that dwell on the land have sentience and agency, and are worthy of respect. People hunt, but they appreciate the necessity to respect the animals they hunt. If the gift of their flesh is not respected, the hunter will not be successful in the future. Using all parts of the animal is one way to show respect. Leaving a clean camp is another way of living properly and being respectful. People believe it is wrong to bother an animal if it is doing you no harm. You should never take the kill of an animal or bird of prey; it's their food and they need it to survive, Gwich'in elder Pierre Benoit told Alestine (pers. comm. August 2000). And the sometimes annoying seagulls, whisky jacks and ravens are not molested. Instead, people leave food for them.

The northern Dene view contrasts with the bounded, fixed tract of land typical of settled, agricultural traditions, and which forms the basis of understanding of land in the Euro-North American tradition. This realization has implications for the intersection of northern indigenous peoples with government policies and land managers. There has been in recent years a great romance with GIS as a tool for organizing and presenting information about land. It is a powerful tool, but is built upon some key assumptions about the nature of land and space (in contrast to place) which may not fit well with traditional knowledges, as Craig Candler eloquently detailed in a presentation at the Canadian Anthropology Society meeting in June of 2000. It is difficult in GIS to render shifting, fluid, unbounded and temporally changing distributions of resources and people, or the nature of the northern land itself, given the magnitude of seasonal change. In the northern Athapaskan world, places are loci of the potential intersection in time, space and probability, and of potential encounter, rather than unchanging things whose characteristics and potential can be simply and unambiguously recorded. I address these themes in more detail in Chapters 10 and 11.

"Land," or *nành'* in Gwich'in, is a key concept for people who make their livelihood from the land, a rich and evocative concept with many layers of meaning. The land is fundamental to northern Athapaskan culture and life.

Land has also been politicized through interaction with the rest of Canada via the land claims process, and resource exploration and development activities. New discourses around land as identity and as economic opportunity are now being elaborated, as hearings and preparation to construct major oil and gas fields and pipeline complexes are heard in the North at this writing in 2007. Because the Gwich'in were highly nomadic peoples, travelling to take advantage of seasonal resources and responsive to the changing patterns of weather and abundance of animal and plant resources, movement was pervasive in the lives of Gwich'in until recently. This perspective of motion still forms the foundation of understanding of the land. Ethnoecologies of northern Athapaskan peoples are engaged rather than theoretical ecologies. Adaptability to real-world situations, and practice, are key to northern Athapaskan understanding of the land. As Alestine said while we worked together in the fish camp at Tree River, "Now you are actually learning our relationship to the land."

Alestine's description of the essence of knowing the land as an engaged awareness, of watching, and seeing what is on the land, is very much what Tim Ingold described in his 1996 paper "Hunting and Gathering as Ways of Perceiving the Environment." Ingold talks about engagement and "enskillment" in learning to see, especially learning to see with a hunter's eyes (Ingold 1996a:142).

Richard Nelson in *Make Prayers to the Raven* (1983) eloquently describes the ethnoecology of another northern Athapaskan group, the Koyukon, in ways that emphasize skilled movement and perception, and attention to the other beings that share the landscape. He writes:

> The Koyukon homeland is filled with places . . . invested with significance in personal or family history. Drawing back to view the landscape as a whole, we can see it completely interwoven with these meanings. Each living individual is bound into this pattern of land and people that extends throughout the terrain and far back across time. (Nelson 1983:243).

Ingold (1996:149) comments "that the activities we conventionally call hunting and gathering are forms of skilled, attentive 'coping' in the world, intentionally carried out by persons in an environment *replete with other agentive powers of one kind and another*" (emphasis added). Nelson (1983) entitles one of his chapters "The Watchful World," prefiguring David Anderson's (2000) phrase "sentient ecology," which emphasizes the perspective of moving in a world "replete with other agentive powers"—all of the animals, plants, the winds, waters and land itself.

Ingold's (1996) remarks on the Pintupi apprehension and interaction with landscape in Australia and his analysis of Hallowell's (2000) presentation of northern Ojibwa (Saulteaux) ontology in Canada lend weight to the notion that significant commonalities exist among peoples who are not cultivators and have special relationships with their homelands. Describing Ojibwa ontology as presented by Hallowell (1960), Ingold writes:

> And these movements, of the sun in the heavens of trees in the wind, of animals and human beings as they go about their everyday tasks, *do not take place against the backdrop of a nature that is fixed, with its locations and distances laid out in advance.* For they are part and parcel of that total life process, of continuous generation, through which the world itself is forever coming into being. In short, living beings do not move upon the world, but move along with it. (Ingold 2000, emphasis added)

This fluidity and flexibility in a world that is not fixed, either spatially or temporally, is equally applicable to the world experienced and described by my Gwich'in teachers and that I experienced. Ingold further comments that Ojibwa world view is,

> to envisage the world from the point of view of a being within it, as a total field of relations whose unfolding is tantamount to the process of life itself. Every being emerges, with its particular form, dispositions and capabilities, as a locus of growth—or in Ojibwa terms, as a focus of power—within this field. Mind, then, is not added on to life but is immanent in the intentional engagement, in perceptions and actions, of living beings with the constituents of their environments. As such primary engagement is a condition of being, it must also be a condition of knowledge . . . (Ingold 2000:108)

When I began my fieldwork with Gwich'in, I was told that I needed to go on the land with knowledgeable people to act as guides in all seasons, that is to learn by experiencing, in order to gain skills. I was admonished to make sure the tea was on and to fetch water. I helped with getting firewood. I tried my hand at cutting dry fish, at cutting the meat off a moose skull, and at checking the fish net solo (and once nearly went backwards down the Mackenzie). I was told how to collect the right snow to melt for tea water, and scolded for inadvertently stepping over meat, a serious act of disrespect. My eyes were guided to see things I would have missed. I was taught to listen and to watch rather than actively question. These elements of "engagement," as Ingold suggests, are conditions for knowledge.

Part of the title of this chapter, "Envisioning Ethnoecology," was drawn from my effort to communicate my experiential learning through use of image, to impart a sense of the land and life on the land through a collage of images, as frozen icons of moving and learning on the land, and to guide my listeners on a journey of virtual understanding of place. Some of those images accompany this chapter, and show the "same" place in different seasons, the clouds to represent the wind, places of good water and berries, and places of power and learning. All of these are important places to understand, requiring respect in Gwich'in ethnoecology. More abstracted images are also included; a map of the Gwich'in settlement region to show where we are in the world, a map showing trails and summer and winter camp locations within an area used by Mary Teya's family, and information about where resources are located. These are the kinds of places referred to in Richard Nelson's quotation above.

8

A Gwich'in Year on the Land

Until relatively recent times, Gwich'in people lived out on the land, moving between seasonal sites in a relatively regular seasonal round. A sequence of different subsistence activities, focused in different locations and at different types of sites, characterized the Gwich'in seasonal cycle. Prior to the past thirty to forty years, villages were occupied for relatively short times, especially at seasonal gatherings such as Christmas, Easter, and Assumption Day or a summer gathering, when visiting and trading were done.

I will begin my description of the seasonal round with "spring," the season when the snow and ice covered landscape is in rapid transition to the summer ice-free state, and the days are rapidly becoming very long. This is a variable period in late May and early June. As travel becomes difficult at this time of year, Gwich'in families had to decide where they would "pass spring." This had to be a site where they could wait out the shift from winter sled (now snow machine) travel to summer boat travel, and high enough above the spring flood and ice jam levels to remain unflooded. Muskrat (*Ondatra zibethicus*) and beaver (*Castor canadensis*) hunting and trapping, and waterfowl hunting, are the principal subsistence activities in a spring camp.

In the summer, after break-up and while the weather is warm, Gwich'in disperse to various locations along the Peel and Mackenzie Rivers, and in the myriad channels of the Mackenzie Delta, to fish for river-running broad whitefish (*Coregonus nasus*), humpback whitefish (*C. clupeaformis*), and inconnu or coney (*Stenodus leucicthys*). Fishable sites are eddies, and locations of productive eddies are known to community members (Figure 8.1). Through an informal network of conversation within communities, people communicate who will be fishing in what areas, and where people will set up their fish camps. Campsites seem to be a form of property, and permission is required to use a site established and improved by someone else who is not a relative. A similar form of family fishing sites is reported for Greenlanders by Peterson (1963). When a family decides to fish an area where they previously had no camp, they are free to establish a new site. Where more than one net is set in an eddy, the nets are set so that they do not interfere with each other and both can catch fish. Areas immediately adjacent to the villages or ferry crossings such as 8 Miles at the Peel River Ferry, and the area below Tsiigehtchic on the Mackenzie River, are areas of common use. Just upstream and across from Tsiigehtchic at Chii t'iet, and the bay just downstream from the western end of the Mackenzie Ferry crossing, are also

Figure 8.1 William Teya pulling coney from net set at eddy below Shiltee Rock, summer 1999

shared areas of common use for people from the Tsiigehtchic community. Figure 8.2 below shows below eddies as solid-shaded areas, along the lower Mackenzie River near Tsiigehtchic, which were fished in the 1999 summer season. Eddies known as fishing and fish camp sites that were used in other years are shown as hollow circles. The Tree River site (Diighe 'tr'aajil) was not used in 1999, but was fished in 2000 (Figure 8.3) as I describe in Chapter 7. This site has been used by Alestine Andre's family for a long time, and has an ancient name commemorating a gambling contest that took place long ago.

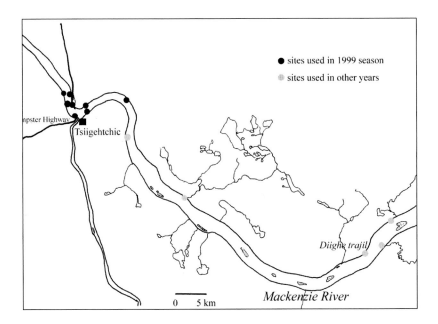

Figure 8.2 Summer fishing sites (eddies) on the Mackenzie River near Tsiigehtchic, Northwest Territories

In the fall, fishing at fish lakes and ice fishing on the Peel and Mackenzie Rivers is carried out. Travel to specific fish lakes was a former part of the Tsiigehtchic seasonal round. "Fish lakes" are lakes in which productive fall fish netting (usually from the ice) can be accomplished. There are also areas of open water such as Travaillant Lake, which has a highly productive crooked back (humpback whitefish) fishery in November. As with rivers, only specific sites are productive (e.g. near inlet streams or off certain points), and

Figure 8.3 Fish drying at the fishing site, Diighe 'tr'aajil, looking across the Mackenzie to Tree River where Hyacinthe Andre had his homestead

one must know both where and when to fish to be successful. People may decline to share the information necessary for successful fishing, especially if they feel would-be fishers may not be adequately respectful of the fish they take. Species taken in lakes include trout (*Salvelinus namaycush*), Arctic charr (*Salvelinus alpinus*), both species of whitefish, loche (*Lota lota*), and northern pike (*Esox lucius*). During the fall fishery on the Mackenzie, broad and humpback whitefish, coney, herring (*Coregonus autumnalis* and *C. sardinella*), loche and northern pike are caught. Fall-caught fish were usually frozen in pits, or made into "stick fish." The whitefish species and coney are the most abundant species. Loche eggs and liver are a delicacy much appreciated by Gwich'in people, as are whitefish eggs.

In the past, serious fall fishing activity was undertaken on rivers and on lakes to catch fish for winter dog feed. A family might cache several thousand fish to ensure an adequate supply (Hyacinthe Andre, Noel Andre, and William Teya, pers. comm.). There are numerous known fish lakes north of the Mackenzie River, north and east of Tsiigehtchic (in the area that will be traversed by the pipeline corridor). Different families accessed specific camping and fishing sites over the years, integrating this movement into their seasonal round (Andre and Kritsch 1992). At present, little concentrated fall fishing is done, because changes in lifestyle associated with concentration into villages and with adoption of gas powered snow machines has eliminated the need for a large dog feed fishery. Fish remain very important as human food, and form a significant part of the diet of contemporary Gwich'in people.

Fall is also a time of caribou hunting and ice fishing on the river. Both Gwich'ya Gwich'in and Teetl'it Gwich'in ice fish in the fall, while Fort McPherson (Teetl'it) people are more involved in fall caribou hunting because of their proximity to the Richardson Mountains where the Porcupine Caribou Herd migrates.

Moose hunting is and was a part of the fall and winter routine of both groups, especially along the rivers and around certain lakes. In addition to the value of the meat, moose hides are important as a source of durable leather. Moose hunting can be combined with trapping activity, also characteristic of late fall through late winter, with a break around Christmas.

Trapping furbearers has been an important economic activity since at least the early 1800s (Krech 1983). Species utilized on traplines include the furbearers that are the focus of the cash economy, and game species for subsistence, and the lake fish formerly procured in the fall for dog feed. Traplines are areas of extensive use in the winter season, and include areas away from the banks of the major rivers. Upland areas are trapped for marten, while Mackenzie Delta areas may be productive of lynx and, in late winter and spring, of muskrat. Beavers have been found throughout the Delta and along the Peel and Arctic Red Rivers. Their numbers have been variable and subject to population crashes. They were trapped in late winter and early spring when sufficiently numerous (Gwich'in Elders 1997:89-95).

People tend to trap in areas familiar to them, or that have been used in the past by family members. According to elders, people had their own trap lines, and they respected the lines of others. Elders stated that you can't cross another trapper's trail, nor use his or her trail in your own trapping activities. Traps may be set, however, in the same general area provided these rules are followed and each trapper elaborates his own trail system (Tony Andre, pers. comm.). These considerations of trapline ownership are similar to those reported for Alaska Gwich'in (=Kutchin) by Richard Nelson (1986). Trapping camps, with requirements for other resources such as dry fuelwood, are also associated with traplines. Trappers can change their areas; the same kind of informal networking among community members that orders the fishing effort also regulates where the trapping effort is focused. As Margaret Donovan of Tsiigehtchic put it, the trappers decide where they are going and who will be concentrating in what area by a kind of "gentleman's agreement." People may decide to try a new area, to give a previously used area a rest, or they may choose to return to an area in which they have worked previously. When Tsiigehtchic had a group trapline, individual trappers decided where to trap within that area. Trappers from Fort McPherson seem to have family traplines, and related people may have lines in nearby areas, such as the Charlie-Tetlichi family and spouses in the Road River area. Some flexibility for people to choose or change a fishing area is allowed, depending on how many people are currently trapping, and choices among several family controlled lines. One can also arrange to trap in someone else's area by talking with them.

Jigging for loche (also known as burbot) through the ice is another winter subsistence activity, and can be done at specific productive sites along the main river systems and Mackenzie Delta channels, and on the lakes.

Caribou are the most important species to Gwich'in identity. A bull caribou, with white neck and antlers held high, adorns the Gwich'in flag. Caribou are the most important animal in the Gwich'in economy, so they are highly valued.

Caribou hunting is another winter activity. Families, especially from Fort McPherson, in the past would follow various routes into the mountains with their dogsleds, and would camp wherever they encountered caribou, to process the meat. There is also a spring caribou hunt, when the caribou are moving north to their calving grounds. People from Tsiigehtchic regularly went up the Arctic Red River to hunt caribou during the fall and winter, where they could access woodland caribou, and in the headwaters, the Porcupine Caribou Herd in the mountains.

Caribou, being vagrant and highly bunched, require different arrangements for their harvest than other large ungulates such as moose. Although the broad outlines of their seasonal cycle and geographic movements are well known, the exact timing and route of movement are notoriously variable. Gwich'in use caribou from the Porcupine Caribou Herd, and the Bluenose Herd of barren ground caribou (*Rangifer tarandus groenlandicus*). Larger and more solitary boreal woodland caribou (*Rangifer tarandus caribou*) are also likely used along the Mackenzie and Peel Rivers (Shaw and Benn 2001; Nagy et al. 2003). The Porcupine Caribou Herd ranges in the northwest extremity of the Northwest Territories, in adjacent areas of the northern Yukon, and on the Arctic Coastal Plane of eastern Alaska, and were more often hunted by the Teetl'it Gwich'in and the Vuntut Gwitchin of the northern Yukon (Gwich'in Elders 1997; Sherry and Vuntut Gwitchin First Nation 1999), than by the Gwich'ya Gwich'in of Tsiigehtchic. Gwich'ya Gwich'in made use of the Bluenose Caribou Herd of the northern Northwest Territories (Gwich'in Elders 1997). People hunted Bluenose caribou where groups were encountered amongst the lakes north of the Mackenzie River in the general vicinity of Travaillant Lake. Bluenose caribou follow different patterns, and they change their route about every 10 to 20 years. As Dan Andre of Tsiigehtchic put it, it is almost like they are aware of how much food they have; they leave a certain area and then return to it later (Johnson and Andre 2001). Another factor influencing their movement to new wintering areas is the occurrence of forest fires, which burn all of the lichens, which are an important food source for caribou. In 1986, the area around Travaillant Lake burned, and the Bluenose caribou are now found in an area to the north of there, where they are relatively remote from Tsiigehtchic.[1] Owing to greater accessibility via the highway, Tsiigehtchic hunters now make more extensive use of the Porcupine caribou instead.

In the past, hunting of the Porcupine caribou involved travel up various trails into the Richardson Mountains, especially trails up the Rat River to

Fish Creek and the Bell River, up Stony Creek to Brass House, up Vittrekwa Creek and Road River across to Rock River, and up Caribou River to the Caribou Lake area (Gwich'in Elders 1997; Bertha Frances, Mary and William Teya, and Neil Colin, pers. comm.) (Figure 8.4). When caribou were encountered, people camped there and processed the meat by making dry meat and caching frozen meat for later use. Some of this dry meat and frozen meat might later be taken to Fort McPherson by dogsled. Communal hunting was often practiced, and information about where caribou were encountered was shared. When caribou are available nearby, people from Fort McPherson preferentially hunt caribou. Gwich'in people required large amounts of meat traditionally; meat is still culturally and nutritionally very important. There is a high degree of sharing of meat, especially of caribou and of moose. When there are no caribou around, Gwich'in people shift to other resources such as moose and rabbits (*Lepus americanus*), and make extensive use of fish. Rabbit and fish are also shared.

At present, Gwich'in from all of the Canadian communities access the Porcupine Caribou Herd from the Dempster Highway. The presence of the highway does ensure that caribou will cross the highway or feed in the highway area at some point during the winter. The relative lack of predictability

Figure 8.4 Rolling slopes of Richardson Mountains in late August, 2000, just as the first of the Porcupine Caribou Herd began moving into the area from their calving grounds to the north

in their movements means that the exact timing and location of encountering huntable caribou varies significantly year to year. This maximizes the value of sharing information about the occurrence of caribou, as well as distribution of the catch. The nature of caribou movement also maximizes the value of dispersing people in predictable areas to make sure that someone encounters caribou, and can communicate to others where the animals are. Communal hunting and a highly developed sharing ethic allow distribution of meat to as many people as possible in the community. This is underscored by the strong Gwich'in belief that generosity in sharing meat is necessary to ensure continuation of good hunting success. Gwich'in consider caribou to be active agents who choose to give themselves to human hunters to enable their survival. Respectful acceptance of the gift, by shooting caribou when possible and sharing the meat if it is more than the hunter's immediate needs, is necessary for that relationship to continue.

Gwich'in livelihood and relations to the land in the early twenty-first century

Contemporary Gwich'in in the Mackenzie Delta region live in the villages of Fort McPherson, Tsiigehtchic, and Aklavik, and in the town of Inuvik. Many people have part-time or full-time wage employment, or live on transfer payments. Oil and gas development dominate the present economy. Few people presently engage in serious trapping, though hunting and fishing for subsistence continue to be important and highly valued activities. Most people spend the majority of their time residing in permanent houses or apartments in town; few spend substantial amounts of time out on the land living in camps in cabins or wall-tents. Those that do, tend to alternate periods of time in town with time on the land. Present subsistence activities are more likely to be within a day's travel of the village, and people may return immediately to town by motorized transportation (truck, boat with outboard engine, or snow machine) with the meat or fish they have obtained.

In the contemporary Canadian context, there are various formal institutions that influence Gwich'in use of land and resources. Since the settlement of the Gwich'in Comprehensive Claim in 1992 these institutions include co-management boards: the Gwich'in Renewable Resource Board (GRRB), the Gwich'in Land and Water Board, and the Gwich'in Land Use Planning Board; the Gwich'in Tribal Council and the Gwich'in Lands Office; community Renewable Resource Councils; local governments; the Porcupine Caribou Management Board; the Northwest Territories Department of

Resources, Wildlife and Economic Development (DRWED) and the Federal Department of Fisheries and Oceans. Comparable Yukon Departments regulate caribou hunting in the Yukon.

A variety of mandates and epistemologies guide the approaches to land and resource management promoted by these diverse organizations. Contemporary Gwich'in ordering of access to land and resources necessarily encompasses the intersection of Euro-Canadian and indigenous perspectives and goals, with these new formal institutions being laid over the highly informal and fluid traditional system. Contemporary Gwich'in find themselves dealing with a global cash economy, the intrusion of other resource values, such as natural gas, tourism, transportation corridors, and other actors, including tourists, resource industries and their employees, non-indigenous government biologists, and other government employees. The Department of Fisheries and Oceans, in consultation with the GRRB and the Renewable Resource Councils, regulates fishing gear, and attempts to collect a series of statistics on all fish caught or released by fishers with commercial licenses.

The conditions and constraints of the comprehensive claim define a bounded Gwich'in Settlement Area, which encompasses much, but not all, of the area traditionally used by Gwich'in of the Mackenzie and Peel Rivers. Within this Settlement Area, some parcels are designated as Gwich'in Private Lands, and other lands are co-managed by the government of the Northwest Territories, through their various agencies, and by the Gwich'in. Which kinds of activities can take place is influenced by the differences between the legal statuses of these types of land. Renewable Resource Councils, the Gwich'in Land Office, the Designated Gwich'in Organizations, and the Co-management boards, DRWED. Furthermore, the Gwich'in Tribal Council review and monitor activities, hold meetings to discuss what courses of action should be permitted, and negotiate the shape of activities on the land, by Gwich'in and other interested parties. Underneath all of this, informal institutions continue to operate as people choose where and when they will fish, hunt or trap. The resilience of all of these institutions, formal and informal, is challenged by the magnitude of proposed and likely changes as pipeline construction proceeds and oil and gas fields are developed in the Mackenzie Delta and perhaps on the Peel Plateau.

Seasonality, flexibility and changing contexts

In an Arctic environment, everything is highly seasonal. Configurations of people and place can change dramatically depending on time of year, and may be renegotiated for each season. Although fishing sites do not change dramatically, people may change the areas they choose to fish. Areas for hunting moose and caribou do change quite a bit from year to year, making it difficult to adequately render habitat on fixed maps. A measure of stability is provided by associations of particular families with specific areas, over periods of at least two to three generations, despite dramatic changes in Gwich'in life.

The changeability of Arctic environment is a major factor in needing flexible organization and the ability to shift spatially in response to shifts in animal populations, unusual weather, and the spatial distribution of stochastic events such as wild fire, which influence furbearer and fish habitats, ease of travel, and plant resources such as berries and firewood. The strong Gwich'in ethic of sharing meat and fish helps to ensure that the variations in harvest are evened out among members of the community, despite variations in the productivity of different areas at different times.

In the contemporary Canadian and global contexts, there are other factors that influence Gwich'in relationships to land. The Mackenzie Delta is part of Canada and the Northwest Territories. The 1992 comprehensive claim settlement dictated various institutional arrangements to accommodate Canadian, territorial, and Gwich'in rights and responsibilities vis-à-vis the land. The global economy continues to influence pressures on the land base by industries such as the oil and gas industry, and the viability of trapping, through the market for fine furs. The renewal of the Mackenzie Pipeline Project in the early years of the twenty-first century, and the frenzied boom in oil and gas exploration, has obvious effects on Gwich'in relationships to land and on participation in the land based economy. The accelerating changes in global climate also influence the Gwich'in homeland, as the Western Arctic is one of the areas which is experiencing significant rise in temperature, with associated permafrost melting and change of ice patterns and seasonal weather (e.g. Maxwell 1997, Nelson et al. 2002, Berkes and Jolly 2001). Indeed, Elders already comment that their ability to predict weather, so important for safe travel on the land, is diminished as weather and winds display novel patterns.

The local subsistence economy continues to be significant, though substantial investments in equipment and fuel are often now required to be able to harvest country foods. The dollar value of country foods, especially fish and wild meats, is very high[2] (cf. Wein and Freeman 1992; Wein 1994) though many people fail to realize their worth. Within this changed context, the local, informal institutions continue to operate, and newer institutions such as the Renewable Resource Councils, the Band Councils, the Designated Gwich'in Organizations, the Gwich'in Tribal Council, the Porcupine Caribou Management Board, and the Gwich'in Co-management Boards monitor land and resource use and debate competing uses for land. Serious questions about the nature of the future landscape in the Mackenzie Delta are hotly debated as of this writing, when Imperial Oil and the other pipeline proponents are waiting for the conclusion of the environmental impact assessment and the decision of the National Energy Board. Concerns regarding the impacts of oil and gas development and of the gas pipeline, and their impacts on key places on the land, temper optimism about badly needed economic development and choices about the Gwich'in future. Concerns about the accelerating impact of global climatic change are also present, and no one is sure how the land, the seasons, or the animals will respond. Though the knowledge of the land may change, and the land and animals themselves may change, relationship to the land remains and will remain a foundation of Gwich'in life, health and identity.

9

Of Nets and Nodes

REFLECTIONS ON DENE ETHNOECOLOGY AND LANDSCAPE

In this chapter I consider landscape and ethnoecology in light of some distinctive aspects of the various peoples who speak Athapaskan languages. I give another perspective on the Witsuwit'en as Dene, and bringing out commonalities between Witsuwit'en and northern Dene.

Athapaskan speakers live across a broad swath of northern North America, from central Alaska to the shores of Hudson Bay, and in the Canadian provinces of British Columbia, Alberta, Saskatchewan and Manitoba. At some time in the past, other Athapaskan speaking groups moved south to become the ancestors of the Apache, Navajo, and small groups of Athapaskan speakers in the Pacific Northwest, according to archaeologists and linguists (Ives and Rice 2003; Ives 2003; Matson and Magne 2007). The north is the homeland of Athapaskan speakers. As we have seen, northern Athapaskans, or Dene, are travelling people. Their traditional subsistence and way of life involved a great deal of movement across the landscape and over the seasons, as they harvested a variety of resources, especially caribou and other large game, various lake and river fish, and berries. I have described how rivers and trails organize movement across the landscape and through the seasons, linking places and areas, and providing a mental template that connects places and seasons, individual histories, and knowledge of the land itself. We can conceive, then, that Dene landscape ethnoecology is organized by a series of anastomosing pathways which form what I call "nets," and by "nodes," focal places along the net of trails and waterways that continue to shape human movement over the land. This way of dwelling in and understanding the world is based on a "traveller's path," the experience of land which arises by moving through it, that differs fundamentally from the notion of land as fixed bounded plots, typical of European based perceptions of the land surface. The sense of the land as bounded areas is the basis of the planometric area-based polygon which underlies most approaches to mapping and Geographic Information Systems (as I discuss in chapters 11 and 12) and relates to concepts of expanses of land as owned, delineated plots. This common approach to organizing space is implicit in resource management paradigms, and explicit in political geography. Tim Ingold calls it "the view from nowhere" (Ingold 1993:155). Dene are always somewhere, and see the land in relationship to where they are, where they have been (backwards along the trail), and where they are going.

In Dene ecology, drainage basins are fundamental units, with the directionality of slope and river flow as basic perceptions (Kari 1989, 1996, 2008). Athapaskan languages are rich with terms that indicate spatial directions of movement of the speaker, or of landscape elements to each other (Moore 2000; Tlen 2006; Basso 1996). Pat Moore explained that the directional terms in Kaska deal with the path of the speaker, refer to places in front or behind the speaker on the trail or river, or to one side or the other; this system is characteristic of all Athapaskan languages (Kari 2008). These can be extended to include areas at the general distance indicated, and can be metaphorically extended to social relationships. (Moore 2002).

The reflections in this chapter integrate insights from my work with the Witsuwit'en of northwest British Columbia, whose ethnogeography and berry patch knowledge I discuss in Chapters 4 and 5, the Kaska Dena of the southern Yukon whom we have met in Chapter 6, the Gwich'in of the Mackenzie Delta, discussed in Chapters 7 and 8, and another northern Dene group, the Sahú'otine of Great Bear Lake, Northwest Territories (Figure 9.1).

Patterns and variations in Dene landscapes

I begin my discussion of specific patterns of Dene landscapes with the Kaska. The first-order shaping of the Kaska land includes the major rivers and lakes, and significant mountains: the Frances River (Tu Chō Tué') flowing out of Frances Lake (Tu Chō Mene) and joining the Upper Liard, and in turn uniting with other tributaries such as the Dease, which enters at Lower Post, and

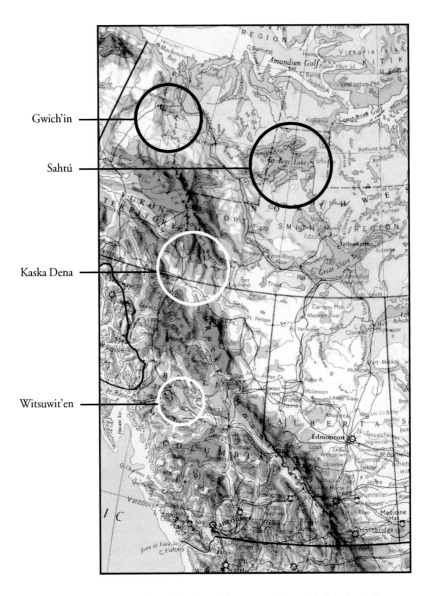

Gwich'in

Sahtú

Kaska Dena

Witsuwit'en

Figure 9.1 General locations of Dene groups discussed in this chapter (basemap from Atlas of Canada and the World second edition Key Porter Books 1997)

the Kechika, which enters above the Grand Canyon of the Liard. As we have seen, significant mountains have names and stories, and are used as landmarks and reference points. Major rivers are all named, and directionality of the rivers and drainage divides has shaped traditional travel. There is a web of trails which connect places on the landscape and through the seasonal round: hunting trails, berrying trails, river travel corridors, and trails for moving over distance such as the Liard-Simpson Lake Trail, which extended from Simpson Lake (Tsē Zul Mene) down to Lower Post BC (Daliyo) in the trading post era. The rivers and the large lakes such as Frances Lake (Tu Chō Mene) are also travel corridors in both summer and winter. The web of pathways forms the "net," the pattern of all of these corridors of travel, these trails, on the landscape. The "nodes" are the places where people converge—the resource patches, camps, or home base areas that focus movement through the seasons—that people occupy or use in transit between seasonal or other resource areas. To give a sense of the flow of the land, I include a sample of my notes travelling a truck trail that parallels the older trapline trail through an area familiar to my teacher Mida Donnessey. As we ascended a ridge:

> Mida explained that fresh moose track is **kéde daga**, uphill is **kúda digé**, and downhill is **kúda ats'á**. **Tlétāgī** is on top of the hill.

> We drove on to Billy Lake [on the top of the hill] for our lunch stop. The old foot trail comes through there, following the ridge. I photographed the trail with two very old blazes, and the camp. The site sits on the ridge top and overlooks the lake. Mida says people sit there and watch for moose in the sedge meadows and wetlands that lie on the western side of the lake. The trail comes up Fish Creek from the place we picked mint. It was her Uncle Liard Tom's trapline, that whole area. Then Frank Tom, who passed away last year, had the trapline.

After stopping at Billy Lake we continued on the old route, passing through an area her Uncles told Mida about, where there is an extensive deposit of red ochre sand, and on toward the confluence of the Rancheria (Tsįh Tue') and the Little Rancheria Rivers, and describing the crossing to the Moose River and the hot springs there.

Fish lakes, alpine hunting areas, river fishing areas, berry picking areas, and places for beaver or moose (*Alces alces*) hunting are some of the nodes on the land.

In the historic period, trading posts and trapline cabins also formed nodes, and family trapping areas centred on trapline cabins and winter camps. In contemporary life, the villages are central places from which people radiate as they travel on the land, and the major highways such as the Alaska Highway, the Cassiar Highway, and the Campbell Highway, facilitate vehicle access to regions adjacent to these arteries.

In contrast, in Witsuwit'en country in west-central and northwestern British Columbia, both the topography and the regional aboriginal political geography combine to make ownership of fixed bounded territories a strong feature of the regional ethnoecology (Figure 9.2). These territories belong to corporate house groups called *yikh*, which themselves are organized into exogamous clans (Gitumden, Tsayu, Laksilyu, Gilhseyu, and Laksamishu). The reciprocal relations between clans of spouses, and therefore clans of fathers and sons, influences access to territory in a manner similar to the Gitksan (Daly 2005; Mills 2005; Johnson 1998).

A well-developed trail net traversed the Witsuwit'en homeland (main trails are indicated by heavy dotted lines crossing the clan territories on Figure 9.2). People travelled in a large seasonal round, alternating time on their winter hunting and trapping territories with coming together to fish and feast in the summer at canyon fisheries. Some families travelled long distances, while other groups had territories adjacent to the summer villages. The late Elsie Tait provided a clear picture of the Witsuwit'en cycle of movement in the early years of the twentieth century:

> Summertime. That's the potlatch, big feast time. They would gather up all of the elders from Nass River and all around. In the old days the people from this Hagwilget Reserve, they all moved in toward Fort Fraser, Fraser Lake, and spread out there. They went to the lakes to fish [for char and whitefish?] and out on their traplines and hunting grounds. In the summer they all came back here. They came by horse and buggies with bundles of smoked meat and half-smoked and dried lake trout . . . They moved back to their houses or set up tents.
> Then the big feast time comes for a couple of months. (Elsie Tait, L.M. Johnson interview notes October 29, 1986)

Each territory had its own trails connecting river to alpine zone, and extending to key lakes, and so on. An interesting aspect of the trail net is that main trails necessary to access one's trapline from the summer salmon

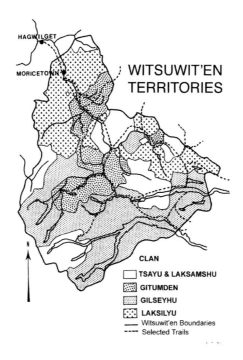

Figure 9.2 Map of Witsuwit'en lands showing clan territories and major trails Witsuwit'en relationship to land is framed in the context of clan and house territories that are fixed and bounded (after Gottesfeld 1993).

fishing village are a kind of no man's land in terms of hunting; Alfred Joseph, Gisde We, affirmed that people travelling along such a travel corridor may hunt in the immediate vicinity of the trail for their subsistence while travelling without infringing the rights of the adjacent territory holders. Certain concentrated resource patches are nodes and access to these resource-rich areas is definitely controlled: alpine groundhog[1] hunting areas were such a resource for the Witsuwit'en, attested in part by vocabulary highlighting the ecotopes which support this resource. Berry patches and fishing stations were other resource nodes for Witsuwit'en. The whole question of territoriality and ownership of resource sites among the Witsuwit'en is related to the discussions of economic defendability (Dyson-Hudson and Smith 1978), and access limitation brought forward by Richardson (1982) for the northern Northwest Coast (Gottesfeld 1993), and applies to Gitksan resource sites and territories as well. Significant resources were spatially restricted and of local abundance, making them "worth" defending; in other words, limiting access by others. In practice, the complex social relations between "mother's" and "father's" sides, and between husbands and wives, makes access to resources very flexible. As with the Yolngu (Williams 1982), the key thing is to ask. The interesting aspect of Witsuwit'en territoriality is that it is overlaid, as it were, on a more fundamental Athapaskan pattern exemplified by Kaska Dena.

Northern Dene—Gwich'in and Sahtú

Gwich'in means "those who dwell here." Gwich'in landscape ranges from flatlands and complex delta environments to the more rugged terrain of the Richardson and Ogilvie Mountains with their extensive rocky areas and alpine peatlands. Gwich'in from Teetl'it Zheh (Fort McPherson) use lands and waterways in the northern Yukon, and have strong social relationships with Gwich'in now settled in Old Crow. The Dagoo who occupied the ranges and rivers draining the ranges and valleys of the Ogilvie and Richardson Mountains settled in more recent times in Teetl'it Zheh, Aklavik, and Old Crow. Routes and passes through the mountains from the drainage of the Peel and the west side of the Mackenzie Delta extend to Old Crow and the Old Crow Basin, and down to meet the Tronjek Hwech'in (Han) in the drainage of the North Fork of the Klondike River near Dawson City. The social net also encompasses Gwich'in from across the border in Alaska, who dwell on the Yukon River and its tributaries and use the slopes of the Brooks Range. Upriver on the Mackenzie, the area of Thunder River marks the contact with the Sahtú people, who speak North Slavey, and now reside in Fort Good Hope and Colville Lake. People from Tsiigehtchic have strong social relations with Fort Good Hope people, as the Mackenzie has been a major travel route, and in historic times they have also shared the Catholic religion. A sense of the movement up and down the Peel from the present site of Teet'lit Zheh is described in Chapter 7.

A bit to the south and east, the Sahtú'otine landscape is dominated by Bear Lake and its pervasive influence on the climate, vegetation, and human mobility. Travel on the lake enables access to many significant areas, but requires knowledge and respect to achieve safely. The inflowing rivers and adjacent lakes are also important, such as the Johnny Ho River. The major trail overland past Hottah Lake, through Rae Lakes to Great Slave Lake to the south, called the Įdaà Trail (Andrews and Zoe 1997; Auld et al. 2005), facilitated strong regional connections, and bypassed the longer and more difficult route up the Mackenzie River. Even in recent times, trips are undertaken along this route to visit Tłįchǫ neighbours in Rae Lakes. The outflowing Great Bear River, connecting the Sahtú people to their relatives at Tulita on the Mackenzie, is also very important.

Rivers—pathways, barriers, and sources of fish

Northern rivers are pathways in the summer and winter seasons, and are barriers to travel in spring and fall, during freeze-up and break-up, and where waterfalls, dangerous rapids or canyons obstruct safe boat or ice travel, quintessential strands of the net. Rivers are also one of the main sources of fish in the summer and early fall seasons. Use of fish is a fundamental Athapaskan Dene strategy. River fishing with traps, nets, and hooks in the open water season has been important in many locations as we have seen in previous chapters. Winter fishing in known and reliable "fish lakes" in winter is also important, especially for more northern groups.

The main fish used by Gwich'in are species of whitefish and arctic charr, and the loche, and they were are still obtained by netting in river eddies in the summer, by net under the fall river ice, on fish lakes, and in spawning areas such as the one described by Hyacinthe Andre by Travaillant Lake. In the past fish were extremely important as dog feed, allowing use of dogsleds to cover large distances and haul meat and the gear necessary for making camp and making northern life possible (L.M. Johnson field notes 1999-2000). Families formerly tended to use dispersed fishing areas consistently, but now people may focus their attention on eddies close the main settlements.

The waters of Great Bear Lake, Sahtú itself, shape the Sahtú'otine fishery. Nets are set from the ice off the shore of the village of Deline, and at other productive locations on the lake (Figure 9.3). Large amounts of huge lake trout are the main species thus caught. There are also net fisheries in bays with inflowing streams, and there was formerly a significant spring fishery at the outlet of the Johnny Ho River at the south end of McTavish Arm, now known to be contaminated by naturally occurring mercury (Auld et al. 2005:24). People know where to fish for grayling along the rivers in the summer season, as at the mouths of some tributary creeks to the Great Bear River. Whitefish are also taken.

The Kaska in the Liard drainage lack local access to salmon.[2] They rely on whitefish runs into fish lakes, and on other fish such as grayling or pike (jackfish) in either rivers or lakes. Formerly, there were encampments in the summer to harvest and smoke-dry the whitefish that lived in lakes such as Simpson Lake, Frances Lake, and Watson Lake. (The construction and improvement of the airstrip, and highway construction have tainted and disrupted the fish in Watson Lake itself, which can no longer be used.) Eddies on the Frances (Tu Chō Tué'), Rancheria (Tsı́h Tué') and other local rivers are productive sites for line fishing for grayling. Fish lakes, sometimes called *thuwe* ('fish') are used throughout the seasons. Kaska elders such as my

Figure 9.3 Tsía, Russell Bay, a productive area for summer lake charr fishing on Sahtú, Great Bear Lake

teacher Mida Donnessey can give an inventory of all of the fish lakes, and what species can be fished from them, along the trails or highways they have frequented over the course of their lives.

For the Witsuwit'en in northwest British Columbia, the Skeena River system provides anadromous salmon, especially the highly prized chinook ("spring") salmon (*Oncorhynchus tshawytscha*) and sockeye (*O. nerka*). The two main Witsuwit'en village sites, Hagwilget (Tse Kya or Tsë Cakh) and Moricetown (Kyah Wiget) are located adjacent to productive canyon fisheries, and formed an annual focus for summer gathering sites.[3] Much has been written about the Skeena River fishery (Morrell 1989; Gottesfeld et al. 2002), including some regarding conservation ideology (Gottesfeld 1994c). Chinook are taken by gaff in canyon sites that constrict the river's flow and force fish to pass in specific areas, where they rest in deep eddies after battling the strong current. Fishing stations were named and owned, and those not destroyed in federal government salmonid enhancement efforts of the 1950s are still used. Trout are also fished from lakes and rivers. Traditionally, other species such as whitefish and sucker fish (*Catostomus* spp.) were also taken in winter through the lake ice, and implements such as willow bark nets were used in such fisheries.

Caribou

Caribou are a key component of northern Dene life. Northern Dene such as the Gwich'in and Sahtú people rely primarily on migratory herds of barren ground caribou, while Kaska, and formerly Witsuwit'en rely on woodland caribou. Caribou movement is key in shaping access to caribou in different regions.

Barren ground caribou are highly migratory, and the probability of encounter is only broadly predictable over their range through the seasons, requiring both mobility and information sharing to ensure that everyone has access to fresh meat. When barren ground caribou are encountered, there are often very large numbers of animals, leading to a premium on sharing information about the location of animals, and of sharing meat. Formerly, Gwich'in in the northern Yukon constructed huge and elaborate caribou fences with snares, a communal activity that intercepted migrating herds and yielded large amounts of meat (LeBlanc 2006; McFee 1981; Roseneau 1974; Warbelow et al. 1975).

For the Sahtú'otine, Great Bear Lake (Sahtú) not only serves for obtaining fish, but also serves as a primary means of accessing caribou. In season, hunters centred in Deline travel by lake to the north end of the lake some 200 km from the community, to the Barren Grounds, for caribou. In the fall when the barren ground caribou of the Bluenose-East Herd (Auld et al. 2005:47) reach the area around the north shore, the lake is still open and the water turbulent even as the surrounding land grows cold. Later in the season, caribou utilize the peninsula across Keith Arm, a much less arduous journey across the lake ice.

Figure 9.4 Boreal woodland caribou hunted by George Kenny and Simon Neyelle along the Bear River, July 2006 and brought to the Deline Plants for Life camp to share

In the summer, barren ground caribou and boreal woodland caribou (Tracz 2006) may be encountered along rivers such as the Mackenzie or Great Bear River as single animals or in small groups, where they are hunted when encountered (Figure 9.4).

Kaska hunt woodland caribou in the mid to late summer in the alpine zone when access up trails or truck trails is good, and when the animals are feeding in relatively lush alpine meadows. This is a contemporary continuation of an ancestral Athapaskan alpine caribou hunting tradition revealed in ice patch archaeology: stone hunting blinds where a hunter could crouch with atl-atl and darts, or bow and arrows, are still evident in the mountains of the southwestern Yukon and the Mackenzie Mountains on the Northwest Territories border, and organic remains of the darts and arrows are melting out of the ice patches (Hare et al. 2004; Farnell et al. 2004; Andrews et al. 2009). In the winter woodland caribou descend from the mountains and roam the lower slopes and valleys, favouring open pine stands (*gǭdze*) with abundant lichens, such as the "white moss" (*ajú*) or turf of *Cladina* species. They can be hunted in such locations, I was told.

Caribou are now nearly absent in Witsuwit'en country, though twenty-five years ago old weathered antlers could still be found in alpine areas they formerly inhabited (Mike Morrell, pers. comm., 1984). Elders such as the late Johnny David (Mills 2005) recalled the time when caribou were hunted and moose yet uncommon in the region. Climate change and perhaps Euro-Canadian settlement seem to have progressively favoured in-migration of moose, which have increased in numbers while caribou precipitously declined. At this time, a very small remnant herd persists in the alpine zone near Telkwa Pass.

Berries

Although animals and fish may dominate Dene traditional economy and shape ethnoecological perception, berries in season also exert their pull. Berries are one of the few productive plant foods of northern latitudes, and often appear in profusion while in season (cf. Parlee et al. 2006; Trusler and Johnson 2008; this work, Chapter 5). In northern communities, berries may suddenly dominate conversation, and children, women and men may all go berry picking when blueberries or cranberries ripen. As described in Chapter 5, the most important berry species for the Witsuwit'en are black huckleberry (*Vaccinium membranaceum*), lowbush blueberry (*V. caespitosum*), and saskatoon (*Amelanchier alnifolia*) and a number of other species such as wild strawberries (*Fragaria virginiana*) are also utilized. The Witsuwit'en, in common with other indigenous peoples in British Columbia and apparently in contrast with northern Dene, managed berry patches by burning, especially harvesting areas for the favoured black huckleberry and lowbush blueberry.

For the Gwich'in, the three main types of berries still widely sought are cloudberries (*Rubus chamaemorus*), locally called yellow berries; blueberries (*Vaccinium uliginosum*); and lingonberries (*V. vitis-idaea*), also called lowbush cranberries. The cloudberries have a very short season at the beginning of August, but may be harvested in large quantities in certain areas at the right time. Blueberries are slightly later than cloudberries, and blueberries and cloudberries may be found in the same places at times. They also have a short season, and do not keep well unfrozen. Cranberries are widely available and highly prized. Although the plants are very common, productive patches are not ubiquitous, and neither can the berry crop be consistently relied upon. According to Parlee, families tend to have more or less private cranberry patches near fish camps (Parlee et al. 2006). The degree of sharing of berries, access control and sharing of information seems to vary in part depending on annual or seasonal patterns of abundance or scarcity.

Certain sites are known as productive berry areas for the Sahtú people. The alluvial fan where Wolverine Creek enters the Great Bear River is one site known for its abundant and productive berry plants, and is easily accessed by those travelling up or down the Great Bear River. (The association of the abundant berries with bears was one reason our group camped at a different location in the summer of 2006.) Bog blueberries (*Vaccinium uliginosum*) and lowbush cranberries are prized berry species.

Kaska also pick bog blueberries, "blackberries" (crowberries, *Empetrum nigrum*) and lowbush cranberries, as well as smaller amounts of several other berry species, including raspberries (*Rubus idaeus*), highbush cranberries (*Viburnum edule*), wild strawberries, soapberries (*Shepherdia canadensis*), and cloudberries. Cranberries are picked in particularly large quantities because they store well. People are attentive to the characteristics of sites with good berries, and also watch where cranberries flower heavily in the spring to predict where the berry crop will be concentrated in the fall, as I describe in Chapter 6. Cranberry patches adjacent to traditional camps or on traplines may to some degree be seen as belonging to the owner, as with the Gwich'in, though at this point anecdotal evidence is only suggestive of access limitation.

Dene patterns: connectivity of nets and nodes

Travelling with Kaska Elder Mida Donnessey, I began to get a sense of some other important focal areas for hunting people. For example, people always talk about licks, mineral lick areas that are visited by animals such as moose, caribou or mountain sheep, particularly when travelling up or down the road or trail that passes a lick area. I learned that lick areas can be spoiled by physical disturbance (e.g. road construction) or by improper behaviour such as failing to retrieve a wounded animal, or fouling the area with entrails (L.M. Johnson field notes 1998-2004). Such areas are of obvious importance for hunters to know about, and may require special care not to disturb the population balance of animals that use the area.

Much further north, along the Dempster highway, the presence of a lick near the road and the river brought thinhorn sheep (*Ovis dalli*) to the slope by the highway just once in several trips up and down the highway, which made me think of my Gwich'in friends' admonition to be constantly watchful, because you never know when you will see an animal (see Figure 9.5).

I also learned about lookouts from travelling with Mida. A lookout is an area along a trail at the top of a bluff or steep hill, which has a view of a productive area below where one may see game. This concept is also shared by Witsuwit'en who call such a place ***coënk'it***; the late Pat Namox described its importance in hunting and its association with seeing (see Chapter 4).

To get a sense of how different sites within an area may be spatially and seasonally related, I would like to return to consideration of what I learned from Mary Teya about her family's use of sites in the Road River area near the Yukon-Northwest Territories boundary. Mary mentioned key resource areas available in different areas near the various camps, including moose country, berry patches, and fish lakes (see Figure 7.3). The river provides reliable access to the area and between sites in summer and in winter. Trapline trails extend along the river or up ridges, converging on the main winter camp, located a few kilometres downstream of the summer fishing camp. Fishing sites, moose habitat, and berry patches all occur near the summer fish camp site. During spring (break-up) or fall (freeze-up), river travel, or indeed much travel at all, is impossible, so camps for spring and fall had to be located where resources could be reached in the immediate vicinity of the camp, as with the spring camp at Three Cabin Creek, where muskrats were available in the wetlands as well as moose in the willow areas.

In Northwest British Columbia, along the drainages of the Bulkley River, the trail net included main trails up and down the main river valleys, and shorter trails up side drainages that connected the main valley with the resources of montane and alpine slopes. The country is precipitous, and in pre-contact times considerable effort was expended in making trails in the mountains, and in making bridges over swift and deep rivers. The Blue Lake area, mentioned at the beginning of this chapter and in Chapter 5 as the site of an important berry patch, is a resource rich montane and subalpine area near the historic village of Hagwilget, where most Witsuwit'en lived for at least some part of the year. After salmon fishing along the main Bulkley River, people travelled up the trail to timberline in the Blue Lake area to access medicines, pick black huckleberries, hunt mountain goat (*Oreamnos americanus*), and dig fern rhizome (**diyii'n**, the rhizome of the spiny wood fern *Dryopteris expansa*) a highly prized carbohydrate food which could be stored for winter, packing down the harvest to the winter village at Hagwilget (Turner et al. 1992). People still sometimes pick berries up in old clearcut patches along a logging road that follows part of the old foot and horse trail. The site also had spiritual aspects, requiring first time travellers to put ashes on their faces, and it is mentioned in some Witsuwit'en narratives as a special place.

The sacred in Dene ethnoecology

The sacred, or spiritually potent, also shapes Dene ethnoecology. The land itself is sacred and things that come from the land, such as medicinal roots or red ochre, must be taken with prayer and payment (Mida Donnessey, L.M. Johnson field notes 1999-2004). The land contains reminders of moral lessons and past events in the relationship of people with place. Shiltee rock is a prominent landmark near Fort McPherson on the Peel River. As described in Chapter 7, this rock formation memorializes a story about a family who camped by the Peel long ago, and what happened when a young girl violated her puberty seclusion. Not only does the place provide a vivid reminder of the consequences of failing to observe the rules of proper behaviour, but it also remains a place of power that demands respect. As Mary and William Teya explained to me, in the late 1980s the community decided to hold a music festival and celebration in a meadow at the base of the slope below Shiltee Rock. Apparently, this was not sufficiently respectful of a place of power, and the following year the meadow area filled and became a lake. People considered that a sign and decided to move the festival to a small lake beside the Dempster Highway, halfway to the mountains. The lake by Shiltee Rock is again dry.

There are many stories about Distant Time and events which occurred long ago, shaping the present form of the world, connecting the distant past with the present in localized places, and providing a geography of power (e.g Andrews et al. 1998). Watson Lake was the site where a rampaging giant elephant was drowned through the quick-witted action of a clever young man, as I describe in Chapter 6. A rocky islet on Great Bear Lake is the frozen remnant of a ferocious giant wolf that used to terrorize travellers that passed by a certain rocky point where its lair was located (L.M. Johnson and C. Fletcher field notes 2005).[4] And red rock formations in Moricetown Canyon are evidence of an ancient tale of infidelity and revenge, also associated with spoiling hunting luck (Madeline Alfred [Dzee], L.M. Johnson interview notes 1988). Further afield, Henry Sharp (1987, 2001) describes giant animals that inhabit dangerous river crossings and other powerful places in the landscape of the Dene Sułine' (Chipewyan) in northern Saskatchewan, Manitoba, and Northwest Territories. Basso (1996a) and Palmer (2006) show similar connection of story to place, and its moral power for the Apache and the Secwepemc of Alkalai Lake, BC, respectively.

Sentient ecology and probabilistic encounter

The Dene world is well described by David Anderson's cogent phrase "sentient ecology" (2000) or Richard Nelson's "the watchful world" (Nelson 1983). For the Dene, the world itself is aware, and people exist in a dynamic and interactive relationship with all of its aspects, threading a careful path across the landscape, alert to all possibilities.

Dene ethnoecology is based on probabilistic encounter, and considers the landscape and the living things that dwell there to be sentient and have agency.[5] It is a moral universe that entails mutual obligations. People cannot take things for granted; they must be alert and perceptive, mentally nimble, ready to take opportunities that present themselves, and ready to avoid dangers. The landscape is not a mosaic of stable fixed areas with hard boundaries, though the exigencies of dealing with contemporary governments and jurisdictions sometimes impose such boundaries on the land.

Dene knowledge of place is rooted in experiential engagement with particular places through the seasons over lifetimes, and through narratives that extend backward through previous lifetimes back to Distant Time. People are keen observers, generalizing on the basis of previous experience of similar places, and quick to apprehend present potentialities. The landscape as well as the plants and animals that dwell within it exist in shifting configurations that form trajectories across the seasons as well as space. The engaged and aware person must be aware of and responsive to these configurations when encountered.

Figure 9.5 Dall sheep along Dempster Highway in the area of Engineer Creek This sheep sighting symbolized "probabilistic encounter" for me.

Reflections and refractions

Thinking about landscape and journeying. . . . I imagine the bubble of here—relationships with landscape experienced from where the journeyer stands—moving with him/her as he/she journeys . . .

Emplacing story on landscape—as relationships move with the journeyer, they are (re-) established in homelands. When people pause in the journey and take up a place as home, stories and relationships are created by dwelling.

The story about the pubescent girl and her father/brothers and/or the dogs turning to stone is emplaced multiple times—at Shiltee rock on the Peel in the homeland of the Gwich'in, and again by Ross river.

Emerging from the moss house[6] into the upper world—and there were monsters, as the Twins found when they emerged into the present world.

The Navajo hogan really is similar to the Gwich'in moss house; they are the "same" kind of dwelling.

Is this the origin of Ket and Navajo stories of emergence from the lower world? Can this emergence also be seen symbolically as birth from the safe lower/inner space of darkness through the empowered hole into a place of light, risk and possibility? Light entails vision and visibility, knowledge and vulnerability.

Thinking about Navajo cosmology and Ket. . . . emerging from a safe lower world to the surface of the land that we know . . . there were monsters to be overcome before the world became as we know it now, relatively safe for human dwelling. All the Dene tell stories about overcoming monsters . . . even Europeans have stories about this . . . memory is long and dwelling on the land is as long as humankind. Kaska have "elephants"; Navajo monsters killed by the Twins; the giant wolverine of Kaska and Dene Tha narrative and others . . . even science acknowledges that there were monsters in that Distant Time when the Age of Ice was waning. . .

These thoughts occur to me after a recent visit to Navajoland, or Dine Bikéya, my first real visit with southern Athapaskan speakers. Connections are even more ancient: it is now apparent that the Ket and Yeniseic speakers of Siberia are far distant kin to the Dene, speaking a language that shows relationship even after thousands of years of separation, and sharing similarly deep ways of understanding the land.

These thoughts also occur to me after reading Spider Woman *by Gladys Reichard (1934), Ed Vajda's (2008) paper "A Siberian Link with Na-Dene Languages," and Ingold's (1993) "The temporality of the landscape." I also give a nod to Moore and Wheelock's (1990)* Wolverine Myths and Visions, Dene Traditions of Northern Alberta, *to Dene Gudeji, Kaska Narratives (1999), and to the stories my Kaska Elder teachers Mida Donnessey and Alice Brodhagen have told me.*

10

Of Named Places

Throughout this book I have referred to named places—rivers, lakes, communities, and the like—as well as to generic place kinds, also called ecotopes. What kinds of places get names? And are there any regularities to which places get singular names, rather than a generic geographic or ecotopic designation? Jett, describing Navajo named places in the American southwest, commented that some features are so unusual as to constitute singularities, that are unique, distinctive, and highly salient features of the landscape, such as Shiprock, Naat'áanii Nééz (Stephen Jett, pers. comm., 2008). Large rivers, and often prominent mountains are named, but not in all cases. Instead, as Hunn commented (1990), smaller features such as resource sites may be named, but a large mountain not named. Areas too may be named, as in the larger regional terms documented by Kari (1989). Instructive differences in the kinds of features names are found in Waterman's descriptions of Puget Sound (1922, quoted in Thornton 1997):

> Waterman observed that "A special name will often be given to a
> rock no larger than a kitchen table while, on the other hand, what
> we consider the large and important features of a region's geography

have no names at all." (1922:178) "Persistent inquiry among the Indians concerning romantic-looking peaks, towering up against the sky arouses no reaction except boredom," he confessed (n.d.a:17). Mountain ranges, rivers, islands, and bays might remain nameless, although dozens, even hundreds of place names might be applied to portions of these features. For example, Yuroks gave Waterman twelve names for places on the slopes of a single mountain, but no name for the mountain as a whole.

Apparently Bainbridge Island, a large island in Puget Sound, had no name at all, but 300 smaller features on the island were named. The size of features named is a question of scales of interest, and distances travelled. If you live on the mountain or island, there may be no need to name the entire large feature. Thornton (1997, 2008) provides an enlightening discussion of named features in the Glacier Bay area of southeast Alaska. In Glacier Bay, Thornton tells us, English place names prominently designate glaciers and mountains, while Tlingit place names often focus on creeks, camping places, and fishing sites.

Obviously not every place is named or worthy of a specific name. There must be some distinctive feature to this forest, that hill, that rock formation, a reason to keep specific places in mind. Food and sources of food are obvious motivators, and numerous place names of indigenous North Americans refer to food resources such as fish or berries (An Sim 'Maa'y, 'black huckleberry on it'; Bik'it digï Ts'oyin, 'we pick black huckleberry on it'; Xsigunya'a, 'Spring Salmon River'). The needs of travellers are another. Kari's detailed investigation of Denai'ina and Ahtna place names suggests one reason to name features—navigation (Kari and Fall 1987; Kari 1989, 1996, 2008). He describes systems of regional place names that encompass the major waterways, routes, and a variety of significant creeks, ridges, peaks, and other features which serve as navigational aids to travellers, enabling people to find safe passes and crossings as they traverse regions for hunting or trade. This resonates with the descriptions of Inuinnait trails with their strings of named places and songs, which help people to remember the landmarks, camps, and resources in areas strung along the trails (Collignon 2006).

Names also record travel hazards or customary activities that take place or formerly took place, at specific sites, such as Chuu tr'idaojìich'uu or Chuw tr'in'aodìich'uu (meaning 'water-rough hateful'), the Peel River Canyon. According to the description on the Gwich'in Place Name Map web page, the canyon, which is both beautiful and dangerous is passable by boat only with a skilled boatman who can "read the water, can avoid eddies and is comfortable with fast flowing water." The canyon requires respect and caution. The description gives a sense of the historic importance of such sites, and why they would be accorded names:

> In early historic times, it [the canyon] was considered so treacherous, that when Teetl'it Gwich'in families who had spent all winter in the upper Peel hunting in the mountains arrived at the canyon in the spring, only the men would take the moose skin boats through the canyon. Each boat had a captain responsible for steering the boat with a large wooden oar and directing the paddlers. The women, children and dogs walked over the portage trail on top of the high cliffs and met the men at the downstream end. If all went well, there was a big celebration here where the best foods would be brought out and a great feast held. After the feast, they would continue their trip down the Peel River meeting other families along their way to Fort McPherson to trade their meat and furs at the Hudson's Bay Company post.
> (http://www.gwichin.ca/Research/placeNamePeel.asp?num=25)

Legat et al. (2001) in their report on Dogrib Tłįchǫ habitats and place names found that river names tended to encode travel hazards, while land place names frequently were rich in ecological information.

Another reason to name specific sites is related to ownership. For Gitksan, knowing the names to features on the territory demonstrates ownership, and also encodes history as it is emplaced on the land. The history itself is an aspect of relationship to and ownership of places on the land. As Dinim Gyet said (see Chapter 3), "You say you own this, your land, most of the place names are all in our language, hey, cause they say that the Creator gave it to us and he give us the names to go with it." In my discussion of the Gitksan storied landscape, I likened the named places to mnemonic pegs on which to "hang" a good deal of information about places and the nature of the land, a metaphor earlier employed by Basso (1990a:128). So, to paraphrase Lévi-Strauss, one might say that names are good to think with, adding specificity and precision to one's recollections of routes and of sites of travel hazard, of sites for specific resources, and through histories and sacred sites, for significant guidance in proper and effective relationships to the land. Or as Thornton would have it, "Toponyms embody both ecological and socio-logical knowledge, and Tlingits learn to *think with the landscape* to achieve a variety of material and social goals" (2008:66, emphasis added).

When I think of "Stekyooden," the magnificent and prominent massif that rises above Hagwilget, Gitanmaax and the Hazeltons in northwest BC, I think about the cautionary tale of the One Horned Mountain Goat, and the necessity for a balanced and respectful relationship with the animals one hunts (Harris 1974). For Gitksan, this story is owned, and versions are part of the House and Chiefly property of two Gisg'aast (Fireweed) Houses. Antgulilbixw, the late Mary Johnson's totem pole in Ansbayaxw has a carving of the one horned goat at the top (Figure 10.1).

For northern Dene such as the Gwich'in, while names for places of habita-tion or special sites along rivers need not signal ownership, they nonetheless signal history and long use. Alestine Andre's fishing site at Tree River, Dighe' tr'aajil, has an ancient name[1] and a history, as does her uncle Gabe Andre's cabin site Tr'inehht'leet'iee about five miles upriver.

Sites such as Shiltee Rock (Shiłdii) also signal history from ancient times, which guide succeeding generations of Gwich'in in appropriate respectful behaviour for the land and the beings who share it with them. The rock is a prominent and unusual rock formation that is visible to all who travel along the Peel River. Other sites of unusual rock formation along the Mack-enzie are also named, and record the deeds of Yamoria from ancient times (Andrews 1990).

Names pertain to places rather than to ecological types. Places often form nodes along the trails and rivers that traverse the landscape. Places vary from sites of very limited areal extent to larger clusters of sites that share names, as Thornton pointed out for Tlingit sites. This is clearly evident for other peoples too: "Road River" (in English) refers to a whole suite of sites along a several-kilometre section of the Peel River, including the winter and sum-mer camps (Figures 7.3–7.6), and the sites of old spring and fall camps and associated berry patches. It does not designate in particular the exact conflu-ence of the Road River with the Peel. This area has extent, but does not have hard boundaries; it is characteristic of places generally that they have areal extent, and lack hard boundaries.[2] Some are broad, such as areas which in Athapaskan languages get special words that indicate 'in the area of' (Kari 2008:12; The Hagwilget [Tse Kya] Band 1995:53), and others are more or less linear features, such as tracks. Rivers, and Australian Dreaming Tracks (*Tjukurpi*) are places with linear extent. Ridges may also be considered linear

Figure 10.1 Totem pole of Antk'ulilbixsxw (the late Mary Johnson) in Ansbayaxw Totem poles instantiate the linkage of House groups to place, through crests which memorialize emplaced history.

places, though not as lengthy as rivers or Dreaming Tracks. I was struck by the cross-cultural encounter revealed in trying to understand these linear places presented in an anecdote by Robert Layton about landscape in the Western Desert of Australia (Layton 1995:213). He wrote:

> The rules of a discourse determine which statements are sensible and which are deemed irrelevant, marginal, or unscientific. The rules specify what is possible. "How wide is a dreaming track?" is, for instance, a nonsensical question within discourse on the Dreaming, though it was one posed at an earlier land claim clearing.

Place names serve as a reflection of how a people view a landscape, and can reveal the kinds of places conceived of by a certain culture. There is an extensive literature on place names, or toponyms in papers (e.g. Tom 1987; Cruikshank 1990a, 1990b; Basso 1990a, 1990b; Correll 1976; Müller-Wille 1983, 1993; Kari and Fall 1987; Kari 1989; Boas 1934; Hunn 1996; Thornton 1997, 2008; Fowler 2009), and a wide range of rich local reports (e.g. Kritsch and Andre 1993, 1994; Greer 1999). As Cruikshank (1990a, 1990b) emphasizes, history is written on the land and is recounted and revisited by mentally travelling over the land, with place as the key to the past, a description very like that given by Dinim Gyet of mentally travelling the trails of his Lax Yip (House territory) under the tutelage of his grandmother. Moral narratives too, are given force by their connection with the land "in this place— it happened *here*" (Basso 1990), as with Shiltee Rock and Stekyooden.

Landmarks along travel corridors are given names, which serve as an orientation system. Apparently in Alaska, a set of consistent place names is widely recognized, and may remain the same across language boundaries, with phonological adjustment and substitution of the variant of generic terms such as 'river' of each language (Kari 1989). Place names can also be used to reveal kinds of places recognized by a culture in the form of what Kari has called "place name generics" (Kari 1989; Kari & Fall 1987), though Kari also comments that not all landscape terms function as "place name generics." He analyses Dena'ina and Ahtna place names to consist of a generic term, plus a modifier, much as plant and animal species are named scientifically. Generics found in Dena'ina include: 'where, place of'; 'the one which'; 'stream, river, creek'; 'river mouth'; 'headwaters'; 'glacier'; 'straight stretch of a river'; 'riverbank'; 'lake'; 'head of a lake'; 'lake outlet, lake outlet stream'; 'land, country'; 'mountain'; 'ridge'; 'hill'; 'flat, clear area, swamp'. With the exception of the first two, which simply specify the domain of 'place', the other terms all have content as types of geographic features with ecological entailments. Other languages may not customarily include a place term generic as the head of place names, though other Athapaskan languages and Gitksan frequently do.

My analysis of a smaller corpus of place names from unpublished files of the Gwich'in Social and Cultural Institute, carried out in 1998, also revealed a series of place kind generics which occurred in the set of 184 place names from two 1:250,000 map sheets (Table 10.1). The types of features named in this set (Table 10.2) reveal that creeks were the most frequently named feature (69), followed by lakes (30), and hills (including "rocks") (15). A number of places were called "place of ___" ("___ *k'it*") but it is not possible to describe what kinds of sites these were as this is a rather artificial grouping of descriptive names of areas. Referents for these place names were quite variable, and included descriptions and characterizations of the sites, people, vegetation, topographic position, fish or animal species, history, dwellings, hydrology, personal names, anatomy, birds, trails, human uses, rivers, or travelling (Table 10.3).

In a study of Gwich'ya Gwich'in place names published by the Gwich'in Social and Cultural Institute in 1993 (Kritsch and Andre 1993:21), the authors list the categories of place names:

- names referring to a Gwich'in person
- places known by two names; the Gwich'in name describing the place and the English one referring to a Gwich'in person
- places known by two names; the Gwich'in name describing a place or a resource and the English name referring to a white trapper and/or trader
- names referring to a white trapper and/or a trader
- names referring to a resource or an aspect of traditional resource economy
- descriptive name
- Ts'ii Dęįį names where the meaning has been lost
- names referring to a legendary place
- names referring to a story

This listing is interesting in that names which refer to use or occupancy by a person, whether Gwich'in or white, are prominent, and a dual naming system encompassing Gwich'in names and an overlapping set of English place names is evident. The importance of description and of the traditional economy in place names is reiterated here, as is the significance of "legend"

Table 10.1 Gwich'in Place Name Generics and Vegetation Terms
(TG = Teetl'it Gwich'in dialect, GG = Gwichya Gwich'in dialect)

Gwich'in term	Dialect	English Gloss	Comments
han	TG	'river'	
han	TG	'channel'	
van	TG	'lake'	
tshik	TG	'creek'	
njik	TG	'creek'	
k'it	TG	'place'	'among, area of' (cognate with other Athapaskan terms; a locative, not a generic)
njuu	TG	'island'	
tshii (chii)	TG, GG	'rock'	
tshii (chii)	TG	'hill'	
vihshraįį	TG	'riverbank'	
vihsraîî	GG	'riverbank'	
thidii	TG	'point'	
thidiyee	GG	'point'	
òk	TG	'eddy'	
nitainlaii	TG	'waterfall'	
nidiilaįį	GG	'waterfall'	
nàn	TG	'hill'	this may really refer to 'land'
ddhàa'	TG	'mountain'	
eyendak	TG	'slough' or 'backchannel'	spelled *iyeendak* in the Gwich'in noun dictionary
git	TG	'glacier'	

Vegetation related terms

tl'oo	TG	'grass'	
dachan	TG	'timber'	
k'àii	TG	'willows'	also 'red willows' (includes shrub willow & alder)
gwahsri'	TG, GG	'meadow'	
gwahsri'	TG, GG	'open place'	
guzrii kak	GG	'barren land'	

from unpublished place name files of Gwich'in Social and Cultural Institute compiled by L.M. Johnson 1998

Table 10.2 Gwich'in Place Name Analysis: Named Feature Types

Feature type	Number named
creek	69
lake	30
places §	15
hill (incl. rock) *	15
island	8
river	6
mountain	4
dwelling	4
river reach	3
high bank	3
fishing site	3
channel	3
small creek	2
rock	2
headwaters	2
eddy	2
dry channel	2
waterfall	1
trail	1
small mountain	1
portage	1
point	1
glacier	1
creek mouth	1
community	1
channel divergence	1
back channel	1
animal habitat	1
Total places	**184**

§ "Places" are areas characterized by a feature, as in ____ k'it.
*One, Shiltee Rock, is also a sacred place

Based on database of Teetl'it Gwich'in Place Names prepared by Ingrid Kritsch.
Canadian NTS Map Sheets 106M and 106L

Table 10.3 Gwich'in Place Name Analysis: Referents for Place Names

Referent	Number of names
description	61
personal area (3 also coded as dwelling)	20
vegetation (7 also coded as description, 1 as animal, 1 as timber, 1 as topography)	19
place	18
position (2 coded also as description)	14
fish	14
history	12
unknown	10
animal (1 coded as history, 1 also as vegetation)	10
dwelling (1 coded as house; several as personal areas, and 1 as community)	6
substrate (3 coded also as description)	5
topography (4 coded also as description)	5
fish harvest (most also coded under fish)	5
hydrology (2 also coded as description)	4
behaviour (2 are fish, and 2 animal, of which 1 is also history)	4
personal name	4
timber	4
anatomical	3
artifacts	3
bird	3
trail (2 also coded as description)	3
confluence	2
culture	1
human use	1
mountain	1
community (also coded as position)	1
river	1
travelling	1
Total referents	**235**

and "story." It is also interesting to compare with Waterman's classification of the corpus of Yokuts place names he recorded in 1922 (page 185). His Table 1 includes the following types of place names:

- Descriptive terms, 202
- References to mythic episodes, 67
- References to animals, 35
- References to food supply, 34
- References to human activities, 33
- Unclassified terms, 49
- Untranslated terms, 137

Kaska place names are similar to the place names discussed by Kari (1989) for the Dena'ina and the Ahtna. Rivers or creeks are apparently often named for the lakes at their head, or lakes may be named for adjacent mountains and then the rivers carry the same name. Kari comments that virtually every lake in a drainage system has a name, unless it lacks fish and is remote from routes of travel or resource harvest. This certainly appears to be the case for Kaska too, where lakes are the most frequently named entities in the sample given in Kaska Tribal Council (1997) (Table 10.4). Mountains in contrast are less frequently named in the Dena'ina/Ahtna corpus. This may also be true for Kaska, but differences in geography make comparison difficult. Mountains and ridges are named in both Kaska and Witsuwit'en, and may have considerable regional or cosmological importance. Elder Mida Donnessey took care to point out three significant mountains and their names from our vantage point by the Tom Creek lookout in 1999, and she mentioned these mountains again on several other trips. Although in the Dena'ina/Ahtna corpus, different sites are infrequently reported to have the same name— Kari 1989 reports five instances of repeated names in a sample of 3200 place names—Kaska naming seems to be more flexible. Three different mountains in the sample of 129 Kaska place names were all called variants of 'Mountain Goat Mountain', two different creeks bore the name 'Lick Creek', and two different lakes, one not associated with a creek of the same name, were called 'Lick Lake'. I also documented a different Tsįh Tué 'Red Ochre River' than the one reported in the Dictionary.

Referents of Kaska place names show similarities with Gwich'in, and also with Witsuwit'en (discussed below). Table 10.5 shows the types of referents in the set of place names in the Dictionary corpus; descriptive names, those which refer to animals, fish, birds, animal habitats, other named features, fish habitat,

Table 10.4 Kaska Place Name Analysis: Types of Features Named

Types of features	Number
lakes	59
mountains	22
rivers	16
creeks	13
meadow areas	2
hills	2
slough	1
settlement	1
animal lick	1
glacier	1
river confluence area	1
Total named features	**119**

animal harvest and anatomy were most important (≥5 examples). History, vegetation, implements and minerals were less significant in place naming.

The phenomenon of sets of linked toponyms, where the stem is the same and the place kind generics vary or where "related parts" are named by reference to the basic place name, is described by Thornton (2008:99) as an "ensemblage." Sets of this sort are evident in Athapaskan place names, especially when dealing with terms relating to integrated drainages. Witsuwit'en Widzin Bin and Widzin Kwikh, the headwater lake and the river of the Morice-Bulkley system, for example, or Kaska Tehkēdenî'ā a mountain whose name means 'Standing Alone,' the associated lakes Tehkēdenî'ā Mené ('Standing Alone Lakes') and the river which flows from them, Tehkēdenî'ā Tuē' ('Standing Alone River') known in English as Ross River, a tributary of the Pelly. In English, the suite of sites designated by "Road River" (the Road River winter camp, the Road River fish camp) would also be an ensemblage of the functional sort given in a number of Tlingit examples.

For the Witsuwit'en, there is a need to recognize landmarks both for orientation and for delimitation of permitted areas for travel and resource harvest. This leads, then, to a sense of the specificity of place. For example, the consequences of being in the wrong place, in pre-contact times, might well be death, giving a high motivation for recognition of boundaries and of one's own place (Mills 1994). The Witsuwit'en had to travel over other Clans' territories to reach their winter trapping grounds. The major trails constituted a kind of 'no-man's land' and one was not guilty of trespass if legitimately travelling along a trail. One could even take animals for one's immediate subsistence in the immediate vicinity of the trail (Gottesfeld 1993:50), but harvest of other resources was not permitted to travellers.

As an aspect of the Territory system, Witsuwit'en place names may be proprietary and therefore relatively few are general public knowledge. The following discussion is based on a small set of names for features of regional importance, a set of place names around Hagwilget compiled in Tsë Cakh Wit'en (The Hagwilget [Tse Kya] Band 1995), and a smaller number of names mentioned to me during interviews. The set of names included in the Witsuwit'en literacy book is, unfortunately, mostly not translated, though indications of what kinds of places are named in the Hagwilget area, and what kinds of names are considered acceptable to share publicly can be gleaned from this list. The name of Hagwilget itself is Tsë Cakh[3] ('under the rock'). Many of the names on the list included in Tsë Cakh Wit'en are small local landmarks, some of which are in the village and in the immediate Hazelton area, and places along regional trails connecting Hagwilget with Babine Lake and the Bulkley Valley. The Babine Trail was a major trade trail,

Table 10.5
Kaska Place Name Analysis: Referents for Place Names

Referent Type	Number
fish	17
animal	11
bird	10
animal habitat	9
other named place	8
fish habitat	6
animal harvest	5
anatomical	5
history	4
locative	4
human reference	4
implement	3
bird habitat	2
vegetation	2
mineral resource	1
personal name	1
Total referents	**135**

which traversed both Gitksan and Witsuwit'en territories and was used as a pack trail in historic times. Many landmarks or resource areas around the Hagwilget area are actually on Gitksan owned territories immediately adjacent to Hazelton, and some of their names are loanwords from Gitksan. I re-analysed this list together with the names I had recorded in more recent years, this time excluding the local and Gitksan derived place names, to get a sense of the content and structure of Witsuwit'en place names.

The most frequently named features in my sample of 71 named places (Table 10.6) are creeks, mountains, hills and berry patches, with camps, lakes, animal habitat and constructed improvements on trails also being noteworthy. This listing is a reflection of the significance of landmarks and the importance of berry patches in Witsuwit'en ecology, but the sample is neither comprehensive nor representative. Naming sites of trail improvement also suggests the significance of maintaining infrastructure. My decision to eliminate places on Gitksan lands, and the current state of the Hagwilget fishery, are responsible for the lack of named places for fishing and smokehouse sites, and the fact I have not travelled in the mountains with hunters causes an under-representation of animal-related named places.

Examining the sample for the referents of the names (Table 10.7) is also instructive. In the Tsë Cakh Wit'en corpus, there are ten local names that are wholly or partially Gitksan in derivation, an unusual situation for Athapaskan languages. The long relationship between the Witsuwit'en and neighbouring Gitksan, and the significance of correct names in the territory system are likely responsible for this. Thirty-six of the remaining names were unanalysed in the Tsë Cakh Wit'en listing, and the meaning of one place name that was independently shared with me was not known to the speaker. Of the remaining names whose referents were apparent to me, nine had a botanical reference, eight were descriptive, and seven referred to animals,[4] animal habitat or animal anatomy. Five names referred to another named place, forming groups with the same base toponym. Three of these ensemblages are evident in my sample of names. Hydrography and 'hydrology' (flow direction), relative size, and position were also features of Witsuwit'en place names. I also analysed place name generics included in the sample of 71 names (Table 10.8). Thirty-seven percent of the names in the sample contained such generics. The four generics which were most frequent were *kwikh* 'creek, river'; *tsë* 'rock'; *dzil* 'mountain'; and *bin* 'lake'.

In Witsuwit'en, as with Kaska and other Athapaskan languages, it seems that drainage systems are perceived as integrated entities, so Wizdzin Kwikh

Table 10.6
Witsuwit'en Place Names: Types of Features Named

Feature Type	Number	other feature types/comments
creek	14	
mountain	13	1 also animal habitat
hill	6	
berry patch	5	also 2 hill, 1 ridge
camp	3	
lake	3	
animal habitat	3	
ridge	3	
constructed trail spot	2	
river	2	
rock formation	2	
trail	2	
vegetation	2	excludes berry patches and wetlands
hillside	1	
creek mouth into lake	1	
grassy slope	1	also animal habitat
flat/mythic site	1	
mountain basin?	1	
lake head	1	
large river	1	
single peak of mountain	1	
foot of mountain	1	
lake narrows	1	also animal habitat
[mountain] pass	1	
small lake	1	
spring	1	
trail end	1	
wetland	1	named for sphagnum
wetland/lake shore	1	named for cattails
Total features	**76**	

rises from Widzin Bin, and carries the name all the way to its confluence with the Skeena River (Ksan) at Hazelton. In contrast, to the English name Bulkley River is given to the river below Houston, but above Houston, "Bulkley" is attached to an easterly tributary stream with a much lower discharge, presumably for historical reasons, as that was the route of overland access by Euro-Canadians into the Bulkley Valley from the south and east. The proprietary nature of place names restricts the possibility of analysing frequencies of types of reference of place names, or of possible repeated names, though the status of place names as indications of rights to defined, bounded Clan territories suggests that repetition would be infrequent.

Table 10.7
Witsuwit'en Place Names: Toponym Referents

Referent	Number
Unanalysed	36
Gitksan	10
Botanical	9
Descriptive	8
Other named place (ensemblage)	5
Animal	5
Hydrology/hydrography	4
Size (big or little......)	4
Positional (under, or standing up)	3
Mythological	2
Flow direction	2
Unknown	1
Substrate	1
Human activity	1
Anatomical	1
Animal behaviour	1
Bird behaviour	1
Animal anatomy	1
Total referents	**95**

Analysis of 2008 sample; n=81; some double indexed

Table 10.8
Witsuwit'en Place Kind Generics

Toponym Generic	Gloss	Number
dzil	'mountain'	4
bin	'lake'	4
kwikh	'creek, river'	6
ts'iy	'ridge'	1
weggiz	'pass'	1
to	'water'	1
kun kët	'camp'	2
tiy	'trail'	2
tsë	'rock'	5
Total names with generics		**26**
Percentage of names with generic		**37%**

*this analysis is based on the 71 name sample which is of Witsuwit'en derivation

2 versions of 1 trail name; uncertain if 'rock' should be substrate referent or place kind generic

As with other Athapaskan groups, Witsuwit'en place names can frequently be descriptive, and may "paint a picture" of the place named, as with 'water flowing from among the cattails', or the name of a flat-topped mountain, 'sawed off bentwood box'. There is also a relatively large number of place names of Gitksan origin which is due to the particular historical circumstances of the location and origin of Hagwilget, Tsë Cakh. The village was established as an enclave in Gitksan territory due to a landslide blocking fish migration further upriver in the 1820s.

Witsuwit'en place names may well be associated with histories, and encounters of a supernatural nature may well be grounded in certain places, such as the 'Stone Beaver Dam' site near Quick. Special places also apparently served for orientation and calendrical reckoning too. The famous "footprints" by the place known in English as Sam Goozley Lake are such a Witsuwit'en place, mentioned to me by two different Elders who were related (on the Father's side) to Namaks, the Chief (Dineza) of that Territory (Alfred Mitchell pers. comm.; Pat Namox, pers. comm.).

It seems clear that Athapaskan speakers in northwestern North America organize their perception of the land as people who travel across the land. Place names and kinds of places both make sense from that perspective. Kari says, regarding Ahtna and Dena'ina understanding of place:

> Clearly the place names are *mental maps* that have been learned by careful memorization, and are a stable, conservative portion of the lexicon. . . .
>
> There are clear principles of *economy* and *memorizability* to the Ahtna-Dena'ina place names system, which make it well suited for long-distance overland travel. (Kari 1989:134-135, emphasis added)

He goes on to discuss travel narrative as a genre in Athapaskan speech, and gives examples which exemplify the linkage between place, individual experience, ecological knowledge, and history.

For other northern Athapaskans such as the Dogrib (Tłįchǫ) and Gwich'in, toponyms, strung together along trails and waterways, serve to link mythos and history, the resource potential of the country, the proper order of the world, and the risks of the lands and waters. These are all expressed through the process of travelling over land to specific places, and the narratives of such travel (cf. Andrews 1990).

Andrews and his co-authors' papers on the Įdaà trail (Andrews and Zoe 1997; Andrews et al. 1998) highlight the importance of the sequence of places along the trail as keys to the sacred, links with the power of the land. Interestingly, formerly important resource sites, such as places of good rock for stone tool construction, are often associated with power places which require ritual acknowledgement along this important travel and trade corridor. Places of harmful power also exist, and require either avoidance or special care to minimize risk. More recent remembrance and personal history may also be associated with particular places along the trail, and portage trails seem to be places especially rich in story. Andrews et al. (1998) write:

> The Dogrib landscape is a mosaic of significant places, all with names and stories attached to them. Place and narrative transform a physical geography into a social geography, where culture and landscape are transformed into a semiotic whole. In Dogrib cosmology, these places represent the physical embodiment of cultural process, which is realized through the combination of *travel* and *story-telling*. By travelling traditional trails, which link places like beads on a string, Dogrib youth are told stories as each place is visited. The stories provide all the knowledge necessary for living within the Dogrib landscape, and in later life *these places become mnemonics for recalling the narrative associated with them*... (emphasis added)

Andrews and Zoe (1997) write:

> The Dogrib landscape is infused with the presence of innumerable entities, or "powers," both benevolent and malevolent. In travelling across the landscape, one must constantly mitigate the impact of personal actions by appeasing these entities with votive offerings, and by observing strict rules of behaviour. For example, at each new water body encountered en route, offerings are left. (page 162)

The *trail* appears to be a preeminent Athapaskan metaphor or organizing principle. Ridington (1990) eloquently expresses the pre-eminence of the *trail* as an organizing principle of experience and understanding for the Beaver (Dane ẕaa):

The Beaver people viewed human experience as a life-sustaining network of relationships between all components of a sentient world. They experienced their world as a mosaic of passages and interactions between animate beings in motion against the backdrop of a terrain that was itself continually in process through the cyclical transformations of changing seasons. *They looked upon the trails of people and animals as a record of these interactions.* Each trail, they believed, continued backward and forward beyond the point at which it could no longer be followed physically. The trails that lay ahead, as well as those that lay behind, could be followed by people in their dreams. The trail of every adult could be followed in the mind back to the point of visionary encounter with a medicine animal, just as the trail of a successful hunter could be followed ahead to his point of encounter with the spirit of an animal. Each actual point of meeting between person and animal was believed to be the manifestation of antecedent meetings in the medium of dream or vision. (emphasis added)

The Witsuwit'en 'kungax' (*cin k'ih*) are "trails of song" (Mills 1994:122) linking past, present and future, and situated in place (Mills 1994; Hugh Brody, address to TC Convention 1987). The *cin k'ih* can be represented by a historical narrative, or can be shown by enactment in the feast hall of the crest of the House Chief, and make publicly manifest the connection of people and Territory. Witsuwit'en stories which relate the early shaping of the world, the stories of Estes, too are linked to places in this world, at least in that they are said to have happened near modern recognized places such as the village of Moricetown (Kyah Wiget and nearby locations), François Lake, or along the Skeena River.

In contrast with Athapaskan languages, Gitksan has to some extent a different logic and structure to its names. Some are similar in structure to Athapaskan names in their descriptive structure, such as Miinhl Sga'nist ('Under the Mountain') for a settlement name. One creek is called Ksa Endilgan ('Creek from the Beaver Dam'). The name of the river, Ksan, is unanalysable, though some derive it from Xsi 'Yeen ('River of Mist'). Communities and settlements commonly are named Git-___ or Kit-___, 'People of _____', as in Gitwingak, 'People of the place of the rabbit'.[5] Similarly, another village is Gitsegukwhla 'people of the sharp pointed peak', and at the confluence of the

Skeena and Bulkley is Git-an-maaxs 'people of the birckbark torches', a name alluding to the story of its founding. Names record boundaries of territories, such as Ensidel Aks in Figure 5.3; resource sites such as berry patches and groundhog hunting area (referred to in Figure 5.3), or the salmon fishery at Xsigunyaa'a[6] ('spring salmon river'); sites of activity such as "Place where you make Wedges" (unpublished Gitksan document, GTO Library); sites of habitation, the names of the villages and other camps; physical or hydrologic features such as Gwat Ts'a'lixs, in reference to the whirlpools at the canyon; and, as Dinim Gyet recalled, specific landmarks on trails which describe features needful to know, such as En sgazel ts'el, the 'eyes' in the wood at the avalanche track crossing. Some locations also had botanical referents. A small creek across the river from my former house is called Xsi Gwin Gaa-nasxw ('water-repellent liverwort creek'), because there is an unusual water repellent leafy liverwort or moss that grows on the ridge near its headwaters.[7] Dinim Gyet could reach into his inventory of place names to pull out land-scape terms, and eloquently demonstrated the linkage of trails, named sites, history, memory and knowledge of the landscape. Gwaans, the late Olive Ryan, told me names of several features on the territory where I lived and gave a sense of their meaning. The little creek flowing into the Skeena just downstream of our former land is called Xsi Gwin Kaiwin ('Seagull Creek'), named as Gull Creek on the highway sign. The fishing site on the flat down-stream of that land was "They Never Sleep at Night," in allusion to its high productivity. The rocks obstructing the main channel just off our upper pasture were Xswinik Xstaat,[8] and mark the area of two oral narratives of the Lax Gibuu (Wolf Clan) recorded by Barbeau (1929 [1973]:129-131). And the prominent red shale outcrop and scree slope above that land recorded the trickster creator 'Wii Gyet's wetting in the river, and gained its colour when he shook off his red dyed cloak, permanently staining the rocks. For Gitksan, the landscape is close grained. Names key very detailed knowledge of ances-tral and more recent history, supernatural occurrence, landmarks on trails, resource sites, and boundary markings. Gitksan presence on the landscape is ancient, and knowledge of the land and its changes is deep. Gitksan travel too, but in a landscape of owned places, where the social environment has as much prominence as the natural, and where proving ownership of resources and territory in the feasthall continues to have relevance.

For the Gitksan, as for the Tlingit, the landscape is crossed with storylines, or trails of story, and the toponyms are keys to a whole network of knowl-edge. Memory is tied to sequences of toponyms which express relationship to land, history and society. As Thornton writes regarding discussion of such storied routes:

> Inevitably this would lead to further reminiscences on the social history of named places, as elders began to connect geographic names to one another and to people in *storylines* of individual and collective experience. Such storylines ultimately weave together in to maps of experience and configurations of **shagóon** ('heritage'), which in resonance and interanimation with the canonical myths and sacred clan histories and geographies (and other **at'óow**) help Tlingits make sense of the world and their place in it. (Thornton 2008:73)

11

Trails versus Polygons

CONTRASTING VISIONS OF THE LAND

The previous chapters describe in detail relationships to land, place naming, and contemporary contexts for a range of northwestern Canadian First Nations. In this chapter, I consider how indigenous conceptions of the Land intersect with approaches to study and classification of landscape in Western scientific traditions. The fundamental unit in most approaches to landscape ecological classification, especially in this era of GIS assisted mapping, is the polygon, a fixed areal extent, defined by some set of criteria, with hard determinate boundaries. A polygon may be defined using nearly any set of spatially distributed criteria, and is a visual rendering of an analytic procedure, or a "mapping." A map composed of polygons typically covers the entire area of interest with a tiling of these discrete and non-overlapping units. This is so natural to those of us familiar with Western mapping traditions as to seem an unproblematic rendering of the real world. As ecologists know, however, the devil is in the details, and tidy map units may be far less clear and useful on the ground. An experience that first gave me an inkling of the issues inherent in generalizing to polygons was an attempt to make sense of the intricate mosaic of floodplain vegetation on the bottomlands of the lower Nass River in northern British Columbia for a forest management project in the early 1980s. There was plenty of patterned vegetation diversity; the difficulty was that the scale was on the order of a few metres in places, far too fine for usable maps. One could determine several discrete sets of site types with associated vegetation, but their spatial occurrence was so intimately intermingled as to be impossible to render as discrete polygons, as it was driven by differences in microtopography, which influenced waterlogging, soil aeration, and soil texture, and flood frequency, and therefore the assemblage of plants in each locale. The best one could do from a polygon perspective was to render the whole area as some sort of mosaic unit—which meant that no inferences could be drawn about any particular spot.

Highlighting the issues involved here was the conflict over reforestation of some of these areas. Though my associates and I struggled through dense tangled thickets of red osier dogwood and stands of young cottonwoods, large volumes of timber had purportedly been removed from the site, and the foresters were attempting to establish spruce seedlings on an 8-by-8 metre grid on one of their supposedly more productive sites, and failing. It turned out that scattered very large spruce trees had existed over the generally low-lying site, germinating on small elevated sites with better soil drainage, such as ancient logs or rootwads or small levees. This was documented by examining large-scale pre-logging air photos, where one could measure the crown of each pre-existing large tree, surrounded by a sea of lower shrubby species and wetlands. Remote sensing experts call this variable grain, as in the graininess of a photograph.

Similar issues of scale and generalizability may be found for many different variables that are commonly rendered in map form. Though polygons appear tangible, natural and concrete, they are, of course, abstractions. The metaphor borrowed for such a tradition of mapping, I would argue, is taken from European systems of land tenure, where a series of fixed bounded and owned plots form a tiling that covers the landscape. Linear features, such as rivers and roads do traverse the landscape, and some features lack areal extent, or are of a much smaller scale, and so are rendered as points and lines. GIS reproduced these conventions through raster and vector data.[1]

The mosaic approach to landscape ecology put forward by Troll (1971), Forman (1982), Forman and Godron (1986), Naveh and Lieberman (1994) and others derives in part from the hard boundaries imposed upon landscape by anthropogenic patterning, especially with relation to property regimes adopted in agricultural and urban cultural landscapes. The boundaries may be far more gradational in landscapes not dominated by human property regimes and transformative activities. When I fly north from Edmonton in western Canada where I live, I quickly pass over the urban sprawl and suburban periphery of greater Edmonton, and then fly for a while over a vast flat patchwork quilt of surveyed mile-square sections, neatly divided by township and range roads, developed as largely quadrangular agricultural fields and punctuated with irregular scrawls of wetland ("sloughs"), ponds, small groves of trees, and small, discrete clusters of buildings. Passing the wide sinuous path of the Athabasca River, the boreal forest coalesces, and the quadrangular tesserae of an agricultural landscape mosaic are left behind. The landscape consists of a dark sweep of coniferous forest, accented by lakes, stream courses and wetlands, and patches perhaps of deciduous trees on gravel ridges or where fires or logging slashes have reset succession. Still further north, multicoloured areas of wetland increase, and forest patches grow more open except, perhaps, along river courses or on steeper slopes. Permafrost, glacial deposits, and bedrock bosses begin to shape the patterning of the land which comes in myriad tones of bronze, gold, ochre, lime green and dark forest green, with large amounts of wetland and water (in the summer season), sometimes dark, and sometimes aqua or reddish. Patterns are sinuous, rounded. The grain of pattern may be fine, at least as it appears from 7000 feet in a small plane. Here I feel more as if I am admiring the complex patterning of a batik scarf, or perhaps the swirling colours of salt dyed silk. Were I to return to these landscapes in winter, the patterning of the landscape would appear completely different, with lakes and wetlands clear roads for travel, and most of the vegetation beneath snow. Features of the winter landscape would not be overly dominated by vegetation communities or limnology, but by wind, snowfall, aspect and exposure. Large woody vegetation—clumps of spruce and tamarack, woodlands of birch, willows or shrub tundra—would influence wind, snow deposition and texture, and feed for animals. The shifts of weather patterns from one year to the next lend a stochastic aspect to exactly where animals may feed, where berry bushes or birch trees may freeze, or whether ice crusts will impede cratering by caribou searching for lichens beneath the snow.

Of trails and places

Tim Ingold (2000) and Beatrice Collignon (2006) have written about issues of mapping, of journeying, and perception of environment and landscape, integrating theoretical and philosophical concerns with anthropological, cognitive and geographic perspectives. I find it interesting (and reassuring) that these authors, working in different contexts and quite independently of my own work, elaborate quite similar conceptions of human relationships with landscapes and environments to those I have laid out (Johnson 1998; Johnson and Hunn 2009; this work). Collignon (2006:96) describes Inuinnait (formerly known as Copper Eskimo) landscape perception in terms of "lines" (routes of travel), "points" or "places" (camps and other significant locales), and zones or areas, that is irregular areas of well-known and well-frequented country surrounding "points." She sees Inuinnait perception of land as being organized "axially" along these routes of travel or axes, and describes way-finding in terms of the memorization of these routes, together with sequences of named and unnamed landmarks, and including the associated histories and stories and remembered experiences which have accrued over the years. These "lines" or routes are remembered through chants, which name the sequence of places to be encountered when travelling the route, strongly reminiscent of the Paiute songs recorded by Isabelle Kelly in the American southwest (Fowler 2009) and the Sahaptin stories of Jim Yokuts reported by Hunn (1996). Collignon finds Nuttall's concept of "memory-scapes" fitting (Nuttall cited in Collignon 2006). Collignon, a geographer, discusses how Inuinnait mapreading replicates the indigenous organization of landscape, describing how people involved in her toponym work oriented on the map by locating a couple of significant places, and then working out the "line" connecting them with reference to the contours of the coast, filling in other places or "points" in between. Elevation data and contours, Collignon tells us, were not used in orienting on the printed National Topographic Series maps. This is quite similar to my experience watching a map interview with my Kaska Elder teacher Mida Donnessey in 1998. She asked the researcher to identify a set of lakes on the topographic map so that she could orient and reproduce a sequence of sites with which she was familiar in that area.[2]

In the 1970s, David Pentland (1975) investigated indigenous maps and mapping of Cree in the Hudson Bay lowlands of northern Ontario in the region of Norway House. His article reproduces several maps drawn by people from this region. Interestingly, what they reveal is a careful depiction of routes; the maps give the details of drainage systems which served as routes of travel, and contain careful depiction of significant landmarks (tributary streams, lakes, etc.) including rapids and portages for which there was a carefully elaborated classification that also included information about fish resources, and "back way" routes, that were parallel streams which could be taken as an alternative way around sections of dangerous rapids. However, large and prominent features, such as nearby rivers unrelated to the route being depicted, were omitted. Pentland's discussion again highlights the significance of routes of travel ("trails") and travel hazards in organizing ways of thinking about the land, and contrasts Cree depictions with the area-based maps produced by the Canadian government.

Ingold's exposition of mapping, mapmaking, wayfinding and navigation is pertinent here. He writes that for the local person, "places do not have locations but *histories*. Bound together by itineraries of their inhabitants, places exist not in space but as *nodes in a matrix of movement*" (Ingold 2000:219, emphasis added). A matrix of movement, I would argue, is the sum of travellers' paths, and Ingold elsewhere describes place as inscribed through journeying. Ingold refers to this "matrix of movement" as a "region," which Collignon or I would refer to as "territory," the homeland or area of use and familiarity, and Australian anthropologists and Aboriginees would refer to as "country." Ingold continues:

> . . . ordinary wayfinding, then, more closely resembles storytelling than map-using. To use a map is to navigate by means of it: that is, to plot a course from one *location* to another in *space*. Wayfinding, by contrast, is a matter of moving from one *place* to another in a *region*. (Ingold 2000:219, emphasis original)

The quintessential devolution from wayfinding, which is based upon nuance and experience, to navigation, that is setting a course between locations, is encapsulated in the recent explosive use of sensitive global positioning system units in everything from aircraft to automobiles to hikers' hands. At this time, the GPS user need not even consult a representation of the landscape of concern in the form of a map, but simply needs to chart a certain set of abstract bearings to reach the location of the carefully geo-referenced destination. "Geo-referenced" refers to highly accurate three-dimensional plotting from navigational satellites, an updating of the abstract astronomically derived grid of the ancient Greeks. This works adequately under most circumstances, as long as the unit continues to function, and assuming that the shortest distance between two points contains no serious obstacles to travel.[3]

"Relational databases" and layers

A corollary of organizing one's sense of the landscape by reference to what I have called "trails" or the "traveller's path," linking nodes comprising a network of specific places, named or not, in that the characteristics (the entailments or affordances) of those places are like a relational database, where toponyms may function as mnemonic pegs on which to "hang" other information about the land. Such information may include safe travel routes, travel risks, places of residence and past residence, gravesites and power places, gathering sites, fishing places and hunting lookouts, and seasonal cycles.

Collignon, describing Inuinnait knowledge of the Land writes:

> A series of places—of points—form a kind of framework on which a mental image of the land can be anchored . . . These points are the places on the land used on a regular basis: the camps (one's own and those of other people), the fishing lakes, streams, plant-gathering areas. They also include all the visible landmarks of the territory such as *inukhuit*, meat caches, fox traps built from a mound of boulders and conspicuous or unusual landforms. But there are also invisible markers: stories and anecdotes that make the places come alive through narrative. The land holds the memory of the Inuit and landscapes are indeed "memoryscapes" . . . (Collignon 2006:92)

Various authors (e.g. Collignon 2006; Hunn 1996; Ignace 2000; Cruikshank 1990b; Kari and Fall 1987; Andrews 1990; Andrews and Zoe 1997; Andrews et al. 1998; Basso 1996; Thornton 2008) have pointed out that place is linked to story. Toponyms key rich associations, including the moral dimension, resources, risks, and recent or ancient history. I have conceptualized the rich net of knowledge tied to place, especially named places, as a set of overlays or layers, all attached through experience and specific knowledge, to place or sets of places that are arrayed along pathways or trails.

Polygons

The polygon has a long and interesting history and is heavily implicated in the creation of space from place (Edgerton 1987; Olwig 1996). Once Europe rediscovered some of the classic works of the Ancient Greek world in the late Medieval period and early Renaissance, the grid system employed by Ptolemy which was defined by the stars—our familiar and unremarked system of latitude and longitude—could be employed in maps of the entire globe, making it possible to precisely designate any space in the absence of any familiarity with a region. Ptolemy's *mappamundi* was organized by ". . .imagining the globe not as amorphous topography but as a *homogeneous surface* ruled by a *uniform geometric grid.*" (Edgerton 1987:13, emphasis added)

Quickly this abstracted space became implicated in the spread of empire, and competing European colonial nations sought economic advantage and hegemony over yet-unknown places. As Edgerton wrote:

> Indeed, a casual look at almost any seventeenth- or eighteenth-
> century map of America reveals the absolute faith Europeans of all
> religious persuasions had in the authority of the cartographic grid.
> Monarchs laid claim to lands solely on the basis of abstract latitudes
> and longitudes. Troops were sent to fight and die for boundaries
> that had no visible landmarks, only abstract mathematical existence.
> (Edgerton1987:46)

Along with the creation of a universal, abstract spatial grid defined by astronomical, not earthly, features, the Alexandrians and then the Romans perfected surveying, enabling the delineation of abstracted polygonal spaces on the earth's surface. A Roman work called the *Corpus Agrimensorum,* authored by Hyginus Gromaticus in 500 AD, laid out how to measure land according to a "molecular grid." According to Edgerton, his job was to survey land in conquered territories into hundred-square units for distribution among Roman colonists. This has strong resonances with the history of colonization in more recent times, when empty gridded space has been dispensed to colonists and concessionaires of colonial and modern state governments (Tsing 2005). Indeed, the Witsuwit'en were dispossessed of their cleared fields, cabins and barns in the Bulkley Valley in northwest British Columbia by just such a creation of empty gridded space from their lived homeland when the colonial government dispensed Crown grants to veterans of the Boer War (Mills 1994:9).

Surveying is also implicated in the conversion of customary tenure and rights systems in Europe. Olwig writes:

> Surveying created a *geometrical, divisible* and *hence saleable* space by
> making parcels of property out of lands that had previously been

defined according to rights of custom and demarcated by landmarks and topographical features . . . (Olwig 1996:638, emphasis added)

This enabled enclosure and the expansion of private holdings at the expense of the commons, creating the array of non-overlapping rectangular bounded plots that became the model for land units in North America and world wide, and which I believe is the basis for the tradition of the bounded polygon as a basic unit of mapping.

Polygons are delimited, bounded generic areas of space, inscribed on the landscape through a specialized mapping methodology. Polygons mark generic classes of landscape, including age and composition of timber cover inferred from air photos, ecological types such as deciduous aspen woodland, mixed forest, wet meadow, and so forth, and inherently involve abstraction and simplification. The bounding of such polygons is of necessity hard; gradational or fuzzy boundaries are not possible to render, and transitional types, or fine-scale mosaics must either be included in other units, or must be broken out as polygons of their own, perhaps rendering smooth gradations in pixel-like mosaic tiles, like jerky animation or low-resolution computer graphics. Polygons are antithetical to flow.

In mapping land for land-use planning, or resource or ecological inventory, a series of different polygons will be delineated to represent the spatial distribution of different categories, such as a set of ratings for moose habitat potential, a layer describing predominant vegetative cover, or a layer that presents soils or surficial geological deposits. Polygons of each layer are often colour coded to facilitate discrimination of types and visual apprehension of spatial patterning of each category of spatial data, a practice that tends to reinforce the sense that the landscape is made up of discrete, bounded patches, that are internally homogeneous and in sharp contrast to adjacent areas, and that the patterns created by these coloured areas are true representations of aspects of the landscape so depicted. The contents of landscape polygons are anchored in gridded space, static and atemporal, unless done as sets of different maps to reflect shifting seasonal arrays or historical change.

Traversing this patchwork of polygons are linear features, such as roads, rail lines, and waterways, unless they are presented on a separate base map of human features or topography. Human settlements are also likely to be indicated as points, or dots of various sizes, unless the landscape being rendered has large areas of urban or residential land. Edge effects from linear features, and the areal extent and nature of settled areas are erased in their collapses to single dimensional lines and dimensionless points, as is their relationship to surrounding areas. Particularity is eclipsed, except by the lettered labels indicating highway numbers, village names, and the names of rivers.

A key question, then, is how to create a conversation between the path-based, rich and localized realm of landscape as experienced by people living in and moving in a region, homeland, or local environment, and the abstracted, spatialized representations of the land which underlie much of the contemporary world's treatment of and relationship to land.

Orientation

Systems of orientation figure in the traveller's perspective and in abstract spatial representations of land alike. Mapping, wayfinding, and narratives about land all require some sort of system of orientation. The concept of four cardinal directions (north always at the top) is so engrained in Western notions of how the world is, that we speak, for example, of driving "up" to Inuvik in the Mackenzie Delta region (latitude 69°N) from Edmonton, located in the prairie region of Alberta (latitude 53°N). In what real sense is Inuvik above Edmonton? Only in that north has become "up" because it is always located at the top of the map page.[4] I found that when I worked in the Mackenzie Delta region, I conceived of northward travel along the Dempster Highway as "up," and spoke of driving "up" to Inuvik. I found it nearly impossible to not say this, despite knowing that for my Gwich'in interlocutors, you travel down to Inuvik from Fort McPherson (it is located about 180 km to the north and east of Fort McPherson). This is because, in Athapaskan orienting systems, upstream and downstream are primary axes in describing and experiencing the Land. Fort McPherson is upstream of Inuvik, which lies downstream to the north, about halfway down the huge Mackenzie Delta.

For many peoples, especially those of forested and mountainous environments, the axes of orientation are formed by properties such as direction on a drainage, and upslope-downslope position, rather than by a set of cardinal directions. This is true for the Gitksan (Johnson 2000), and for the Witsuwit'en. For Gitksan speakers, their dialects, rendered as "Eastern" and "Western" in English, are instead *gigeenix* 'upstream' and *gyeets* 'downstream.'

James Kari has described systems of orientation and topographic knowledge for Athapaskan speaking peoples in northwestern North America (Kari 1989, 1996; Kari and Fall 1987), showing how place names are markers within regions, facilitating travel and exchange across regions. Specific stems for 'river,' 'lake' and 'mountain' are shared within these regions, though variation in the shape of the words derived from the common stems will occur between languages.[5] Drainage basins, with their associated mountains, are fundamental in Athapaskan perception of land, and terms for upstream-downstream, and upslope-downslope are found in all of them, while abstract terms for cardinal directions are absent. These perceptions are related to travel and orientation while moving on the land; direction of river flow is significant to ease of travel, and helps one to parse the grain of the land. Which way are things moving? Slope and current require neither technology nor visibility to be perceived, and accord well with the motion and action centered sense of Athapaskan languages. When one cannot see the northern horizon or the pole star, and nothing in the landscape comes in straight lines, "north" is an abstraction that does not relate to embodied experience.

An extension of this orientation system, I believe, is the complex set of locational prepositions that Athapaskan languages draw on when describing landscape. Moore (2000, 2002) and Hargus (n.d., 2007) carefully present the terms used to indicate directions in Kaska and in Witsuwit'en. 'Up,' 'far ahead,' 'down,' 'further down,' 'to the side,' 'across' (often rendered in English translation as "across-side") can describe directions in relation to both slopes and rivers, and be extended metaphorically to indicate closeness of social relationship, as Moore explains (2000, 2002).

In the far north, as at sea, the winds can be significant in orientation. Where prevailing winds tend to blow from consistent directions, and especially if other clues to direction may be obscured, knowing the winds and parsing their signs can help the traveller to know what direction he or she is travelling. Collignon (2006) and Aporta (2000), and Aporta and Higgs (2005) describe the significance and names of the winds for Inuinnait and Inuit in the Canadian Arctic. When I was working with Gwich'in in the Mackenzie Delta region, the names of the winds and something of their patterning was one of the things I was taught as important for orientation, and also for predicting winter temperature and visibility, thus significant in terms of snow quality and overflow on river ice, along with the expressed concern that the wind patterns were becoming less predictable in this period of rapid climate change. Aporta (2000, 2009) describes the wind system of the Ingloolik Inuit as a system of cardinal directions, with axes of WNW, NNE, ESE, and SSW. He writes:

... the Inuit of Igloolik designate four primary winds: Uangnaq (WNW), Kanangnaq (NNE), Nigiq (ESE) and Akinnaq (SSW) [MacDonald, (1998):181]. MacDonald points out that these winds constitute two pairs of counterbalancing winds, "one on the Uangnaq-Nigiq axis, the other on the Kanangnaq-Akinnaq axis" [ibid.]. He also points out the symbolic value of these opposites, especially in the pairing of Uangnaq and Nigiq, which "are said to retaliate against each other" [ibid.]. As I will show now, this opposition (and the understanding of its occurrence) goes beyond the symbolic to play a leading role in predicting the mood of the moving ice. (Aporta 2009)

Here too, the wind both allows orientation, and as an agent in the landscape, also causes conditions which have implications for safety and hunting opportunity.

In places such as the Alberta prairies, the absence of landmarks and the subdued grain of drainage and topography render reckoning by the sun a natural and effective strategy, and the four cardinal directions created by the apparent passage of the sun—east, south, west then north—have deep importance in cosmology as well as in orientation. In the sundance, dancers move in a sun-wise direction (clockwise) (e.g. Anonymous 1996). In this northern region, the directions are also associated with seasons, and cycles of beginning, ending and renewal.

Orientation with reference to cardinal directions may be derived from the need to navigate (here we are reminded that a root of navigate is *nave-*, boat) in places or regions that lack strong grain of slope and current. Adelaar (1997) comments about contrasts in orientation systems of Austronesian language speakers who dwell in interior regions, versus the orientation systems of those who dwell along the coasts. Interior peoples orient in relation to rivers and mountains, while coastal dwellers tend to have orientation systems based on some sort of cardinal direction system. Which direction is "up" or "upstream" when you are out of sight of land, at sea? Here celestial navigation can be important, as the pattern of the stars varies only by time and latitude, if they are visible, and the path of the sun is a consistent guide, when it is visible. Goodenough (1996) describes the complex navigation system of mariners in the Western Carolines, Micronesia, who have created a 32-point sidereal compass, using Polaris (at the northern horizon) and the Southern Cross (on the southern horizon) as its poles, with a series of paired stars whose rising and setting marks the other directions. Goodenough writes:

> These thirty-two points, like the points on the European wind rose, form a conceptual compass, and serve as the directional points of reference for organizing all directional information about winds, currents, ocean swells, and the relative positions of islands, shoals, reefs, and other seamarks. Every point has another that is conceptually diametrically opposite to it. These diametrical opposites are seen as passing through a point at the center of the compass, and a navigator thinks of himself or any place from which he is determining directions as at this central point, just as western navigators do when using a magnetic compass.

In practice this system required finesse and practical experience to account for the inexact spacing of the actual rising and setting of stars, and student navigators had to memorize large amounts of information about the nearest objects lying along each of the star paths for every island, a practice called "Island Looking." Navigators also named "sea roads" between various islands and reefs, along with the reciprocal star directions on which they lie, and so on.

A variant of the upslope-downslope orientation appears on islands. For Polynesians, "toward the mountains" (Hawai'ian *mauka*) contrasts with "toward the sea" (Hawai'ian *makai*). Winds are important for dwellers on islands and for mariners, too. In Hawai'i in my youth, the sense of which side of the island was windward and which leeward was part of my understanding of place; the consistent trade winds create significant differences in distribution of precipitation and therefore of vegetation on Oahu. This is apparently an ancient concept in Austronesian languages, and becomes transmuted to upriver/downriver in interior groups such as the authoctonous peoples of interior Borneo (the Dayak) (Adelaar 1997). Sets of terms relating to this upriver/downriver orientation system have a strong similarity to the set of terms found in Athapaskan languages (Adelaar 1997:69-70).

A dichotomy appears to exist in traditional descriptive words for positions; whether these reference the speaker's position and body (right/left, above/below, front/back) or are tied to some system of cardinal directions (Brown and Levinson 1993). The perception of body-centred position description as the "natural" way to speak about positions is naturalized in European and

American concepts, and may be inherent to Indo-European languages, while in other language families, absolute reference may be employed even when speaking of the positions of features or objects near the speaker, as in Guugu Yimithirr (Haviland 1993) or Tzeltal (Brown and Levinson 1993).

Among the impetuses to the development of absolute systems of reference for European cultures were the demands of seafaring, as was also the case for Austronesian and Polynesian mariners (Adelaar 1997). The European compass or wind rose encodes 16 (or 32) specific directions, which can be used to plot a course. Once navigational instruments advanced to include magnetic compasses, the direction of north could be told even without being able to sight on stars or see the sun. Maps could then be drawn using the abstract grid of latitude and longitude, using north, south, east and west as derived from the courses of sun and stars, and people could navigate to places or positions they had never before seen.[6]

12

Implications

At present we are in the midst of a revolution in the way we as humans experience and think about the world. The new tools of the Internet and ever more pervasive and sophisticated computers impact everything we do. In this context, I would argue, the potential transformation of indigenous landscape ecological concepts by mapping, based in European conventions of the nature and representation of space, and by the seductive and powerful tools of contemporary geographic information science and GIS must be carefully considered. What is the impact of GIS representation, and of global positioning units, on the experience and understanding of place?

An uncritical use of GIS to record local knowledge of land has the potential to transform that knowledge in the image of standard international and national geographic understandings of landscape and cartographic conventions, as Rundstrom (1995) cautions. As I suggest in Chapter 9, some types of knowledge are very difficult to render in GIS. GIS naturalizes, for example, an aerial bird's-eye view, which may or may not be "natural" to the community whose knowledge is being represented; a traveller's path mediated by known landmarks may better represent the emic perspective.[1] Similarly, locales which shift or have indefinite or gradational boundaries, what one might call "ephemeral patches" or "fuzzy patches," respectively, cannot be adequately represented by the conventions of GIS, being neither points, polygons, or vector lines, nor a specified set of geo-referenced cells. The probability that caribou may be encountered in a given area of the Richardson Mountains, for example, is neither spatially nor temporally determinate, but rather is probabilistic, though it may have considerable significance to the prepared and aware Gwich'in hunter.

This has caused considerable difficulty in some of the applications of GIS, as, for example, attempting to delineate polygons that should be avoided in mining exploration in the Sahtú region in the Canadian Northwest Territories (Boran Tracz, pers. comm., December 2006). Landscape effects are crucial here, but specific localities may, and often do, shift through seasons, and do so with less predictability over longer periods of time. Seasonality causes relatively predictable shifts in northern landscapes; a river as a concept is a "permanent" year-long feature, but the meaning and nature of a river in practice may shift dramatically over the seasons and even over shorter time periods, as the flowing river is covered by a mantle of ice of various characteristics which are significant for travellers and fishers, or gravel and sand bars are submerged or above water and the navigable channel shifts. The suite of relevant features along a drainage is also dynamic over longer periods of time, as sloughs are cut off, new channels formed across old wetlands or forested islands, and so on.

Despite these caveats, GIS and mapping have been widely embraced by local indigenous groups, partly as a way to legitimize and render visible their interest in the land and their knowledge of it, as in land claims or environmental impact contexts; and partly to engage in land-use planning and co-management with government and industry representatives or in the management of indigenous-owned lands and resources. Mapping was significant in the Gitksan-Wet'suwet'en land claims case *Delgamuukw vs the Queen*, where an atlas representing Gitksan and Witsuwit'en interests in the land was an important part of the plaintiffs' evidence. The Gitksan organization the Strategic Watershed Analysis Team (aka SWAT) and the successor Gitxsan GIS Department have logged large amounts of information about the biophysical and cultural resources and sites of the traditional territories. Their efforts required them to make decisions about landscape units on the basis of received categories, such as biogeoclimatic units as developed by the BC Forest Service, as well as deciding how to code and delineate relevant categories, such as grizzly bear habitat or berry potential, in ways comprehensible to the British Columbia Forest Service and other agencies, obviously imposing a certain level of abstraction and analysis in the production of resulting maps.

After the appeal decision in the Delgamuukw court case recognized unextinguished aboriginal rights in areas of British Columbia where treaties had never been signed, a number of British Columbia First Nations undertook projects to attempt to make evident their interests in the land, most while continuing to pursue land claims in order to gain a stronger and more lasting recognition of their special relationships and rights to their homelands. As with legislated efforts to integrate TEK (traditional ecological knowledge) in northern Canada (Nadasdy 1999, 2003; Stevenson 1998), the parameters of the projects, the language of communication if you will, was set by resource management agencies, and involved standard mapping and planning paradigms. As previously discussed, it is difficult to render experiential knowledge, or a "dwelling perspective" as Ingold (2000) would put it, through such abstracted spatialized mapping conventions. Another issue that arose was who would be able to access this detailed but decontextualized knowledge. Issues of fuzzy boundaries (Ignace 2000), and appropriateness of sharing sensitive or sacred knowledge were complicating factors. How, for example, do you prevent a landing for yarding timber to be constructed at a sacred site if you don't want to tell those who do not understand its significance exactly where it is? Or how do you prevent non-local hunters from coming in and hunting out your moose if you reveal where mineral licks or good hunting lookouts are? Detachment of knowledge from its social and cultural context may allow its unauthorized or inappropriate use by outsiders or the government (cf. Weinstein 1998). This results in strategies to deliberately obscure exact locations of significant places, which has the unfortunate effect of distorting the understanding of landscape possible from the maps and associated spatial databases, and which may, therefore, reduce discussions to vague generalities. The reasons for this are certainly valid, but the maps' usefulness is then limited for efforts such as educating community members about the land, which underscores the problems that result from people no longer being able to move on the land as a way of gaining knowledge about it.

Several local groups have experimented with innovative ways to render traditional information about their homelands or traditional territories through GIS, especially GISs enhanced with multimedia, one of a range of technical approaches called "qualitative GIS" (Elwood 2006). The Confederate Salish and Kootenai Tribal Preservation office has shown its approach to rendering seasonal information in its GIS in a conference presentation at the American Anthropological Association meeting and at the ESRI Users Conference (Cross 2000; Sam 2005). The Tulalip Tribe in the Puget Sound Region of Washington State is another group that has made creative use of GIS and related multimedia technologies, for planning purposes and to communicate about the land and its history to Tribal members (Metzler et al. 2002; Tulalip Tribes n.d.). The Wimidji Cree of the James Bay region in Quebec have recently been involved in a participatory GIS project with researchers from McGill; coming to grips with the basic and abstract set of "feature types" in the local geographic ontology has proved a sensitive and challenging aspect of the work which is foundational to the applications which may be made of GIS in local contexts (Sieber 2008).

However, for the most part it appears that representation of indigenous perspectives may indeed be constrained by the framework of the technology and the institutional framing of interaction between indigenous peoples and government. The Aboriginal Mapping Network is a group that facilitates communication among indigenous users of GIS and mapping. A recent perusal of their website (http://www.nativemaps.org/) suggests that at present there is a considerable discussion of technical aspects of GIS, sharing of databases, and of techniques for interfacing with government and company "referrals," but little critical content. ("Referrals" are requests for input in various planned development efforts on lands where local aboriginal groups hold interests, that is, their traditional homelands, residences, trails and harvesting areas.) Effectively, the site presents a relatively mainstream approach to GIS as a tool in dealing with government, other users, and administration of indigenous reserves or homelands. Little about the present constitution of the site consisted in critique of GIS paradigms, or discussions of how better to render indigenous understandings of and interests in land through GIS technologies, though they have sponsored several conferences that have dealt with such issues in past years.

GIS does have the effect of divorcing people from land, through mediated, abstracted and indirect experience. GIS eliminates experiential knowledge of land, which is deeply held by indigenous peoples to be the most important way that people must learn about the land. GIS makes land an abstracted thing, a representation, not a locus of power and agency. This is a deep quandary to cultures that are based in the experiential human relationship to homelands. Rundstrom's (1995) arguments about loss of control of the recipients of knowledge of the land, when it is configured as "spatial data" in GISs, are important. This loss of appropriate context and control in the transmission and access to knowledge about land abrogates moral elements of the human–land relationship, which lies at the heart of many indigenous cultures, ways of life, and world views. Rundstrom's discussion of performative and inscribing cultures is also of interest, highlighting the performance of knowledge of the land in the transmission process through such media as contextualized storytelling, dance, or song, versus a technological artifact of geographic knowledge that exists as a disembodied and de-contextualized representation accessible to anyone under a wide range of circumstances and in many contexts.[2] More recently Renee Puilani Louis (2008) has made similar points about the performative nature of Native Hawai'ian cartography.

These are quandaries for contemporary indigenous people. In the unequal cross-cultural encounter with states and their various bureaucracies and organs of government, and with industries and other outside interests, supposedly culture-free and universal, "objective" portrayal of the land is the common language imposed, as are the epistemological underpinnings of local knowledge, just as national languages such as English or French are also imposed in these dialogs. This means that pressure to produce technically trained and locally connected indigenous people who can frame their own knowledge in a language that can participate in these unequal dialogs is overwhelming; the hope is that local people will be able to find a way to represent their important truths in a medium that is fundamentally inimical or antithetical to the truths that need to be represented, and in an absence of social and experiential context. The kicker is that if indigenous people do not participate, they will be deemed to have had no interest in the land, and others will take or impose at will in accordance with their institutional mandates or for corporate or personal gain.

Therefore, various tribal consultants, lands and resources departments, and so on, have attempted to find ways to use GIS and other tools of contemporary political negotiation and land management to meet their collective goals (e.g. Ping 1995; Roddan and Harry 2000). In the transformed context of sedentary reserve, village, or community life, many efforts seek ways to retain and transmit essential truths about culture, language and homeland through alternative media, such as computer multimedia applications and enriched GIS renderings of the locations and spatial and temporal patterning of aspects of the land. Some of these efforts have the inherent difficulties that Nadasdy (1999, 2003, 2005) has pointed out in his cogent, and rather discouraging, discussions of resource co-management and use of TEK in the Yukon.

To some degree, as Rundstrom (1995) reminds us, adoption of GIS is strongly encouraged or almost imposed by agencies such as the United States Bureau of Indian Affairs (BIA), who adopt a modernist perspective on abstracted planning (e.g. employing contemporary land-use planning and urban-town planning paradigms) that requires a decontextualized objective dataset to be able to make "rational" decisions. Adoption of GIS by indigenous groups is also explicitly encouraged and facilitated by ESRI, the leading GIS commercial software company, who may donate initial software and training to enable tribal or First Nation groups to adopt GIS. Roman and Carruthers (2000:3) write:

> Unlike industry or government's gradual embrace of GIS tech-
> nologies, First Nations are not being given the time to adapt the
> technology for local applications. There is currently intense pressure
> for native groups in the province to "hit the ground running" and
> become proficient with GIS tools overnight. Whether it is for treaty
> negotiations, litigation, cultural, or resource management applica-
> tions, First Nations are becoming creative in how to deal with
> these pressures, adapt the technology, and tell their own stories
> through maps.

A romantic and romanticized depiction of the past does not serve con-temporary indigenous peoples, who have to live with the hard realities of the present, including the shifts in social and economic contexts and complex interactions with numerous outside forces and peoples, including interna-tional markets, powerful corporate actors, and national as well as regional or local governments. Change may bring opportunities as well as challenges. New technologies, though inevitably transformative, may be considered vital tools for present and future self determination. However, the nature of the transformations induced by new technologies must be carefully considered and recorded, and an evaluation of what is lost or gained in translation must be carried out so that implications and alternatives may be explored, and foundational and/or deeply significant insights regarding the land and human relationship with it are not lost.

Some groups have worked with professionals who have tried to create database structures that will work for the recording of cultural information, including land information, typically in formats that include multimedia. One such collaborative project from western Australia is described by Andrew Turk and Kathryn Trees (2000). Other groups innovatively develop what will work for them, within the inevitable constraints of human, technical and financial resources (e.g. Roddan and Harry 2000), sometimes as facilitated by other indigenous groups such as the Aboriginal Mapping Network, as described by Roman and Carruthers (2000). A group of Native Hawai'ians is active in creating culturally sensitive place databases and in spearheading the reclaiming of Native Hawai'ian place names in the Islands (Louis 2008).

Various groups in the Canadian Northwest Territories have used GIS and multimedia digital technology to render aspects of local understanding of landscape. The Sahtú Atlas (Auld et al. 2005) and the Prince of Wales Northern Heritage Centre's Idaà Trail interactive website are two such efforts, which combine images of land, animals, and people and text stories. Other ways of presenting the storied landscape digitally through the Internet can be seen with the virtual museum display from Doig, BC, which is not based in GIS. It too features hyperlinked text, images, sound files and video in an attempt to convey local history and values in land, prominently including Elder's voices (Attachie et al. 2006; Hennessy 2006; http://www.virtualmuseum.ca/Exhibitions/Danewajich/). The Dane-zaa have their own history of maps, depictions of trails to heaven, one of which is figured on a prophet's drum head and its story is one of the highlights of the site.[3]

Nonetheless, there is evidence that the presentation and understanding of the landscape are being changed through the necessity of communicating local interests to non-local parties in ways they can comprehend, and by the adoption of "tiling"-based mapping conventions. Communication with younger generations about the land is also using more mainstream modes based on written texts, multimedia, and mapping, although northern Elders continue to express the value of experiential learning through being on the land as superior to virtual learning about the land. In the case of the Sahtú Atlas, for example, the mapping tools and GIS expertise of the professionals influenced the ways that information about the land was conceptualized and shaped for communication with Sahtú beneficiaries and other readers of the atlas. Photographs, and written versions of some key "located" cultural information, accompany maps where deemed relevant. Complexities of the territory system or local land knowledge can be obscured by tidy maps comprised of colourful polygons with firm boundaries. Nesting of different types of resource sites, for example, such as berry patches or fishing sites, may be obscured by attribution of large areas to a single group, quite aside from more subtle factors such as contested areas, which belong more to the internal political arena. When boundaries were originally learned by memorization of named places and their associated stories from relatives and Elders, reinforced over many years, and by travel over the land to the named sites as Dinim Gyet describes (Chapter 3), and then reinforced in the feasthall, the resulting understanding has a different and much finer grained character than transferring mapped boundaries to a site on the ground via GPS. Subtle and progressive shifts, such as shifting gravel bars and resulting fishable eddies, or the exact location of harvestable berries or roots are not well described by georeferenced and bounded polygons or GPS points, though their location and significance can be plain on the ground to those who know how to locate them.

Often significant sites are best understood and located by reaching them from the old trails or waterways and can be missed by those (such as myself) attempting to locate them from mapped localities printed out from GIS databases, using a GPS for navigation from contemporary logging roads. A disconnect develops between recorded stories and the place-on-the-ground. The example that comes to mind is my attempt to locate the named site Milkst ('Crabapple') along the Telegraph Trail, a major access trail to the Upper Skeena in the late nineteenth and twentieth centuries. In the 1990s a logging road was pushed through past the formerly isolated village site of Kuldo (Galdo'o), obscuring the old trail and its landmarks. Although my companion and I found the general flat below Kuldo Creek and walked around for several hours, we were unsuccessful in locating any crabapple trees, and it appeared that we had not actually reached the site where Beverley Anderson and Mike McDonald had interviewed the late Geoff Harris Sr. (Luus) and videoed him talking about the area in 1987. It remained unclear upon reviewing the videotape whether they had actually been at the site with crabapple trees when the tape was originally recorded.

Tim Ingold's discussion of wayfinding, navigation, mapping and map-making is relevant here (Ingold 2000, Chapter 13). I was navigating using a GPS, combined with an understanding of topographic maps, travelling with a companion who had walked the old and now obscured Telegraph Trail, but who was, like myself, not Gitksan, and who did not have stories and experience to guide us to the place we sought. I subsequently flew up the Skeena in a float-plane, recognizing the flat and what we had seen on the ground and inferred from the maps from the air, briefly achieving the bird's-eye view.

I still could not locate crabapple trees. Claudio Aporta (Aporta and Higgs 2005) has interesting comments on the use of GPS in Igloolik in the eastern Canadian Arctic, and on traditional wayfinding skills. Aporta (pers. comm., 2002) investigated Inuit wayfinding and navigation skills for his PhD dissertation, and also engaged in a community place name and trail mapping project, using a GPS and simple computer program for recording place and trail information. Among the topics he investigated while in Igloolik was the ways that GPS units were used by local people. He found that they were widely accepted, as compasses are useless in the area because it is too close to the magnetic pole, and poor visibility often makes travel difficult or impossible if landmarks (or "icemarks") cannot be discerned. Though younger men not skilled in the exacting Inuit science of wayfinding might be quite dependent on GPS units to locate themselves or travel to specific destinations, older men had a more nuanced use of the units. While they appreciated the ability to know where they were when visibility was poor, they used their traditional knowledge of wind, current, and ice conditions to choose travel routes that were easier and faster than straight line routes, avoiding difficult traverses of rough or dangerous ice. For them, the GPS complemented rather than replaced traditional knowledge of land and ice, and how to travel.

In part, the widespread adoption of GIS and Western mapping conventions by Canadian indigenous people can be seen as the result of a power imbalance and the people's need to present their knowledges in a language and form that can be understood and accommodated by governments and industry (e.g. Aboriginal Mapping Network website; Native Geography, 2000). Such presentations are required for land claims, and are the language of land-use planning. None of the groups I work with have strong control of much of their traditional homeland, but must work within settlement terms, and within the authority of provincial or territorial and federal governments. The process of interacting with governments, of presenting claims and then pursuing management or co-management objectives, allows some things to be said and understood, and others not (cf. Nadasdy 2003, 2005). It also creates the need for local people to become technically trained and conversant with various approaches to managing land and economic development. This creates a group of people who have perhaps shifted to or internalized a mapped—rather than storied—approach to the Land, converting homelands and places at least in part into bounded spaces and labelled dots and lines.

Local GIS departments, renewable resource councils and other local infrastructure begin to use these admittedly powerful tools for their own purposes, and in the process, knowledge is inevitably transformed (cf. Rundstrom 1995) though it is difficult and perhaps inappropriate to pass judgment on this process in the abstract. Recognizing the non-relational and abstract character of the standard geographic and topographic paradigms on which standard GIS and mapping conventions are based (Rundstrom 1995; Goodchild et al. 2007; Couclelis 1992; Usery 1993) local groups have made innovative attempts to find ways to use these tools to represent the complex realities of a local and indigenous world view and sense of the Land through the seasons (e.g. Cross 2000; Sam 2005; Metzler et al. 2002; Tulalip Tribes n.d.; Roddan and Harry 2000; Burda et al. 1999; Collier and Rose 2000), as have other local organizations described in the "participatory GIS" literature (cf. Elwood 2006). Some groups have pioneered the use of interactive maps that use multimedia to attach narratives, toponyms and photographs to specific sites, creating "cultural atlases" to convey information about the land through multimedia on websites or CD ROMs (e.g. Prince of Wales Northern Heritage Centre Įdaà Trail website and Inuvialuit Place Names website; Gwich'in Social and Cultural Institute Place Names Map; Navajo presentation at 1996 Dene Language meeting; Topkok 2000; Attachie et al. 2006; Hennessy 2006; Fletcher 2001), as a surrogate, to some degree, for being able to visit the site with knowledgeable people through direct experience.

The mapping efforts produced by indigenous groups attempting to have greater leverage in their interactions with states and industry are sometimes described as "countermapping." The Strategic Watershed Analysis Team, a Gitksan GIS and mapping unit, was explicitly engaged in a countermapping project, to assert, assess and make evident Gitksan knowledge of their traditional territories, inscribe both names and the social system on the map, and to create the technical expertise necessary to regain control of resources or effectively intervene to protect Gitksan interests in the land in the face of government and industry activities. To this end, a huge amount of creative field time was undertaken, and a great deal of mapping done. The unreliability of technology such as GPS units under trying field conditions, and the difficulties of logistics and funding, made the undertaking challenging, and the complex internal and external political climates further affected the ultimate use of much of the mapping. I interacted with SWAT in the 1998-2000 period, spending time in the field, and discussing questions of how one might input traditional resource values, as well as examining some of their output maps. High-profile publications and appearances underscored the potential of the culturally grounded approach they championed (Burda et al. 2000; Collier and Rose 2000; Pinkerton 1998), but ultimately, lack of resources and funding, and political climate, limited the impact of their mapping in inscribing alternative visions of the land and its development "on the ground" in northwest BC. Although considerable mapping was done, dramatic consequences in terms of economic development and empowerment proved more elusive.[4]

Sui and Goodchild (2003) present the concept of GIS as "media for communication" and employ a McLuhan-based "tetradic" analysis of it as media, which Crumplin (2007) extends to examination of two specific case studies, one in an American city (Minneapolis) neighbourhood, and the other a complex landscape-level land-use study in Kerala State in India, involving both peasant settler farmers and *adivasis* (tribal peoples), and government and technical agencies. A medium for communication may be seen as a "language"; the kicker is that language shapes what can be (easily or readily) said. This is in effect another instance of the weak form of the Whorfian hypothesis,[5] and relates once again to issues of cross-linguistic communication. One could see the shift of geographic knowledge to GIS as yet another type of language shift impelled (largely) by government policies and the need to interact with these (cf. Roman and Carruthers 2000), this time in the arena of land claims, planning efforts, and dealing with referrals regarding corporate initiatives to engage in development on indigenous lands, particularly with regard to impact-benefit analyses and environmental impact assessments. One can only do analysis in terms of what can be input to the system; otherwise participants simply talk past each other, to paraphrase Crumplin (2007). There are fundamental tensions between personalized, experiential "trail-based/storied" knowledge of land and abstracted spatialized depictions generated on computers.

It is nonetheless true that where information is culturally very relevant and input with categories that correspond to local ones, people, especially elders, may very quickly apprehend the potential of, for example, a laptop computer with GPS input of local place names (Aporta presentation to NS 390 class, fall 2002). Many important questions remain regarding both the impact and desirability of converting traditional knowledge, including knowledge of land, to new media, and transmitting it in new ways. The desirability of doing this depends very much on specific situations and contexts, community values, and alternatives for carrying knowledge forward.

Many efforts that are ostensibly community-driven may not deeply question received paradigms of representation in GIS or in web-based representations, either because GIS experts or information technicians are non-local, or because local people have been trained in systems that do not reflect local categories and ways of presenting information as "the" way of doing GIS or computer multimedia. Lynn Usery (1993), in an early theoretical paper on feature-based GIS that employed Rosch's category theory[6] (e.g. Rosch 1981), comments that the features of a GIS need to be the basic level categories of the user group, a point also made in a seminal paper on geographic ontologies by Mark and Turk (2003). The persistent and insistent need to respond to data and situations framed by outsiders, and to configure knowledge in ways comprehensible to these outsiders, framed often as "science" and seen as "modern," drives communities toward relatively standard ways of using GIS, often with the addenda of elders meetings, interviews carried out by community interviewers, and attractive photos of people and land. This qualitative information may be variably reflected in the GIS, but might not impact the analytical approach deeply enough to reflect more fundamental local ways of understanding and valuing the land. Some aspects are simply incommensurable with the empiricist presumptions of scientific methodologies that underlie GIS. Inconsistency and under-resourcing, and divides between technically trained and leadership (i.e. "elites") and other community members, can create problems for the stability and effectiveness of local control over, creative reconfiguring, and use of GISs.

Nadasdy's perceptive and unsettling analysis of incorporation of traditional ecological knowledge into resource and land management in the Yukon raises concern about whether participation in resource co-management actually extends state power into indigenous communities by enforcing the boundaries of the problems under negotiation, and constraining the kinds of input and connections among them which could be received (Nadasdy 1999, 2003, 2005). Similar questions certainly can be raised about the effects of mediating knowledge of the land through computer databases and GIS generated maps. In my own experience, there is a huge difference in being on the land with an elder, learning about place through observation, movement, and story, and attempting to recreate such experience through computer screen mediated graphics and sound bites. Elders and knowledgeable people in Deline, Northwest Territories, though they appreciate the utility of GIS and other technical tools in interfacing with government and outside interests, strongly believe that the way to preserve and transmit their land-based knowledge is, simply, on the land (cf. Johnson et al. 2005). This was also the way that Gwich'in advisors felt was appropriate for me to learn about

Gwich'in knowledge of the land, as I describe in Chapter 7, travelling on the land, experiencing it in different seasons, in the company of people who know the land from a lifetime of experience, and through the words of their elders. In Traditional Knowledge, the importance of the skill, knowledge and intelligence of the "viewer" or knower is what create informed analysis, a nuanced understanding of land.

Indigenous people have long employed representations of land, often contextualized with story, or sometimes drawing maps in snow or dirt to illustrate story. In one of the few studies of "cultural cartography," Pentland (1975) presented and analysed northern Algonquian mapping traditions. The maps he reproduces are detailed and nuanced depictions of riverine travel routes, and there are clear differences in attention to aspects of the land and waters in the features that Cree from the Hudson Bay lowlands around Norway House chose to include in their maps, in comparison with standard NTS maps of the same area. Pentland discusses the significance of the Cree maps in terms of wayfinding and navigation, including alternate routes of travel and a nuanced classification of rapids. The classes of rapids also included information about fish resources. Rundstrom (1990) described Inuit and Inuinnait (aka Copper Inuit) maps as "performance," that is, as a quintessential use of mimicry to communicate the nuances of land. The accuracy and extent of Inuit maps amazed Europeans, who used them widely for navigation and as a base for their own mapping efforts. Kaska guides depicted the route up the Liard River from Lower Post, BC to Frances Lake for geologist George Dawson in 1887, drawing a map on a canvas canoe cover, and naming all of the lakes and tributary streams (Dawson 1987:105B). Moore (2002:233-234) comments that these names are still in use today.

Indigenous maps, as with some historic Medieval European mapping conventions (Edgerton 1987), may also serve spiritual purposes and express spiritual understandings of the nature of the world. The Dane-ẕaa (Beaver or Dunne Za) tradition of visionary depictions of the trail to heaven, often painted on leather drum heads as in Figure 3 in Ridington (1981:354) and Doig River First Nation (2007), is one such indigenous mapping tradition. In his classic ethnography *Maps and Dreams*, Brody (1988:259-269) describes the amusing yet poignant cross-cultural encounter between white and native maps and mappers during a community hearing to discuss pipeline routing.

Ingold (2000) argues that the person at home on the land, in their home land, does not need a map, and he argues with the convention of describing the knowledge of place held by those who dwell there a "mental map." He argues that a map implies abstract space, which separates people from the land and from the knowledge of region accumulated through movement along many pathways of experience and memory. Ingold calls the movement through place "mapping," which he distinguishes from any end-product artifact, that is, a map.

Craig Candler (2000) in his talk "Maps, Dreams and GIS" gave a thoughtful critique of the constraints of relying uncritically on GIS for First Nations in the same area described in Brody's ethnography, detailing ways that GIS could constrain or transform how people understood the land. My concerns with representation of traditional knowledge through GIS are several: I am concerned that it reifies knowledge, pins it down, in the same manner as Agrawal (1995) described for traditional knowledge databases. Moreover, as I and others have described, locales may shift in precise georeferenced terms, but nonetheless retain their importance and essential characteristics. One may need to know a precise point to be able to encounter power, or know the site where a particular supernatural event is recorded, but need to designate a large polygon to avoid encroachment on such a power site by industrial activity or those without knowledge. One may need to know the exact location of a resource patch to be able to harvest a particular plant such as spiny wood fern, and generalized associations of the species with, say, a land or forest cover type is useless to the would-be harvester. The level of abstraction and generalization is totally inappropriate to the activity. Most likely a harvester would need to know a set of sites and the social rules of access, as well as seasonal considerations and also the access routes to get to the sites, in order to be able to harvest the plants. A skilled harvester would also be aware of characteristics of the sites where the fern rhizome or a valued medicine is found, and would be alert to potential resources of similar sites if he or she needed to find the plant, showing the resourcefulness of the engaged person on the land. In other instances, large and indefinitely bounded areas may be the relevant level of specificity, as when Marianne Ignace (2000) described a whole set of special sites, connected by the travels of a supernatural ancestral figure and explicated in traditional narratives, in the Marble Canyon/Fountain Lake area east of Lillooet, BC. This too was difficult to input into the TUS (Traditional Use Study)[7] database for GIS output required by the traditional use study format set by the BC Forest Service.

Another realm of difficulty is mapping the sacred, as in the example discussed by Ignace (2000) above. Given that there are strong concerns about how and to whom to communicate sacred knowledge (see Rundstrom 1993 and Gulliford 2000 for thought-provoking discussion of these issues), such information is often not recorded on maps or in GISs, or is presented in such a way as to diffuse actual locale, to protect sites from inappropriate or dangerous intrusion (cf. Weinstein 1998). It may well be that such knowledge is incommensurable with databases and hard rendering on Western style maps. If GIS-mediated depictions supplant more experience near understanding of land, there is a risk that the sacred will drop out of sight, or will be rendered in such a distorted and blurred way as to mislead. The depiction of land that is shared with outsiders and reified through electronic and printed maps and data may offer an incomplete picture. Interestingly, when Davidson-Hunt and Berkes (2003) sought to render Shoal Lake Anishinabeg landscape terms on landscape drawings, the community members rejected depictions that did not include both sites of human activity and supernatural associations, underscoring the risks of presenting only secular data. In my own Gitksan research, I have been told about sacred kinds of sites, but Dinim Gyet warned that it was dangerous to indicate the locations of such sites, as the unprepared might be at significant risk if they encountered a *sbi laxnok̲*. Although mapping specific sites is inappropriate, Gitksan understanding of landscape definitely includes the notion of powerful places, and that must not be overlooked simply because it does not appear on the map.

Although I express concerns for how translations into GIS-compatible terms may affect traditional knowledge of the land, one can also see the adoption and use of GIS and Web technologies as another instance of the resilience of indigenous peoples in the face of new contexts, needs, and opportunities. Thinking about GIS and the effective use of GIS-generated maps and databases in contemporary land claims and co-management contexts made me think of the use of maps in an earlier era to communicate essential aspects of indigenous homelands, as the carefully labelled maps by Michael Inspiring Bright and other Gitksan presented in *Tribal Boundaries in the Nass Watershed* (Sterritt et al. 1998).

According to Crumplin and others, GISs have the potential to empower and democratize, as well as to disadvantage and alienate (e.g. Crumplin 2007; Pickles 1995 and authors therein; Elwood 2006; Rundstrom 1995). As the critical and participatory GIS literature (Elwood 2006; Crumplin 2007; Duncan and Lach 2006) makes clear, what can be expressed or recorded through GIS is at least in part a question of database and study design, and group goals; if the community controls how data is recorded and structured, there is a real possibility of ownership and empowerment. A remarkable multifaceted community driven study of habitats and toponyms in the Northwest Territories shows the potential that such studies can have in sensitively exploring the nuances of environmental knowledge without being dominated by the constraints of the technology (Legat et al. 2001). This Dogrib (Tłįchǫ) study of habitats and environments in the West Slave area of the Northwest Territories was inspired by concerns for the potential impacts on a large area of sensitive tundra and taiga on the Canadian Shield when the diamond prospecting boom of the early1990s suddenly made real the possibility of widespread industrial impacts on very sensitive environments which are the homeland, and source of caribou and other foods, for the Dogrib people. The study initiated by the Dogrib Treaty 11 council was entirely community run, and almost all of the researchers were also Dogrib, including language experts and the GIS coordinator, and unfolded over a period of four years. The importance of careful linguistic work, recording of narratives, and visits to significant areas chosen by community members in each of the community areas gives a real richness and authority to the information recorded. The information recorded places the highly specific site information into contexts of narrative, of general habitat types, of travel routes and needed resources for travel, and in relation to caribou, the most important animal for the Tłįchǫ people. It also enfolds all within the concept of *dè*, the Land. They describe *dè* as

> a term which is usually translated as land, however the concept is much broader. Dè is much closer to the scientific concept "ecosystem," except where ecosystem is based on the idea that living things exist in association with non-living elements, the Dogrib term dè is based on the idea that everything in the environment has life and spirit. (Legat et al. 2001:3, footnote 12)

The material will form the basis of a long-term monitoring effort to assess the environmental health and integrity of the region, and identify any impacts from industry or climate change.

Still, in the balance, GIS cannot replace the landscape of experience, though it may offer complementary perspectives, and we must be cautious of uncritically accepting the representation and novel analyses while letting the reality slip away. As of yet, GIS, though useful and powerful in its own right, cannot convey the depth and power of the storied landscape, which unites knowing subjects with a rich and powerful land that embodies history, and which through the strength of direct experience, teaches both about itself and the person who lives, moves, camps, and dwells there. The bandwidth of virtual perception is so much less than the multisensory and effortful engagement with the land itself. The richness of social context which includes other people and other beings on the land, and the immediate consequences of action, are likewise absent from the representation, of which we are largely passive audience.

13

The Ecology of Knowing the Land

We come full circle. The book itself is a trail or a journey, an exploration of knowing the land, of living with and on the land. For Dene and others such as the Gitksan, the Land encompasses much more than a mere extent of the earth's surface, or any area of soil. As Legat and her co-authors (2001) remind us, the concept of land held by Dene differs considerably from the concept of land or terrain that is the underpinning of contemporary mainstream European and North American society, and forms the basis of our legal concepts of land tenure. For the Gitksan and for other groups of Canada's Northwest Coast, the land too is much more than real estate or a source of resources; it is the locus of history and of identity, the centre of a web of relationship that encompasses all beings in a moral framework, and provides both living and home. This very different worldview is eloquently communicated by indigenous authors such as Umeek, A. Richard Atleo (2004), and non-indigenous authors who have worked long and closely with indigenous teachers and communities (e.g. Turner 2005). The challenge of trying to communicate across epistemologies, in shifting contexts, and in fields of power relationships is immense (cf. Nadasdy 2003).

The problem is how to bring *space* into communication with *place*. In contrast to the patchwork quilt of polygon based mapping, the virtual bird's-eye view alluded to by Ingold in his discussion of mapping and mapmaking (Ingold 2000, Chapter 13), many local people experience the Land as a series of trails, which can be extended metaphorically to the trail through life, or to walking the trail as the proper way of living and relating to the Earth. The metaphor of *walking* as a skilled way of being in the world, of moving through the world, encapsulates the embodied, experiential way of knowing and doing. Walking, Tilley (1994:29) writes, is ". . . simultaneously an art of consciousness, habit and practice, that is both constrained by place and landscape and constitutive of them. Walking is the medium and outcome of a spatial practice, a mode of existence in the world." Robert Wishart also takes up the theme of walking (Wishart n.d.). Wishart tells us that to walk well, for a Gwich'in man, means a man is competent to move in the frequently difficult and challenging world of his low-Arctic homeland, understands place and moment, and knows how to best make his way across the landscape, is able to hunt and to return with meat to family and others who need it. Landscape is a medium, imbued with meaning, a partner in the business of living, and skilled walking is a way of competently moving through it.

Living on the land implies identity, and wellness. Naomi Adelson (2000) explicitly draws the connection between skilled movement on the land and wellness, for the Cree of the James Bay region. Dene Elders also often see the Land, being on the land in appropriate relationship and with skill, as the path to health and well-being.

In aboriginal Australia, the Dreaming Tracks, which record in the frozen substance of the Land itself the activities, transformations and metamorphoses of the ancestors, are reminiscent of the understandings of the land held by indigenous peoples of North America, though the system of trackways and power charged sacred places seems more comprehensive and deeply developed in Australia than among Canadian First Nation peoples, and more directly linked to specific social groupings than among the Dene. When I read of Australian understandings of land (Strang 1997; Rose 2000; Ingold 1996a:137-139), I am particularly reminded of the travels of Yamoria or Yamózah in the Mackenzie region, and the landforms that bear testament to his activities and adventures (Andrews et al. 1998; Andrews 1990). Considering what I have read of Australia, I also think of those places of power and danger in the Canadian North, rapids where giant animals are said to dwell, and which require special care to cross (cf. Sharp 1987); the stories told by my Kaska Elder teacher Mida Donnessey, where she alludes to the places where giant animals were overcome; or the sentient landscape revealed by Julie Cruikshank (2005) as she explores indigenous understanding of the surging glaciers of the Kluane-Saint Elias-Glacier Bay region of the Alaska-Yukon border.

In indigenous concepts landscape has agency. This perspective implies a relationship between humans and other entities of the land, and the Land itself, different than that prevalent in European cultures. Indigenous North Americans stress the necessity for respect in relations with other entities on the land (e.g. Bastien 2004). People are enjoined to follow the "Dene way" (***Dene k'eh***, in Kaska) or warned of the consequences of failure to respect, in powerful narratives. Lessons are instantiated in the form of the land itself, visible and memorable for those who have been taught the stories. Shiltee Rock standing above the Peel River remains forever a warning about the consequences of failing to follow the appropriate rules of respect, and continues to be a place of power (L.M. Johnson field notes 1999, 2000; Gwich'in Social and Cultural Institute, Place Name Map, Peel River, No. 2). Stekyooden, looming above Hagwilget and the Hazeltons, remains a visible reminder of when the mountain goats took revenge on careless ancestors for overhunting and disrespect (Harris 1974). The red rocks in Moricetown Canyon are a reminder of the grisly consequences of infidelity, and the repercussions that such acts have in the balance of power and ability to successfully hunt (Madeline Alfred Dzee, L.M. Johnson interview notes 1988).

Landscape ethnoecology

One aspect of knowledge of the land I have focused on in this work is the place kinds that people recognize in their local landscapes. At this detailed level of knowledge of the land, one can gain insights into the subtleties of people's understandings, which illuminate aspects of relationship to the land and what is needful to be able to travel safely on and live from it. All of the groups of people I have worked with recognize many kinds of landscape features, and features of waterways, in their homelands. The lists of English glosses of feature types recognized show many similarities among the groups I have worked with, though reasonably comprehensive landscape and water feature lexicons have only been recorded for Gitksan, Witsuwit'en and Kaska. The range of terms include physiographic features (mountain, pass, slope, slide area, etc.), water features (spring, creek, river, lake and parts thereof), complex features such as "swamp" which are both hydrographic and vegetation types, vegetation, snow and ice terms, substrates, features defined on the basis of animal behaviour, features related to human use (camp, trail, grave), and sacred or powerful sites. This last, owing to its sensitive nature, has neither been explored nor presented in detail, though the sacred and powerful aspect of the land must always be borne in mind. The list is rather heterogeneous, as colleagues such as Eugene Hunn (pers. comm.) have pointed out. Hunn prefers to separate out ecotopes of evident biophysical character from those less determinate in terms of physical features, and consider the latter to be "special purpose" categories (cf. Hunn and Meilleur 2009). I argue that, though the list is indeed heterogeneous, it is artificial and obscures important connections to decide a priori which kinds of features are "really" landscape features with ecological content, and set the others aside.

For all groups I have worked with, recognition of vegetation variants is frequently descriptive or offered in terms of a few dominant types, though people have good ideas of where to find particular plants of interest and when to pick or harvest those wanted for foods, medicines, or materials. The correlation of plant occurrence with various aspects of habitat can be described, as when Elders were asked to list plants occurring on shorelines, *tamā*, or in the alpine zone *héskage*, at a Kaska language meeting (Johnson 2007, this work). In contrast to the exposition of plant occurrence in correlation with distinct habitat types characterized by physiography and substrate or soil types, as obtained by Legat and her co-authors, I did not gain much explicit connection of plants and soils in the work that I did. Perhaps if I had framed my work in a different way, such connections would have emerged. The methodology and purposes of Legat and her co-authors was quite different from that which I employed, and focused on careful description of a set of named places chosen by Elders of the various Tłı̨chǫ communities, with the intention of establishing environmental baseline conditions and presence of biotic resources in the face of probable future resource development.

It is also instructive to consider the kinds of features and processes recognized by a group of people in a given area and to consider their similarity or difference from the geographic ontology of other groups of people. Understanding the patterns of seasonal change of environments, seasonal use of habitats and places by animals, successional change after disturbance, and phenological cycles of plants and fruiting are all dynamic aspects of people's pragmatic landscape knowledge. Davidson-Hunt and Berkes (2003, 2009) give some particularly cogent examples of the understanding of burn cycles and fruiting cycles in their work with the Shoal Lake Anishinaabe.

Gitksan and Witsuwit'en understanding of burn cycles, and how to manage land through burning in connection with berries, was discussed at length in Chapter 5. Deep knowledge of the movements of animals through the seasons, and in what kinds of places they may be encountered is a salient aspect of Kaska, Sahtú'otine and Gwich'in knowledge of the land.

The sense of the dynamic and shifting landscape, with trails or paths of connection focusing at spatio-temporal nodes, is also extremely important in the understanding of the northern landscape. As with contemporary landscape ecology, landscape ethnoecology deals with dynamic landscapes, fluxes and connections, as well as more static patterning of categories in local classifications. As Roy Ellen (2009), and Tim Ingold (1996b), in their different ways have asserted, knowledge may not be lexicalized or cognized, but may instead be embodied and demonstrated as needed, in context. Reading Ingold's work, I reflected that Dene knowledge of land involves training in observation, replication, and creative problem solving informed by rich layered traditions that require active engagement to tease out their relevance to the situation at hand, a characterization that also reflects the understanding of the storied landscape communicated by Dinim Gyet and other Gitksan and Witsuwit'en elders and knowledge holders.

The view from elsewhere

There are commonalities among the understandings of landscape in different regions of the world, despite large differences in the biophysical environment itself, and there are, as it were, local flavourings. As I read studies of others' landscape knowledge, I found myself considering the kinds of entities named, the relations attended to, and the integration of the sacred or spiritually powerful, with other aspects of the lived world. In many societies beyond those of northwestern Canada, the Path as organizing principle is apparent.

Strong similarities between the landscape perceptions of indigenous peoples of Siberia and those of the northern regions of Canada are evident, though the inscription of the Soviet period on Siberian lands and societies has given a different trajectory to landscape relations of the past century. Most Siberian peoples are traditionally herders (of reindeer—domesticated deer of the same species as caribou—or cattle) rather than strict hunters, but the taiga landscape of their homeland and the north Canadian environment are similar. Vitebsky (2005) writes about the paths taken by Eveny herders and their reindeer, and the spirits of place. Despite the strong changes induced by Soviet state policies, successful herders retained a perspective of the sacral landscape, of path and season. Gravesites on the land remain sacred places. Relations of respect with animals sound similar to Koyukon in Alaska or Dane-ẕaa in Canada, except a supreme lord of animals called Bayanay directs the animals and decides whether they will offer themselves. He is at once the owner of the animals, and is incarnate in all the animals. This is a somewhat more personified relationship than apparent in most Dene or Gitksan discussion of relations with animals. Vajda (2007) writes of Ket landscape perception in the upper Yenisei River. Rare among Siberian indigenous peoples, Ket were traditionally hunters and gatherers until Soviet collectivization during the 1930s forced change. Their landscape perceptions were organized along the Yenisei River north-south axis, with upriver south:

> . . . a source of positive energy, goodwill, and economic benefits as was the sky itself. The downriver north was a realm of cold, ill will, and death that merged with conceptions of the underworld. The east, the point of the rising sun, was likewise a source of life, whereas the west, where the sun disappeared was associated with extinguishment of life. (unnumbered pre-print)

As with other northern peoples, strong seasonal contrasts existed in terms of which portions of the landscape were used, with summer activities focused by the riverbank, and winter hunting activities in the forest. Vajda (2008) reports that the Ket conceived of time as a repeating cycle of birth and rebirth. Their cosmography was relatively elaborate, with seven layers of the sacred sky, and seven levels of the underworld (which was the abode of the dead), and the ordinary land in between. The Ket recognized a region of stony land (**_tynbang_**) and a region of watery land (**_ulbang_**) within their homeland. Trees were symbolically important to Ket, and "cedar" (*Pinus sibirica*) was considered sacred. The similarity of Ket and Athapaskan conceptions of landscape may be indicative of ancient relationship as well as similarity in environment and way of life; recently Vajda and other linguists have provided evidence of deep genetic relationship between Yeniseic and Na-Dene languages (Vajda 2008).

King (2002, 2006) has written about the relationship to sacred and storied land in Kamchatka, emphasizing the integrated view of people and land held by native Kamchatkans. He coins the term "culturescape" to encapsulate his sense that the people, their social relations and cultural understandings, and the landscape are not analytically separable. His exposition attends particularly to symbolic systems and meanings, and includes instances of rocks as power places and sites of transformation, and to the layered cosmography with an upper world, the quotidian world of ordinary human life, and an underworld. This perspective of land, as for other indigenous Siberian peoples, has vertical dimensions, similar to the medieval European landscape Tuan (1974) described, where the layered world is more significant than vast horizontal expanses.

Collignon's (2006) exposition of Inuinnait geographic knowledge is discussed extensively in Chapter 10. Here too was a traditional seasonal opposition between where people wintered and where they summered, which for the Inuinnait was the time of the ice and the time of the land, respectively. Collignon evokes the succession of named places associated with stories, which lie along the traditional routes of travel between camps and hunting areas.

Stephen Feld (1996), describing a very different environment emphasizes Bosavi perception of landscape through sequences of acoustic landmarks in the highlands of New Guinea, and Joseph Bastien's (1978) eloquent analysis of the significance of *ayllu* as a social, spiritual and ecological organizing principle in the Bolivian Andes near the border with Peru provides a strong example of the explicit integration of the sacred into local ecological understanding in a South American agrarian context.

While these studies discuss habitation, broad environmental orientation, and aspects of hunting and fishing ecology, narratives, cosmography, and the integration of the sacred, there is relatively less discussion of the ecotopic level, and the kinds of place recognized in local geography, especially plants and habitats. This is partly because of the interests and skills of those who have recorded the traditional geographic knowledge and partly because of the obvious and overwhelming importance of animals and knowledge about animals in the north.

Ethnographer Peter Dwyer wrote a piece that compared and contrasted the landscape perceptions of two nearby groups in Highland New Guinea, which had different degrees of agricultural intensification, population densities, and degrees of contact with the larger world. The description of the Kubo world presented by Dwyer (1996) and the importance of the network of trails, different resource sites, and locations that indicate human activity pervasive on the landscape, is strongly reminiscent of Dene and Gitksan perspectives of the land. He writes, "The invisible world permeates the land. Fabulous beings are associated with specific environmental zones or even particular places . . ." (Dwyer 1996:168). He continues:

> The visible and invisible worlds are co-extensive. In each, the
> significance of particular places is pre-eminent but always transient.
> Through time, places of current significance drift across the land.
> The two worlds converge in a mutual dynamic that facilitates their
> intercommunication. (Dwyer 1996:169)

Alice Legat and her co authors (2001) write about the relationships of
place names and landscape knowledge for the Dogrib (Tłįchǫ) of the Northwest Territories, showing the linkages between ethnoecological and cultural
knowledge of different types, in ways that resonate with the understandings I
have gained over the years of working with different Canadian First Nations:

> . . . patterns associated with Tłįchǫ placenames suggest that names
> that contain topographic and water flow terms have the primary
> purpose of describing safe understandable travel routes, whereas
> the primary purpose of the placenames containing biological terms
> seem to indicate locations with various resources or biodiversity.
> Placenames stimulate oral narratives that contain knowledge of
> socio-political relationships, social behaviour, resources, ancestral
> use, graves and obstacles while traveling and camping in the area.
> Often a placename will be mentioned to stimulate the listener's
> memory, hoping to encourage them to think and act in a
> certain way.

Keith Basso (1996) has described the use of place names for the same purposes among the White Mountain Apache, Athapaskan speakers who live in
the mountains of the desert Southwest of the United States.

Various authors such as Beatrice Collignon (2006) have commented
on trails linking named places, which in turn may be both point and surrounding region. I also discuss this in Chapter 3 in considering the Gitksan
storied landscape. People can and do generalize about places and extrapolate
knowledge from known places to similar new exemplars. However, most
people carry an inventory of named sites that serve for wayfinding, locating resources, and to integrate information about place from and within
narratives. Cruikshank (1990b, 1998, 2005) and others (e.g. Hunn 1996;
Fowler 2009; Rosaldo 1980; Johnson 2000) have commented on how history is written spatially, as it were, on the land, rather than as a dislocated
chronological listing, for many small-scale, land-based societies, especially
those without a written literate tradition or formal calendrical reckoning.

The comments made by Legat and her co-authors (2001) about the kinds of places named resonate with my own understanding of kinds of place on the landscape. Place names and kinds of places that are significant reflect the requirements of travelling people. They show a concern with features needful to know in order to travel safely and effectively, knowledge about the locations, or potential locations, of resources (useful plants, animals, etc.), a geography of power and the sacral, and place knit together by story.

The nature of nature

Understanding the nature of nature is an implicit background to the differences in perception and understanding of the landscape between many indigenous peoples, cosmopolitan science, and many strands of contemporary Western culture. In a holistic view, nature and the human inhabitants of the land form a seamless, interrelated whole, while the analytical perspectives which predominate Western thought and science have tended to separate the human and the natural, seeing them in opposition and often, as with the writing of the Romantics in the nineteenth century, holding up Nature as a mirror to reflect the purity and virtue missing in polluted and soul-less human society (e.g. Thoreau 1854/1849; Muir 1912, 1915; Cronon 1996). Previously, the imposition of human order upon the unseemly messiness of raw nature was seen as a virtue, for example as in the discussion of the ecological transformation of New England by eighteenth century commentators in Cronon (1983:5-6).

Many authors (e.g. Ingold 2000; Johnson 2000; Turner 2005, other references; Nadasdy 2003; Davidson-Hunt and Berkes 2003; Cruikshank 1998, 2005; Dwyer 1996; Strang 1997; Rose 2000, 2005; Roberts and Wills 1998; Fienup-Riordan 1990, 1999), including indigenous commentators (Atleo [Umeek] 2004; Kawagley 1995; Colorado 1988; Merculieff 2002; Burda et al. 1999), have commented upon holistic indigenous conceptions of humans-in-nature that are prevalent in many small-scale local and indigenous communities. Others such as Kay Milton (2002) have considered perspectives on nature of contemporary environmentalists in Euro-North American contexts.

Arturo Escobar (1999, 2001) looks at the interrelationships of nature and culture from the perspective of political ecology, regarding conceptions of both—as opposed to the underlying "biophysical reality," which he characterizes as prediscursive and presocial—from a constructivist perspective. Escobar considers conceptions of nature, and of culture, to reflect political power and hegemony, resistance and hybridity. Escobar comments:

... we might be witnessing—in the wake of unprecedented
intervention into nature at the molecular level—the final decline
of the modern ideology of naturalism, that is, the belief in the
existence of pristine Nature outside of history and human context
... We are talking here about nature as an essential principle and
foundational category, a ground for both being and society, nature
as an "independent domain of intrinsic value, truth, or authenticity"
... (Escobar 1999:1)

Lessons for the present and future

During this time of great change in the relations of peoples with homelands
and other lands, of increasing population and broad human impact on the
planet, its climate, and its chemical contamination, as rapid globalization
casts planet-wide webs of connection while severing and dislocating local
ones, how shall we learn from the storied landscape? How can we express
and share the insights of the traveller's path in the contemporary world, and
perpetuate knowledge among cultural, social and linguistic communities
whose demography and ecology may be shifting rapidly? Nature and culture,
for many, slip into imaginaries, and as Escobar points out (1999, 2001), conceptions of nature and culture are tools of domination, resistance, or identity
construction, which are communicated and experienced in mediated forms,
often through mass media. The World Wide Web allows communication of
localities to an undefined world-at-large, and of imagined and imaged culture
to Self, within the community to local people, their children, and others.
What exists on the ground can be transformed at the stroke of a metaphoric
pen, by states and transnational industries, lending an unreality to what was
previously a solid, factual, empirical world and world view (cf. Tsing 2005).
Or transformation in the relations of people and land can come through war
and civil unrest, or civil or inter-ethnic strife.

GIS and electronic representations of land and landscape—media? mediation? transformation? useful tools?

Contemporary technologies such as GIS, remote sensing, and GPS units
collaborate in transformations of understandings and of land. As various
authors have pointed out, GIS is both method and medium. As such, it has
been widely used by indigenous groups and those working with them, to

represent indigenous knowledge(s) in a number of contexts, often disseminated or accessed via websites. The hypertext and linkage patterns of websites, together with their multimedia capabilities, allow presentation of traditional information about land in a relatively rich, if virtual, manner. Storytelling and trail can both be accommodated, although the bandwidth of such virtual experience, and the ability to contextualize tellings and experiences according to season, place, and social relations, is far less than "real" experience.

A website that works hard to reproduce a traditional experience of land and its meanings is the Įdaà Trail website, produced by the Prince of Wales Northern Heritage Centre. The organization of Įdaà trail website is explicitly a "virtual" trail or traveller's path; while Web access allows entry at any point, the *body* is not experiencing the land, nor is the listener actually present as the audience of the recorded story, which cannot shift in the way live telling does depending on context and listener, as Cruikshank describes in *The Social Work of Stories* (1998). However, in an electronic fashion, the essential features of the storied landscape, travelled by a trail that links places is preserved, and enables a range of people to experience this through multimedia. Given an enriched context, as, for example, in a northern classroom, such websites can contribute significantly to the transmission of traditional understandings to the young, and also give a sense of the northern sense of land to non-local audiences worldwide.

GIS representations familiar to most of us as non-specialists are computer-generated maps which draw on centuries of mapping conventions developed in Europe. GIS theorist Donna Peuquet writes:

> Since maps are human-derived representations of geographic space,
> it can be inferred that this image vs. structure duality also holds
> for how humans perceive geographic space, corresponding to the
> world as seen (image) and the world as understood (structure) . . .
> The fundamental difficulty with attempting to develop an overall or
> uniform representation for geographic space is that there can never
> be a single representation of or view of the world that incorporates
> every possible viewpoint. (Peuquet 1988: 378)

This last I would urge people to keep in mind as local understandings, indigenous or other, are all reconfigured to be "processed" and "output" in GISs, digested and homogenized to make apprehension of geographic information easier and more effective.

As geographic information systems and GPS units become ubiquitous, at least among elites in more technological countries, and among scientists and resource managers, there are implications for how we understand landscape and how we deal with it (e.g. Aporta 2009; Aporta and Higgs 2005). We leave further behind the embodied travel across land, the skills necessary for wayfinding, the particularity of place, and the ability to deal with shifting or ambiguous positions and fuzzy boundaries. If you can't geo-reference it, does it exist? GPS and remote sensing change ability to deal with spatial information. They are enormously powerful tools, but are not designed to deal with ambiguity. They are inherently reductionist. GIS cannot include information about place in database without precise georeferenced positions. As with other types of quantitative data analysis, imprecise data cannot be entered, however significant. Daily lived experience is often difficult to quantify precisely. As of this writing, the ability to express shifting or unbounded areas lies at theoretical cutting edge of GIS (Goodchild et al. 2007; Peuquet 1988), and as yet far from routine practice. But we risk missing the proverbial "elephant in the room" if we cannot deal with ambiguous or poorly bounded information and relationships and so simply leave them out. We may miss essential aspects of indigenous landscape ethnoecology and local experience altogether. As with the difficulty of dealing with the value of beauty or nature in economic terms, it is not yet possible to georeference a sense of place, though the insights garnered with GISs have been very powerful and, some have argued, empowering for indigenous peoples and other less advantaged groups such as inner city residents (Elwood 2006).

Roy Wagner (1977), in a comparison of scientific and Papuan conceptions of the innate, commented that, analogous to the quantum dilemma of position and motion, if you focus on relationship, then the identity of the objects is not significant and is not the focus, while if you focus on objects then the relationships recede. Wagner sees Western science as focusing on the objects (a particularly strong aspect of geographic information science), and Papuan worldviews as focusing on relationship. Relationship is not something that GIS does well. As Peuquet (1988) commented, with raster[1] data, attributes are attached to located cells and spatial patterning or relationships are only implicit.

Difficulties with GISs as representations of indigenous knowledge of the land arise on several levels. One I dwell on at length is the removal of knowledge from the realm of direct experience and of storied social context. Another issue is the reductionist and abstracting nature of quantitative analysis itself, necessary before one can construct databases and carry out analyses informed by them. However, the fact remains the GISs are powerful tools, and can help to reduce unmanageably complex relationships to something that one may be able to apprehend. As Weinstein points out in his 1992 report to the Ross River Dena Council (a Kaska community) on ecological and social impacts of mine development, without GISs and some forms of abstraction and generalization in analysis, spatial data are far too complex and multifaceted to allow full use to be made of graphic results of qualitative research such as map biographies, the sine qua non of land-use and occupancy studies. These are familiar issues in the complementary and contradictory natures of qualitative and quantitative research within western research paradigms.

Where methodologies of landscape research and practice are adequately collaborative, creative syntheses that serve local communities can result. One of the underpinnings of successful collaborative syntheses is genuine power sharing, and such efforts, occurring as they inevitably do in dialogue between systems of thought, involve translation and careful explication. In January 2008 I was fascinated to hear a presentation by Gabrielle Mackenzie-Scott, then Chair of the Mackenzie Valley Environmental Impact Review Board at the Northern Truths forum at the University of Alberta. Mackenzie-Scott is a Tłı̨chǫ woman, and her eloquent exposition of the role that indigenous members of the environmental review board played in interpreting the significance of traditional knowledge to more scientific and industry oriented colleagues suggested ways that holistic perspectives and local spiritual perspectives on land can be integrated in important real-world decisions (Struzik 2008).[2] Aporta's work on community use of the mapping potential of a simple GPS program in Igloolik, Nunavut also suggests ways that new technologies can serve to continue indigenous knowledge of land (Aporta 2003). The collaborative Whitefeather Forest initiative is a multifaceted and multi-partner initiative to document a boreal forest cultural landscape in northern Ontario. This initiative pioneers cross-cultural methodologies to further the aims of the Pikangikum First Nation in stewardship of their homeland (Davidson-Hunt pers. comm., n.d.; http://www.whitefeatherforest.com/).

For the communities with whom I have worked, it is difficult to present a clear picture of innovative and creative approaches to documenting and managing the land and its resources. The landscape, so to speak, of successful approaches to landscape management is complex and can change quite quickly. There have been interesting Gitksan initiatives, such as the Strategic

Watershed Analysis program (Burda et al. 1999; Darlene Vegh, pers. comm.) and the La<u>x</u> Skiik plans for the Fiddler Creek territory (Art Loring, pers. comm.), but it is a bit more challenging to say what is happening in 2009. The Gitksan GIS department is largely associated with the Gitxsan Watershed Authority, which primarily focuses on fisheries-related issues. It has been engaged in innovative training and in representations of traditional territory, continuing a counter-mapping effort which was developed in the Delgamuukw land claims case; however, these efforts do not appear to have much influence on forestry development planning on the territories (A.S. Gottesfeld, pers. comm.). The Kaska efforts around land use are similarly complex, and have been marked by political success in terms of joint agreements and impact benefit agreements; how this articulates with other qualitative efforts to document and preserve knowledge is difficult to assess. The Gwich'in Renewable Resource Board has institutionalized co-management based largely on western paradigms of data collection and analysis, though considerable community direction, consultation and participation in the research is also standard in their procedures. How their efforts coordinate with the innovative talking maps (http://www.gwichin.ca/Research/place-NameMap.html) and other traditional knowledge initiatives of the Gwich'in Social and Cultural Institute is not clear.

Further reflections

Peuquet (1988:378-379) writes that "a geomorphologist's view of a mountain would be different from a climatologist's or a botanist's. Yet all would recognize the same entity as a mountain." I would add, keeping Mark and Turk (2003) in mind, at least within a Western cultural and linguistic context. She further comments, "A mountain may look very different in summer from how it does in winter but would still be recognized as a mountain. Some necessary invariant qualities must therefore identify these objects . . ." (Peuquet 1988:379). Again, Mark and Turk (2003) and Mark and his co-authors (2009) might comment on the difficulties of establishing the boundaries of the mountain-as-object, and here also seasonality enters in: depending on the type of feature, and what qualities one needs to keep in mind, the mountain may still be a mountain, but its meaning in late summer, mid winter, or spring may be significantly different. When Witsuwit'en or Gitksan Elders speak of travelling in the mountains in the springtime, it is a time of great danger of being swept away by avalanches of heavy snow from far above, a risk Dinim Gyet spoke of when he discussed the Gitksan term for "slide," describing the faces in the trees which must be exposed by snow melt before a passage of the trail could be attempted (Chapter 3). When Kaska Elders speak of mountains in late summer, it is with anticipation of ascending to the alpine zone to look for caribou in the fall hunt.

Geographer Yi-Fu Tuan wrote about this about "mountain" and "valley" in his classic monograph *Topophilia*, reminding us that topographic terms have connotations, entailments, and connections with the moral:

> As scientific terms, "mountain" and "valley" are types in a topographical category. In metaphorical thought, these words carry simultaneously the value-laden meanings of "high" and "low," which in turn implicate the idea of male-female polarity and antithetical temperamental characteristics. (Tuan 1974:141)

A mountain in the distance has different meanings than a mountain up close. As Mark et al. (2009) write, "a mountain *qua* mountain is *away* from us, in the visual landscape, and when we stand on it, our proximate environment is filled not with 'mountain,' but with rocks, trees, snow etc." (emphasis added). Their conception of "ethnophysiography" is more concerned with the distance than the proximity. A mountain in the distance can have myriad meanings: as a symbol, a method of wayfinding, the abode of deities, scenery, an emblem of wilderness, and so on. A mountain up close, when you are, as Gitksan and Dene languages alike phrase it, "on mountain," is a different matter. Then one may well be concerned with places and place kinds of smaller scale, such as trails, berry patches, lookouts, passes, avalanche tracks, alpine meadows, cliffs, scree slopes, or snowfields. These too are ecotopes, may be named, have meanings, may be sacred or ordinary, integrated in daily life, of seasonal significance, or are perhaps to be avoided. Eugene Hunn's *Nch'i-Wána, "the Big River," Mid-Columbia Indians and Their Land* (Hunn with Selam and family1990) comments that Sahaptin often name these smaller, more local features rather than focusing on mountains-at-a-distance.

This book has been an exploration of landscape ethnoecology based on fieldwork in northwestern Canada. My approach integrates detailed delineation of local knowledge of place kinds, or ecotopes, with the overarching domain of meaning and combines ethnoscience, visual, and narrative traditions. I have reflected extensively on relations of local landscape knowledges to science, geographic information systems, resource management and government policy. Relationships between land and culture are mutually constitutive. Identity and polity are rooted in the ways people understand and act upon land. The environmental relationships and economies created through this understanding may be sustainable or ephemeral. Understandings of land also underlie the complicated dance of development of natural resources, and even the concept of "resource" as it is negotiated between local populations and larger socio-political and economic forces, states, and the global market. In this time, both environment and economies are undergoing rapid change, and sustainability of either is an open question. Resilience of the land and of human societies will be key in shaping the future.

ENDNOTES

CHAPTER 1

1 The release of the United Nations report *Our Common Future* by the World Commission on Environment and Development in 1987 marked a turning point in popular global awareness of a number of interrelated issues of environmental quality and economic development. *Our Common Future* brought the concepts of sustainability and sustainability development into every day discourse. It is often known Brundtland Report in acknowledgement of the role of former Norwegian Prime Minister Gro Harlem Brundtland as Chair of the Commission when the report was released. Its publication set the stage for the 1992 Earth Summit and the adoption of Agenda 21, a blueprint for sustainable development, the Rio Declaration on Environment and Development, and the Convention on Biological Diversity which together established the international framework for promotion of sustainable development and which were signed by more than 178 governments. (Agenda 21 for Change, a Plain Language Version of Agenda 21 and the other Rio Documents, http://www.iisd.org/rio%2B5/agenda/default.htm.)

CHAPTER 2

1 This conception of "the Land" is in sharp contrast to "land" as a quantifiable mass noun as discussed in Ingold 1993:153, where he contrasts generic, quantifiable "land" with qualitatively rich, lived-in "landscape."

2 In the same vein, I was recently struck by a statement in Scott (1998), where he muses on nature, free gifts of nature, and natural resources. Scott writes,

> . . . utilitarian discourse replaces the term "nature" with the term "natural resources," focusing on those aspects of nature that can be appropriated for human use . . .

> But the moment it [common property] becomes scarce (when "nature" became "natural resources"), it became the subject of property rights in law, whether of the state or of the citizens. The history of property in this sense has meant the inexorable incorporation of what were once thought of as free gifts of nature: forests, game, wasteland, prairie, subsurface minerals, water and watercourses, breathable air, even genetic sequences into a property regime. (1998: 39, emphasis added).

3 A recent paper by Istomin and Dwyer (2009) explores contrasting theoretical perspectives on mapping and mental maps, and reports significant empirical studies of orientation and mapping in two adjacent reindeer herding groups in Russia, finding significant differences in mapping between the Komi and Nenets, and between genders within each group.

4   Two strong examples of this phenomenon are given in Tsing 2005 and Scott 1998. Tsing details the transformation of the Meratus Dayak homeland in Kalimantan, socially and ecologically, into a "resource frontier." Scott provides a detailed and informative case history of the transformation of the German forests into monocultural managed *Normalbäum* growing timber for the state, completely eradicating the relationship of local communities to the previous diverse old growth forest landscape.

CHAPTER 3

1   The spelling of "Gitksan" is somewhat problematic; this was the former standard spelling. Gitxsan was used by the Gitxsan Treaty Office and is frequently found in publications, but Gitxsan (Gigeenix dialect) and Gitksen (Gyeets' dialect) are also frequent, and are the spellings used by the Gitksan Dictionary Committee.

2   In other published works (e.g. Marsden 2008) and in the Delgamuukw Court Case documents, this name is spelled T'enim Gyet. The orthography I use here is a newer practical orthography used by the Gitksan Dictionary committee, and is the spelling I have used in previous works.

3   For a detailed discussion of Gitksan social structure, traditional governance, and economy, see Richard Daly's 2005 *Our Box Was Full, an Ethnography for the Delgamuukw Plaintiffs*.

4   The two spellings given are for the eastern or Gigeenix dialect, and the western or Gyeets' dialect.

5   Art Mathews, Dinim Gyet, explained that the Elders prefer to keep that knowledge secret, because these are places of risk and power, and people who do not understand or respect such places, like most Whites, may "mess around" with them—which could harm themselves or others, or the land.

CHAPTER 4

1   The name is pronounced roughly "Wadzín Kwah." My orthography follows linguist Sharon Hargus.

2   The name Hagwilget is a Gitksan word that means 'quiet man'; the Witsuwit'en name Tse Cäkh (often spelled Tse Kya) means 'under the rock.'

3   The Court Case referred to here is the landmark land claims case *Delgamuukw vs. the Queen*.

4   This term is spelled three different ways in the excerpts from the interview transcript, reflecting my uncertainty about the correct transcription. The spelling of this term has not been checked by a trained Witsuwit'en linguist.

5   The spelling in brackets is the corrected spelling provided by Dr. Sharon Hargus.

6   The new white inner bark of the lodgepole pine is edible and nutritious (Gottesfeld 1995). It is called **k'inih** in Witsuwit'en, and often referred to as 'pine sap' in English.

CHAPTER 5

Some of the material in this chapter was previously published in a co-authored article with Scott Trusler entitled "'Berry Patch' as a Kind of Place—the ethnoecology of black huckleberry in Northwestern Canada" *Human Ecology* (2008). I have cited that work where pertinent.

1   Productivity for black huckleberry is high in the Gitksan and Witsuwit'en territories. Burton (1998) reports yields of 200 grams per square meter in for sites with 60-80% full sunlight, almost ten times the productivity reported by Minore et al. (1979) for Washington state.

2   This map represents a general overview, as it is not a complete inventory of traditional berry patches, nor does it show several village sites that are no longer occupied, nor the numerous fishing sites and smokehouse locations along the rivers.

3   One of the factors that is not clear is whether "packloads" refer to fresh or dried fruit. The volume ratio of fresh-to-dried fruit is 10.25:1, which could create a 10-fold error in the projections. However, ethnographic information from interviews suggests that in the nineteenth and early-twentieth centuries, fruit was usually processed and dried on site and transported in dry form (L.M. Johnson field notes; People of Ksan 1980).

4   Spellings of Witsuwit'en place names here are after the spellings in the Delgamuukw court case documents and do not represent the current practical orthography for Witsuwit'en. Other Witsuwit'en language terms are represented in the practical orthography. I acknowledge the assistance of Dr. Sharon Hargus of the University of Washington with spellings; any errors that remain are my own.

5   As I describe in Chapter 4, the fishing site at Hagwilget Canyon was first utilized when a rockslide blocked migration of salmon to the falls on the Bulkley River at present day Moricetown in the 1820s. Since the Federal Department of Fisheries blasted the rock that made fishing possible in Hagwilget Canyon in a misguided salmonid enhancement project in the late 1950s (Cassidy 1987), the Witsuwit'en fishery takes place only at Moricetown. Spring (chinook) salmon are the most important fish resource of the Witsuwit'en at present. Sockeye from the Nanika Lake stock have dwindled over the past century (Gottesfeld et al. 2002:95).

6   *Digï* is the correct spelling of the name for huckleberry in the present practical orthography.

7   *Sis Kwikh* is the spelling of the Suskwa River in the Tsë Cäkh Wit'en book (The Hagwilget [Tse-Kya] Band 1995).

8   I believe Maryann is referring here to the hunting sequence in the film Hugh Brody released in 1988 about the Gitksan-Wet'suwet'en Land Claim.

9   This spelling is in the Gigeenix dialect. It is *Ksa'endilgan* in the Gyeets dialect.

10 Thornton (1999, 2007) explicitly discusses Tlingit berry patch ownership and enhancement in terms of economic defendability.

11 Moss also discusses the influence of gender and status on the prominence of shellfish utilization among the Tlingit in the ethnographic record. It is possible that gender bias has also contributed to the relatively low emphasis in the traditional ethnographic record for berry resources as opposed to more male and charismatic enterprises such as salmon fishing and, for coastal peoples, sea mammal hunting. Gendering of knowledge around berry patch management and harvesting would be an interesting topic to investigate; to date, only scattered and suggestive data on this topic are available for Gitksan or Witsuwit'en. It appears that women may have had substantial input into deciding when a patch needed to be renewed by burning, and perhaps that men usually carried out burning of montane berry patches, possibly in the course of hunting activities as suggested by Sim'oogit Tsii wa's narrative. Women and children are certainly prominent among harvesters, but I did not get the sense that men avoided picking. In mixed resource utilization from montane or alpine base camps, it is likely that women would be more likely to pick berries while men were engaged in hunting mountain goats or procuring groundhogs, as suggested by Mary Ann Austin's narrative.

CHAPTER 6

1 Elephant is the term consistently used in English for this fearsome monster.

2 A version of the Sisters Who Married Stars told by Mida's cousin Clara Donnessey, with whom she was raised, is included in *Dene Gudeji, Kaska narratives* pp. 358-367 (Patrick Moore, Ed, 1999).

CHAPTER 7

1 William Teya tragically disappeared in 2005, and Alice Andre passed away in 2006. I honour their memory and am grateful for time shared on the land.

2 Alestine Andre earned a Masters in Environmental Studies at the University of Victoria in 2006, and in 2007 received an Aboriginal Achievement Award for her research in Gwich'in traditional knowledge of land, culture and healing, and her efforts to ensure that this knowledge will be available to future generations.

CHAPTER 8

This chapter is based upon a co-authored paper written with Daniel Andre, originally presented at the 2000 IASCP meeting at Indiana University, and has been updated to reflect subsequent changes in the economy and resource development.

1 These changes highlight the sensitivity of caribou to landscape disturbance. Such changes will be of significance if, or more likely when, the proposed Mackenzie Valley pipeline is constructed. The route crosses the entire area from the Inuvik area to the eastern edge of the Gwich'in Settlement Area, where the course of the Mackenzie resumes its southward course, and passes close by the northern edge of Travaillant Lake, which the Gwich'in have proposed be designated a protected area.

2   The figures for country food consumption by Inuvialuit from Aklavik, a Mackenzie Delta village that also has a large Gwich'in population are indicative of the importance of country foods in local nutrition(Wein and Freeman 1992). The replacement cost figures for Yukon First Nations given by Wein (1994) can be taken as an indication of the magnitude of the dollar value country foods represent for Northern peoples.

CHAPTER 9

1   This is the hoary marmot or 'whistler,' *Marmota calligata*, locally called "ground-hog," a formerly important food species of comparable significance to the "gopher" or Arctic ground squirrel *Spermophilus parryii* in the economy of Dene in the Yukon.

2   Although there is no local access to salmon in the Liard River system, Pacific salmon run in the Yukon River and its tributaries and in the Stikine River. Kaska and Tutchone fish for salmon on the Pelly River, and Tahltan have access to chinook and sockeye salmon on the Stikine River below the Grand Canyon of the Stikine, enabling people with social connections to obtain fish from people in these adjoining regions.

3   In the 1950s dynamiting of The Rock in Hagwilget Canyon in a misguided salmonid enhancement effort completely eliminated the productive fishing sites that had prompted the establishment of the village in that location (Morice 1904; Morrell 1989).

4   Many more storied places are detailed in the Sahtu Atlas, a compilation of land-based knowledge published for the people of the Sahtú region (Auld et. al 2005). See also the website for the Įdaà Trail, Prince of Wales Northern Heritage Centre http://www.lessonsfromtheland.ca/IndexLng.asp

5   The sense of a dynamic world with agency, and the necessity to treat the world with respect to avoid dangers is eloquently explored in the recent monograph by Julie Cruikshank entitled *Do Glaciers Listen?* which describes Tlingit and Tutchone (another Dene nation) interactions with the glaciated landscape of the Glacier Bay/ Mt St. Elias region.

6   A Moss house is a traditional Gwich'in dwelling, which is constructed of poles covered with moss, and partially dug into the ground. It was a warm winter dwelling in the period before log cabins, and canvas tents with stoves (Andre and Kritsch 1992).

CHAPTER 10

1   These names are Ts'ii Dęįį or "Stone Age" names, names in an older form of the language; the meanings of such names are not entirely understood by contemporary Gwich'in speakers.

2   Tim Ingold (1993: 156) commented, "places have centres—indeed it would be more appropriate to say they *are* centres—they have no boundaries."

3   There have been shifts in the popular orthography in Witsuwit'en; the terms formerly written Cakh and Kwah are now written Cikh and Kwikh.

4   I include mammals in the term "animal" and exclude fish and birds.

5   Interestingly, the term 'rabbit' here is a loanword from Athapaskan languages, as are other important animal terms such as that for moose, which speaks to long contact between language groups in the region (Rigsby and Kari n.d.).

6   *Xsi-* is a variant of the term for water which translates as 'creek, river.'

7   Dinim Gyet described how the water repellent liverwort or moss could be used and thought it resembled a particular leafy liverwort figured in a plant guide; the plant remains unidentified.

8   In Barbeau's text the spelling is Kwunekstaet.

CHAPTER 11

1   Raster data, in geographic information systems, is data coded to cells of a regular gridded field, like pixels, while vector data consists of points, lines, and formally defined polygonal spaces. Converting data from one type to another, or matching layers of vector and raster data is an important area of geographic information systems (GISs), and much has been written about the implications of choosing one type of representation or the other, and on the resolution of spatial data coded in raster form.

2   Angela Wheelock and Pat Moore were conducting land use and occupancy work for the Liard First Nation.

3   For a careful discussion of the social effects of introducing GPS, its benefits and downsides, and the effect on self-sufficiency of powerful but expensive units that cannot be locally repaired, see Aporta and Higgs 2005.

4   It is so naturalized in the contemporary world that in the rare instances when north is not depicted at the top of a map of an area of the land , it can make a statement, the momentary disorientation the map reader feels serving to challenge received truths and graphically emphasize that a distinct perspective is being represented. The plaintiffs in the Delgamuukw court case used this tension to give impact to the Atlas they presented as evidence regarding their occupancy and ownership of their lands.

5   For example, river or stream in Witsuwit'en is *–kwikh*, while for Dalhkeh or Carrier, the cognate form is *–ko*.

6   This is of course, a rather glib simplification of a complex process of technological development. For further discussion of the steps involved in the 'cartographic revolution' see David Turnbull's *Mason, Tricksters and Cartographers* (2000), Chapter 3. Accurate chronometres that would work at sea also had to be developed to

measure travel in an east/west direction to be able to determine longitude, and continued refinement of navigational instruments and techniques has taken place from the Renaissance to the present, when the GPS/GIS revolution is supplanting earlier techniques of navigation. GPS/GIS can deliver very accurate positions with the aid of satellite data and highly sophisticated computer software, and has become the norm for navigation in the air and at sea, and is quickly becoming widespread, at least in Europe and North America, for navigation on the ground.

CHAPTER 12

1 Ingold (2000) discusses these issues at length in his chapter on mapping and mapmaking, where he asserts that mapping is fundamentally different from mapmaking, and that the metaphor of a bird's-eye view actually obscures the work and movement that go into producing a map, rather than being a "natural" way to represent landscape. I wonder, in this era of GoogleEarth and mapping derived from satellite view if this any longer strictly true. Since the invention of the airplane and aerial photography, it has in fact been possible to view, and map, the landscape from this disembodied, disengaged perspective.

2 Nadasdy (2003) terms maps and databases which transform traditional ecological knowledge while purporting to preserve and record that knowledge, "TEK artifacts."

3 Another prophet's drumhead design depicting the Trail to Heaven is figured in Ridington 1981, page 354, Figure 3.

4 GIS and mapping subsequently moved to the Gitxsan Watershed Authority, and have been employed particularly in fisheries issues, and for some specific Chiefs' House territory planning.

5 The Whorfian hypothesis, also often referred to as the Sapir-Whorf hypothesis, deals with the notion that how we think and understand the world is influenced by aspects of the structure, grammar and lexicon of our languages. This is in fact one of the arguments for the need for the conservation of the diversity of the world's languages, as it implies that unique ways of understanding the world may be conditioned by the particularities of structure and vocabulary of the language one uses to think about and communicate about the world. In its "strong" formulation, it would be impossible to think in ways novel to the speaker's language, or to translate between languages, a notion no longer considered credible, but in its "weak" formulation, the Sapir-Whorf hypothesis suggests that language structure and lexicon influences or facilitates certain ways of understanding the world, and makes others less natural.

6 Eleanor Rosch, a psychologist at the University of California at Berkeley, pioneered a theory of category formation based on prototypes, rather than on definitions comprised of lists of traits, which has been very influential in subsequent cognitive and ethnoscience research.

7   When the decision of Justice McEachern in the original Delgamuukw case judgment was appealed, the Court of Appeals ruled that the Gitksan and Wets'uwet'en
did not retain title to the land, but stated that they did have unextinguished use
rights in the land. In its implementation of this ruling in the early 1990s, the
Province of British Columbia undertook a program to facilitate the identification
by British Columbia First Nations of sites of aboriginal significance for heritage or
land use which related to their unextinguished aboriginal use rights. The Province
provided funding to Bands for these studies, called Traditional Use Studies, and
universally referred to as TUS.

CHAPTER 13

1   In GIS, raster data is the form of spatial data that exists in the form of a geo-
referenced grid of cells, which is a very frequent form of GIS and remote sensing
data. The other main form of GIS data is vector data, which is comprised of an
array of points, lines and polygons, that is, of geographic objects.

2   Mackenzie-Scott was replaced as Chair of the review board in March 2008,
shortly after I heard her speak, suggesting the fragility of such hopeful efforts. Her
replacement followed the rejection of two mining developments (Drybones Bay and
Upper Thelon) by the MVEIRB in 2007, primarily because of the strong cultural
significance of the areas where development was proposed. Concern regarding the
loss of her voice on the committee was expressed by the office of Dennis Bevington,
MP for the Western Arctic.

REFERENCES

Aboriginal Mapping Network, www.nativemaps.org.

Adelaar, K. Sander. 1997. An Exploration of Directional Systems in West India and Madagascar. In *Referring to Space: Studies in Austronesian and Papuan Languages*, ed. Gunter Senft, 53-81. Oxford Studies in Anthropological Linguistics. Oxford: Clarendon Press.

————. 2000. Orientation systems in Western Austronesian Languages. Anthropology Seminar, University of Alberta, March 20.

Adelson, Naomi. 2000. *'Being Alive Well', Health and the Politics of Cree Well-Being*. Toronto: University of Toronto Press

Agrawal, Arun. 1995. Dismantling the divide between indigenous and scientific knowledge. *Development and Change* 26:413-439.

Alcorn, J. 1981. Huastec noncrop resource management: implications for prehistoric rain forest management. *Human Ecology* 9:395-417.

Allard, E. 1929. Notes on the Kaska and Upper Liard Indians. *Primitive Man*, 2(1/2): 24-26.

Anderson, David. 2000. *Identity and Ecology in Arctic Siberia: The Number One Reindeer Brigade*. Oxford: Oxford University Press.

Anderson, Eugene N. 1996. *Ecologies of the Heart, Emotion, Belief and the Environment*. Oxford: Oxford University Press.

————. 2009. Managing Maya Landscapes: Quintana Roo, Mexico. In *Landscape Ethnoecology: Concepts of Physical and Biotic Space*, eds. Leslie Main Johnson and Eugene S. Hunn, pp. 255-276. New York: Berghahn Books.

Anderson, M. Kat. 2005. *Tending the Wild, Native American Knowledge and the Management of California's Natural Resources*. Berkeley: University of California Press.

Andre, Alestine, and Ingrid Kritsch. 1992. *The Traditional Use of the Travaillant Lake Area Using Trails and Place Names of the Gwichya Gwich'in from Arctic Red River, N.W.T.* Final Report, on file at Gwich'in Social and Cultural Institute, Tsiigehtchic, NT.

Andrews, Thomas D. 1990. *Yamoria's Arrows: Stories, Place-names and the Land in Dene Oral Tradition*. Unpublished report, for National Historic Parks and Sites, Northern Initiatives, Canadian Parks Service, Environment Canada Contract no. 1632/89-177.

Andrews, Thomas D., Glen Mackay and Leon Andrew. 2009. *Hunters of the Alpine Ice: The NWT Ice Patch Study*. Blurb Creative Publishing Service.

Andrews, Thomas D., and John B. Zoe. 1997. The Įdaà Trail: Archaeology and the Dogrib Cultural Landscape, Northwest Territories, Canada. In *At a Crossroads: Archaeology and First Peoples in Canada*, eds. George P. Nicholas and Thomas D. Andrews, 160-177. Burnaby: Archaeology Press, Archaeology Dept., Simon Fraser University.

Andrews, Thomas D., John B. Zoe, and Aaron Herter. 1998. On Yamòzah's Trail: Sacred Sites and the Anthropology of Travel. In *Sacred Lands: Claims, Conflicts and Resolutions*, eds. Jill Oaks, Rick Riewe, Kathi Kinew, and Elaine Maloney, 305-320. Occasional Publication No. 43. Edmonton: Canadian Circumpolar Institute.

Anonymous. 1992. List of toponyms and names extracted from materials prepared for *Delgamaukw vs. the Queen* (Gitksan-Wet'suwet'en landclaims courtcase). Manuscript on file, Gitksan Treaty Office Library, Hazelton, BC.

Anonymous. 1996. The White Buffalo Woman. Originally published in *Share International Magazine*, September 1996, reproduced on *White Buffalo* webpage; http://www.merceronline.com/Native/native05.htm.

Antoine, Francesca, Catherine Bird, Agnes Isaac, Nellie Prince, Sally Sam, Richard Walker, and David B. Wilkinson. 1974. *Central Carrier Bilingual Dictionary*. Fort St. James, BC: Carrier Linguistic Committee.

Aporta, Claudio. 2000. Life on the ice: understanding the codes of a changing environment. *Polar Record* 38(207): 341-354.

———. 2003. New ways of mapping, using GPS software to plot place names and trails in Igloolik, Nunavut. *Arctic* 46(5):729-754.

———. 2009. Life on the Ice: Understanding the Codes of a Changing Environment. In *Landscape Ethnoecology, Concepts of Biotic Physical and Space*, eds. Leslie Main Johnson and Eugene S. Hunn, pp. 175-199. New York: Berghahn Books.

Aporta, Claudio, and Eric Higgs. 2005. Global Positioning Systems, Inuit wayfinding, and the need for a new account of technology landscape. *Current Anthropology* 46(5):729-754.

Ashmore, Wendy, and A. Bernard Knapp. 1999. *Archaeologies of Landscape, Contemporary Perspectives*. Maiden, MA and Oxford: Blackwell Publishers.

Atleo, E. Richard (Umeek). 2004. *Tsawalk, A Nuu-chah-nulth Worldview*. Vancouver: UBC Press.

Attachie, Billy, Madeline Oker, Kate Hennessey, Julia Miller, and Patrick Moore. 2006. Dane-zaa Jíge, *Beaver Land: The Virtual Museum of Canada "Dane Wadagish" and Volklwagen Foundation "Beaver Knowledge Systems" Projects*. Presentation at Special Session on Internet Resources, Land and Language Online, 2006 International Dene Languages Conference, June 12-15, Yellowknife, Northwest Territories, Canada.

Atran, Scott. 1993. Itza Maya tropical agro-forestry. *Current Anthropology* 34(5):633-700.

Auld, James, Robert Kershaw, Melonie Dyck, Deborah Simmons, Miki Promislow, Alasdaire Vietch, and Jody Snortland. 2005. *The Sahtu Atlas, Maps and Stories from the Sahtu Settlement Area in Canada's Northwest Territories*. Deline: The Sahtu GIS Project.

Bandeira, Fabio Pedre S. de F., Jorge Lopez Blanco, and Victor M. Toledo. 2002. Tzotzil Maya ethnoecology: landscape perception and management as a basis for coffee agroforest design. *Journal of Ethnobiology* 22(2):247-272.

Barbeau, Marius. 1929. Totem Poles of the Gitksan, Upper Skeena River, British Columbia. Bulletin No. 61, Anthropological Series No. 12. National Museum of Canada. Page references are to the 1973 facsimile edition. Ottawa: National Museum of Man, National Museums of Canada.

Basso, Ellen. 1976. The enemy of every tribe: "bushman" images in Northern Athapaskan narratives. *American Ethnologist* 5(4):690-709.

Basso, Keith. 1990a. Stalking with stories: Names, places and moral narratives among the Western Apache. In *Western Apache Language and Culture*, ed. Keith Basso, 98-137. Tucson: the University of Arizona Press.

————. 1990b. Speaking with names: Language and landscape among the Western Apache. In *Western Apache Language and Culture*, ed. Keith Basso, 138-173. Tucson: the University of Arizona Press.

————. 1996a. *Wisdom Sits in Places, Landscape and Language among the Western Apache.* Albuquerque: University of New Mexico Press.

————. 1996b. Wisdom sits in places, notes on a Western Apache landscape. In *Senses of Place,* eds. Steven Feld and Keith H. Basso, 53-90. Santa Fe: School of American Research Press.

Bastien, Betty. 2004. *Blackfoot Ways of Knowing, the Worldview of the Siksikaitsitapi.* Calgary: University of Calgary Press.

Bastien, Joseph W. 1978. *Mountain of the Condor, Metaphor and Ritual in an Andean Ayllu.* St. Paul, MN: West Publishing Co.

Beaucage, Pierre, and Taller de Tradiccion Oral del CEPEC. 1997. Integrating Innovation: The Traditional Nahua Coffee-Orchard (Sierra Norte de Puebla, Mexico). *Journal of Ethnobiology* 17(1):45-67.

Bender, Barbara, ed. 1993. *Landscape, Politics and Perspectives.* Oxford: Berg.

Benn, B., and J. Shaw. 2001. Mountain Caribou (*Rangifer tarandus caribou*) Survey in the Northern Mackenzie Mountains, Gwich'in Settlement Area September 2000. Gwich'in Renewable Resource Board, Inuvik, Northwest Territories. Report 01-03. pdf, http://www.grrb.nt.ca/publications_author.htm.

Berger, Thomas R. 1977. *Northern Frontier, Northern Homeland, the Report of the Mackenzie Valley Pipeline Inquiry.* Page references are for 1988 Revised Edition. Vancouver/Toronto: Douglas & McIntyre.

Berkes, Fikret, and Dyanna Jolly. 2001. Adapting to climate change: social-ecological resilience in a Canadian western Arctic community. *Conservation Ecology* 5(2): 18, http://www.consecol.org/vol5/iss2/art18.

Blackstock, Michael D. 1996. *Gyetim Gan: Faces in the Forest.* MA Thesis, University of Northern British Columbia.

Boas, F. 1934. Geographical Names of the Kwakiutl Indians. Columbia University Contributions to Anthropology, Vol. XX. New York: Columbia University Press.

Boyd, Robert, ed. 1999. *Indians, Fire and the Land in the Pacific Northwest.* Corvallis: Oregon State University Press.

Brody, Hugh. 1988. *Maps and Dreams, Indians and the British Columbia Frontier.* Vancouver/Toronto: Douglas & McIntyre.

Brown, Cecil H. 1976. General principles of human anatomical partonomy and speculations on the growth of partonomic nomenclature. *American Ethnologist* 3:400-424.

Brown, Penelope, and Stephen C. Levinson. 1993. "Uphill" and "Downhill" in Tzeltal. *Journal of Linguistic Anthropology* 3(1):46-74.

Burda, Cheri, Russell Collier, and Bryan Evans. 1999. *The Gitxsan Model, An Alternative to the Destruction of Forests, Salmon and Gitxsan Land.* Victoria: Eco-Research Chair of Environmental Law and Policy, University of Victoria.

Burton, P. 1998. Inferring the Response of Berry-Producing Shrubs to Different Light Environments in the ICHmc. Final Report on FRBC Project SB96030-RE. Prepared for the Science Council of BC. Symbios Research and Restoration, Smithers BC.

Campbell, Robert. 1958. *Two Journals of Robert Campbell (Chief Factor, Hudson's Bay Company), 1808 to 1853,* ed. John W. Todd, Jr. Seattle: Shorey Books.

Candler, C. 2000. Telling stories with new technology: maps, dreams and GIS. Paper presented at Canadian Anthropology Society. Société canadienne d'anthropologie 27th Congress, May 4-7, Calgary, Alberta.

Casey, Edward. 1996. How to get from space to place in a fairly short stretch of time, phenomenological prolegomena. In *Senses of Place*, eds. Steven Feld and Keith H. Basso, 13-52. Santa Fe: School of American Research Advanced Seminar Series.

Cassidy, Maureen. 1987. *The Gathering Place, a History of the Wet'suwet'en Village of Tse-Kya.* Hagwilget, BC: the Hagwilget Band Council.

Clément, Daniel. 1990. *L'Ethnobotanique Montagnaise de Mingan.* Collection Nordicana, No. 53, Cerntre d'études nordiques. Quebec: Unitersité Laval.

Colding, J., T. Elqvist, and P. Olsson. 2003. Living with disturbance: Building resilience in social-ecological systems. In *Navigating Social-Ecological Systems, Building Resilience for Complexity and Change*, eds. F. Berkes, J. Colding, and C. Folke, 163-185. Cambridge: Cambridge University Press.

Collier, Russell, and Martine Rose. 2000. The Gitxsan model: A vision for the land and the people. *Native Geography, Annual Magazine of the ESRI Native American/First Nations Program.* Printout, page 2, posted on-line at http://www.conservationgis.org/native/native2.html.

Collignon, Béatrice. 2006. *Knowing places: The Inuinnait, Landscapes, and the Environment.* Translated by Linna Weber Müller-Wille. Circumpolar Research Series, No. 10. Edmonton, Alberta: Canadian Circumpolar Institute Press.

Colorado, Pam. 1988. Bridging Native and Western science. *Convergence* 21(2/3):49-68.

Conklin, H. 1961. The study of shifting cultivation. *Current Anthropology* 2:27-61.

Correll, T. C. 1976. Language and location in traditional Inuit Societies. In the report, "Inuit Land Use and Occupancy Project, Vol. 2. Supporting Studies", ed. M. Freeman. Department of Indian and Northern Affairs Publication QS 8504-002-EE-A1, Ottawa, pp. 173-179.

Couclelis, Helen. 1992. People manipulate objects (but cultivate fields): beyond the raster-vector debate in GIS. In *Theories and Methods of Spatio-Temporal Reasoning in Geographic Space International Convergence GIS—From Space to Territory: Theories and Methods of Spatio-Temporal Reasoning, Pisa, Italy, September 1992 Proceedings*, eds. A. U. Frank, I. Campari, and U. Formentini. Lecture Notes in Computer Science 639:65-77. Berlin: Springer-Verlag.

Cronon, William. 1983. *Changes in the Land, Indians, Colonists and the Ecology of New England*. New York: Hill and Wang.

———. 1996. The trouble with Wilderness; or, getting back to the wrong Nature. In *Uncommon Ground, Rethinking the Human Place in Nature*, ed. William Cronon, 69-90. New York: W.W. Norton and Co.

Cross, Marcia. 2000. The Confederate Salish and Kootenai Tribal Preservation Office: Preservation and Perpetuation. Presentation at the 99th Annual Meeting of the American Anthropological Association, San Francisco, November 15-19, 2000.

Cruikshank, Julie. 1990a. *Life Lived Like a Story*. Vancouver: University of British Columbia Press.

———. 1990b. Getting the words right: perspectives on naming and places in Athapaskan oral history. *Arctic Anthropology* 27(1):52-65.

———. 1998. *The Social Life of Stories: Narrative and Knowledge in the Yukon Territory*. Lincoln and London: University of Nebraska Press.

———. 2001. Glaciers and climate change: perspectives from oral tradition. *Arctic* 54(4):377-393.

———. 2005. *Do Glaciers Listen? Local Knowledge, Colonial Encounters and Social Imagination*. Vancouver: UBC Press.

Crumplin, William W. 2007. Geographic Information Systems as media and society: does GIS wear a white or black stetson? *Cartographica* 42(1):65- 86.

Curtis, J. T. 1959. *The Vegetation of Wisconsin*. Madison: University of Wisconsin Press.

Daly, Richard. 2005. *Our Box Was Full, an Ethnography for the Delgamuukw Plaintiffs*. Vancouver: UBC Press.

Darby, Melissa. 2005. The intensification of wapato *(Sagittaria latifolia)* by the Chinookan people of the lower Columbia River. In *Keeping it Living, Traditions of Plant Use and Cultivation on the Northwest Coast of North America*, eds. Douglas Deur and Nancy J. Turner, 194-217. Seattle: University of Washington Press and Vancouver: UBC Press.

Davidson-Hunt, Iain. 2003. Indigenous lands management, cultural landscapes and Anishinaabe People of Shoal Lake, Northwestern Ontario, Canada. *Environments* 31(1): 21-41.

———. n.d. Documenting the Whitefeather Forest Cultural Landscape: A Case Study in Landscape Ethnoecology. Unpublished draft report in possession of author.

Davidson-Hunt, Iain, and Fikret Berkes. 2003. Learning as You Journey: Anishinaabe Perception of Social-Ecological Environments and Adaptive Learning. *Conservation Ecology* 8(1), http://www.ecologyandsociety.org/vol8/iss1/.

———. 2009. Journeying and Remembering: Anishinaabe Landscape Ethnoecology from Northwestern Ontario. In *Landscape Ethnoecology, Concepts of Physical and Biotic Space,* eds. Leslie Main Johnson and Eugene S. Hunn, pp. 222-240. New York: Berghahn Books.

Dawson, George. 1987. *Report on an exploration in the Yukon District,* reprint by The Yukon Historical and Museums Association, Whitehorse [original publication 1888-1889].

Deur, Douglas, and Nancy J. Turner. 2005. *Keeping it Living, Traditions of Plant Use and Cultivation on the Northwest Coast of North America.* Seattle: University of Washington Press and Vancouver: UBC Press.

Doig River First Nation. 2007. Dane Wajich, Dane-ẕaa Stories and Songs, Dreamers and the Land [English Version]. Virtual Museum of Canada. http://www.virtualmuseum.ca/Exhibitions/Danewajich.

Duncan, Sally L., and Denise H. Lach. 2006. GIS Technology in Natural Resource Management: Process as a Tool of Change. *Cartographica* 41(3):201-215.

Dwyer, Peter. 1996. The Invention of Nature. In *Ecology, Culture and Domestication--Redefining Nature,* eds. Roy Ellen and Katsuyoshi Fukui Eds, 157-186. Oxford: Berg.

Dyson-Hudson, Rada, and Eric Alden Smith. 1978. Human territoriality: an ecological reassessment. *American Anthropologist* 80: 21-41.

Edgerton, Samuel. 1987. From mental matrix to *Mappa mundi* to Christian Empire: The heritage of Ptolemaic cartography in the Renaissance. In *Art and Cartography: Six Historical Essays,* ed. David Woodward, 10-50. Chicago: University of Chicago Press.

Ellen, Roy F. 2009. Why aren't the Nuaulu like the Matsigenka? Knowledge and categorisation of forest diversity on Seram, eastern Indonesia. In *Landscape Ethnoecology, Concepts of Physical and Biotic Space,* Leslie Main Johnson and Eugene S. Hunn, pp. 116-140. New York: Berghahn Books.

Elwood, Sarah. 2006. Critical issues in participatory GIS: Deconstructions, reconstructions, and new research directions. *Transactions in GIS* 10(5):693-708.

Entrikin, J. Nocholas. 1991. *The Betweenness of Place: Toward a Geography of Modernity.* Baltimore, MD: Johns Hopkins University Press.

Escobar, Arturo. 1999. After Nature, steps to an antiessentialist political ecology. *Current Anthropology* 40(1):1-30.

———. 2001. Culture sits in places: reflections on globalism and subaltern strategies of localization. *Political Geography* 20:139-174.

Farnell, Richard, P. Gregory Hare, Erik Blake, Vandy Bowyer, Charles Schweger, Sheila Greer, and Ruth Gotthardt. 2004. Multidisciplinary investigations of alpine ice patches in Southwest Yukon, Canada: Paleoenvironmental and paleobiological investigations. *Arctic* 57(3):247-259.

Feld, Steven. 1996. Waterfalls of song, an acoustemology of place resounding in Bosavi, Papua New Guinea. In *Senses of Place,* eds. S. Feld, and K. H. Basso, 91-135. Santa Fe: School of American Research.

Feld, Steven, and Keith H. Basso. 1996. *Senses of Place*. (School of American Research Advanced Seminar Series.) Santa Fe: School of American Research

Fienup-Riordan, Ann. 1990. *Eskimo Essays, Yup'ik Lives and How We See Them*. New Brunswick, New Jersey: Rutgers University Press.

―――. 1999. *Yaqulget Qaillun Pilartat* (What the Birds Do): Yup'ik Eskimo Understanding of Geese and Those Who Study Them. *Arctic* 52(1):1-22.

Fletcher, Christopher. 2001. Learning From the Land: Ashkui April 2001. Interactive CD-ROM for Innu school children based on project research.

Forman, R. T. T. 1982. Landscape elements: A core of landscape ecology. In *Perspectives in Landscape Ecology, Contributions to research, planning, and management of our environment*, eds. S. P. Tjallingii and A. A. de Veer, 35-48. Wageningen: Centre for Agricultural Publishing and Documentation.

Forman, R.T.T., and M. Godron. 1986. Landscape Ecology. New York, NY: John Wiley and Sons, Inc.

Fowler, Catherine S. 1992. *In the Shadow of Fox Peak, an Ethnography of the Cattail-Eater Northern Paiute People of Stillwater Marsh*. Fallon, Nevada: Cultural Resource Series Number 5, US Department of the Interior Fish and Wildlife Service, Region 1, Stillwater National Wildlife Refuge.

―――. 2009. What's in a name? Southern Paiute toponymy as a key to landscape perception. In *Landscape Ethnoecology: Concepts of Physical and Biotic Space*, eds. Leslie Main Johnson and Eugene S. Hunn, Chapter 11. New York: Berghahn Books.

Frecchione, John, Darrel A. Posey, and Luiz Francelino da Silva. 1989. The perception of ecological zones and natural resources in rhe Brazilian Amazon: an ethnoecology of Lake Coari. In *Resource Management in Amazonia: Indigenous and Folk Strategies*, D. A. Posey and W. Balée, 260-282. Advances in Economic Botany Vol. 7. Bronx: New York Botanical Garden.

Galois, Robert. 1993-1994. The history of the Upper Skeena Region, 1850-1927. *Native Studies Review* 9(2):113-183.

Gisday Wa and Delgam Uukw. 1989. The Spirit in the Land: The Opening Statement of the Gitksan and Wet'suwet'en Chiefs in the Supreme Court of British Columbia, May 11 1987. Gabriola: Reflections.

Gleason, H. A. 1939. The individualistic concept of the plant association. *American Midland Naturalist* 21(1): 92-110.

Goodchild, Michael F., May Yuan, and Thomas J. Cova. 2007. Towards a general theory of geographic representation in GIS. *International Journal of Geographical Information Science*. 21(3): 239-260.

Goodenough, Ward. 1996. Navigation in the Western Carolines, a traditional science. In *Naked science: anthropological inquiry into boundaries, power, and knowledge*, ed. Laura Nader, 29-42. New York: Routledge.

Gottesfeld, Allen S., Ken A. Rabnett, and Peter E. Hall. 2002. *Conserving Skeena Fish Populations and Their Habitat, Skeena Stage I Watershed-based Fish Sustainability Plan*. Hazelton, BC: Skeena Fisheries Commission.

Gottesfeld, Leslie M. Johnson, ed. 1991. *Plants That We Use, Traditional Plant Uses of the Wet'suwet'en People.* Moricetown, British Columbia: Kyah Wiget Education Society.

———. 1993. *Plants, Land and People, a Study of Wet'suwet'en Ethnobotany.* MA Thesis, Anthropology Department, University of Alberta.

———. 1994a. Wet'suwet'en ethnobotany. *Journal of Ethnobiology* 14:185-210.

———. 1994b. Aboriginal burning for vegetation management in Northwest British Columbia. *Human Ecology* 22(2):171-188.

———. 1994c. Conservation, territory and traditional beliefs: an analysis of Gitksan and Wet'suwet'en subsistence, Northwest British Columbia, Canada. *Human Ecology* 22(4):443-465.

———. 1995. The role of plant foods in traditional Wet'suwet'en nutrition. *Ecology of Food and Nutrition* 34:149-169.

Gotthardt, Ruth. 1993. *Frances Lake, Traditional and Archaeological Sites.* A Report to the Liard First Nation, Heritage Branch, Government of Yukon.

Gow, Peter. 1995. Land, people and paper in western Amazonia. In *The Anthropology of Landscape, Perspectives on Space and Place*, eds. Eric Hirsch and Michael O'Hanlon, 43-62. Oxford: Clarendon Press.

Granö, Johannes G. 1997. *Pure Geography.* Baltimore, MD: Johns Hopkins University Press. (Book originally published in German in 1929 and in Finnish in 1930.)

Greer, Sheila. 1999. *Ehdiitat Gwich'in Place Names Research.* Report on file, Gwich'in Social and Cultural Institute, Tsiigehtchic, NT.

Gulliford, Andrew. 2000. *Sacred Objects and Sacred Places, Preserving Tribal Traditions.* Boulder: University Press of Colorado.

Gwich'in Elders. 1997. Nành' Kak Geenjit Gwich'in Ginjik, *Gwich'in Words About the Land.* Inuvik: Gwich'in Renewable Resource Board.

Gwich'in Social and Cultural Institute. Place Name Map. http://www.gwichin.ca/Research/placeNameMap.html.

Hare, P. Gregory, Sheila Greer, Ruth Gotthardt, Richard Farnell, Vandy Bowyer, Charles Schweger, and Diane Strand. 2004. Ethnographic and archaeological investigations of alpine ice patches in Southwest Yukon, Canada. *Arctic* 57(3):260-272.

Hargus, Sharon. 1999. Witsuwit'en Hinic Dec'enï Bik'iydïzdle: *Witsuwit'en Topical Dictionary.* Manuscript in files of author.

———. 2007. *Witsuwit'en Grammar: Phonetics, Phonology, Morphology.* Vancouver: UBC Press.

Harris, Ken. 1974. *Visitors Who Never Left, the Origin of the People of Damelahamid.* Vancouver: University of British Columbia Press.

Haviland, John B. 1993. Anchoring, iconicity, and orientation in Guugu Yimithirr point gestures. *Journal of Linguistic Anthropology* 3(1): 3-45.

Hawkes, K., K. Hill, and J. F. O'Connell. 1982. Why hunters gather: optimal foraging and the Aché of eastern Paraguay. *American Ethnologist* 9:379-398.

Hennessy, Kate. 2006. Decolonizing geographies: language, place and participatory digital ethnography. Paper presented at American Anthropological Association 105th Annual Meeting November 15-19, San Jose, California.

Hirsch, E. and M. O'Hanlon, eds. 1995. *The Anthropology of Landscape: Perspectives of Space and Place.* Oxford: Clarendon Press.

Honigmann, John J. 1949. *Culture and Ethos of Kaska Society.* Yale University Publications in Anthropology, Volume 40. New Haven: Yale University Press.

Hornborg, Alf. 1998. The Mi'kmaq of Nova Scotia. In *Voices of the Land: Identity and Ecology in the Margins,* eds. Alf Hornborg and Mikael Kurkiala, 135-172. Lund Studies in Human Ecology 1. Lund: Lund University Press.

Houseknecht, S., S. Haeussler, A. Kokoshke, J. Pojar, D. Holmes, B. M. Geisler, and D. Yole. 1986. *A Field Guide for the Identification and Interpretation of the Interior Cedar-Hemlock Zone, Northwestern Transitional Subzone (ICHg), in the Prince Rupert Forest Region.* Land Management Handbook Number 12. Victoria: BC Ministry of Forests.

Hunn, Eugene S. 1996. Columbia Plateau Indian place names: what can they teach us? *Journal of Linguistic Anthropology* 6(1):3-26.

Hunn, E. S., and B. A. Meilleur. 1992. The utilitarian value and theoretical basis of folk biogeographical knowledge. Paper presented at the 3rd International Congress of Ethnobiology in Mexico City, November 10-14.

———. 1998. Toward a theory of ethnobiogeographical classification. Paper presented at the American Anthropological Association conference in Philadelphia, December.

———. 2009. Toward a theory of landscape ethnoecological classification. In *Landscape Ethnoecology, Concepts of Physical and Biotic Space,* eds. Leslie Main Johnson and Eugene S. Hunn, pp. 15-26. New York: Berghahn Books.

Hunn, Eugene S., with James Selam and Family. 1990. *Nch'i-Wána, "the Big River", Mid-Columbia Indians and Their Land.* Seattle: University of Washington Press.

Ignace, Marianne. 2000. Secwepemc notions of place and possession of land, and their representations in public discourse. Paper presented at Canadian Anthropology Society/Société canadienne d'anthropologie 27th Congress May 4-7, Calgary, Alberta.

Ingold, Tim. 1993. The temporality of the landscape. *World Archaeology* 25(2)152-174.

———. 1996a. Hunting and gathering as ways of perceiving the environment. In *Ecology, Culture and Domestication—Redefining Nature,* eds. Roy Ellen and Katsuyoshi Fukui, 117-155. Oxford and Herendon, VA: Berg.

———. 1996b. The optimal forager and Economic Man. In *Nature and Society, Anthropological Perspectives,* eds. Philippe Descola and Gísli Pálsson, 25-44. London and New York: Routledge.

———. 2000. *The Perception of the Environment, Essays in Livelihood, Dwelling and Skill.* London and New York: Routledge.

Istomin, Kirill V., and Mark J. Dwyer. 2009. Finding the Way, a critical discussion of anthropological theories of human spatial orientation with reference to reindeer herders of Northeastern Europe and Western Siberia. *Current Anthropology* 50:29–50.

Ives, John W. 2003. Alberta Athapaskans and Apachean origins. In *Archaeology In Alberta, A View from the New Millenium,* eds. Jack W. Brink and John F. Dormaar, 256-281. Medicine Hat, Alberta: Archaeological Society of Alberta.

Ives, John W., and Sally Rice. 2003. The Apachean Departure from the Subarctic: I. Linguistic and Human Biological Evidence. Paper presented at the 5th Biennial Rocky Mountain Anthropological Conference, Estes Park, Colorado.

Johannes, R. E. 1981. *Words of the Lagoon.* University of California Press, Berkeley.

Johnson, Leslie Main. n.d. Sacred Land and Biodiversity: Implications of the Relationship of Indigenous Peoples of Northwestern Canada and Their Land. Unpublished manuscript in files of the author.

———. 1997. *Health, Wholeness, and the Land: Gitksan Traditional Plant Use and Healing.* PhD Dissertation, Department of Anthropology, University of Alberta.

———. 1998. *Traditional tenure among the Gitxsan and Wet'suwet'en: its relationship to common property, and resource allocation.* 1998 IASCP Conference Papers, http://www.indiana.edu/~iascp/iascp98.htm.

———. 1999. Aboriginal burning for vegetation management in northwest British Columbia. In *Indians, Fire and the Land in the Pacific Northwest,* ed. R. Boyd, 238-254. Corvallis: Oregon State University Press.

———. 2000. "A place that's good," Gitksan landscape perception and ethnoecology. *Human Ecology* 28(2):301-325.

———. 2005. Parsing a Subarctic Landscape- an exploration of Kaska Dena landscape ethnoecology in the southeastern Yukon Territory, Canada. Paper presented at the 35th Annual International Arctic Workshop, March 11, 2005 (Abstract, https://arcticworkshop.onware.ca/prothos/onware.x/conf/000000982/papers/submitted.p?!=public=11493070941785=15=27160772.)

———. 2008. Plants and habitats—a consideration of Dene ethnoecology in Northwestern Canada. *Botany* 86:146-157

———. 2009. Visions of the land: Kaska ethnoecology, "kinds of place" and "cultural landscape". In *Landscape Ethnoecology, Concepts of Physical and Biotic Space,* eds. Leslie Main Johnson and Eugene S. Hunn, pp. 203-221. New York: Berghahn Books.

Johnson, Leslie Main, and Daniel Andre. 2001. "People, Place and Season: Reflections on Gwich'in Ordering of Access to Resources in an Arctic Landscape." Presented at the Eighth Conference of the International Association for the Study of Common Property, "Constituting the Commons: Crafting Sustainable Commons in the NewMillenium", Bloomington, Indiana, USA, May 31-June 4 2000. Published in Digital Library of the Commons (abstract and pdf) http://dlc.dlib.indiana.edu/documents/dir0/00/00/02/82/.

Johnson, Leslie Main, and Sharon Hargus. 2007. Witsuwit'en words for the land—a preliminary examination of Witsuwit'en Ethnogeography. In ANLC Working Papers in Athabaskan Linguistics Volume #6, eds. S. Tuttle, L. Saxon, S. Gessner, and A. Berez. Fairbanks, AK: Alaska Native Language Center, University of Alaska.

Johnson, Leslie Main, and Eugene S. Hunn, eds. 2009. *Landscape Ethnoecology— Concepts of Biotic and Physical Space.* New York: Berghahn Books.

Karamanski, Theodore. 1983. *Fur Trade and Exploration, Opening the Far Northwest 1821-1852*. Norman: University of Oklahoma Press.

Kari, James. 1989. Some principles of Alaskan Athabaskan toponymic knowledge. In *General and Amerindian Ethnolinguistics, in Remembrance of Stanley Newman*, eds. Mary Ritchie Key and Henry M. Hoenigswald, 129-149. Berlin, New York: Mouton de Gruyter.

———. 1996. A preliminary view of hydronymic districts in Northern Athabaskan prehistory. *Names, A Journal of Onomastics* 44(4): 44(4):253-271.

———. 2008. A Case Study in Ahtna Athabascan Geographic Knowledge. Pre-conference readings, Landscape in Language Workshop, Albuquerque New Mexico and Chinle Arizona, October 9.

Kari, J., and J. A. Fall, eds. 1987. *Shem Pete's Alaska: The Territory of the Upper Cook Inlet Dena'ina*. Fairbanks, AK: Alaska Native Language Center, University of Alaska.

Kaska Elders. 1997. **Guzāgi Kúgé,** *Our Language Book: Nouns, Kaska, Mountain Slavey and Sekani*. Volume 1. Kaska Tribal Council.

Kawagley, A. Oscar. 1995. *A Yupiaq Worldview, A Pathway to Ecology and Spirit*. Prospect Heights, Illinois: Waveland Press.

King, Alexander D. 2002. Reindeer herders' culturescapes in the Koryak Autonomous Okrug. In *People and the Land, Pathways to Reform in Post-Soviet Siberia*, ed. Erich Kasten, 63-80. Berlin: Dietrick Reimer.

———. 2006. Koryak necromantic landscapes, or how to walk your dog to the next life. Paper given at the American Anthropological Association 105th Annual Meeting, San Jose California, November 15-19 (ms in files of author).

Krauss, Michael. 1992. The world's languagues in crisis. *Language* 68(1):4-10.

Krech, Shepard, III. 1983. The influence of disease and the fur trade on the Arctic drainage lowlands Dene, 1800-1850. *Journal of Anthropological Research* 39(1):123-146.

Kritsch, Ingrid, and Alestine Andre. 1993. *Gwichya Gwich'in Place Names up the Arctic Red River and South of the Mackenzie River, Gwich'in Ssettlement Area, N.W.T.* Tsiigehtchic, NWT: Gwich'in Social and Cultural Institute.

———. 1994. *Gwichya Gwich'in Place names in the Mackenzie Delta, Gwich'in Settlement Area, N.W.T.* Tsiigehtchic, NWT: Gwich'in Social and Cultural Institute.

Krohmer, Julia. 2009. Landscape perception, classification and use among Sahelian Fulani in Burkina Faso (West Africa). In *Landscape Ethnoecology, Concepts of Physical and Biotic Space*, eds. Leslie Main Johnson and Eugene S. Hunn, pp. 49-82. New York: Berghahn Books.

Kuhnlein, H. and N. J. Turner. 1991. *Traditional Plant Foods of Canadian Indigenous Peoples, Nutrition, Botany and Use*. Food and Nutrition in History and Anthropology vol. 8. Gordon and Breach Science Publishers, Philadelphia, Reading, Paris, Montreaux, Tokyo and Melbourne.

Lawrence, Denise, and Setha M. Low. 1990. The built environment and spatial form. *Annual Review of Anthropology* 19:453-505.

Layton, Robert. 1995. Relating to the country in the Western desert. In *The Anthropology of Landscape: Perspectives of Space and Place,* eds. Eric Hirsch and Michael O'Hanlon, 210-231. Oxford: Clarendon Press.

LeBlanc, Raymond. 2006. Communal Caribou Hunting Systems of the Northern Yukon Gwitchin. Talk given to Circumpolar Students Association Northern Speaker Series, University of Alberta, 21 March.

Legat, Allice, Georgina Chocolate, Madelaine Chocolate, Pauline Williah, and Sally Ann Zoe. 2001. *Habitat of Dogrib Traditional Territory: Placenames as indicators of Biogeographical Knowledge—Final Report.* Submitted by Whàehdòǫ Nàowo Kǫ̀ Dogrib Treaty 11 Council to West Kitikmeot Slave Study Society, Yellowknife, NT, March 2001.

Lehtola, Veli-Pekka. 2002. *The Sámi People—Traditions in Transition.* Aanaar-Inari: Kustannus-Puntsi.

Lepofsky, D., D. Hallet, K. Lertzman, R. Mathewes, A. McHalsie, and K. Washbrook. 2005. Documenting pre-contact plant management on the Northwest Coast, an example of prescribed burning in the Central and Upper Fraser Valley, British Columbia. In *Keeping It Living, Traditions of Plant Use and Cultivation on the Northwest Coast of North America*, eds. D. Deur and N. J. Turner, 218-239. Seattle: University of Washington Press, and Vancouver: UBC Press.

Louis, Renee. 2008. Hawai'i, Toponyms and GIS. Presentation at Landscape in Language Workshop, October 30, 2008, Thunderbird Lodge, Chinle, Arizona.

Low, Setha M., and Denise Lawrence-Zúñiga, eds. 2003. *The Anthropology of Space and Place, Locating Culture.* Malden, Maine: Blackwell Publishing.

MacDonald, John. 1998. *The Arctic Sky: Inuit Astronomy, Star Lore, and Legend.* Toronto, ON: Royal Ontario Museum and Nunavut Research Institute.

Mack, C. A. 2001. A burning issue—Native use of fire in Mount Rainier Forest Reserve. Paper presented at the Society of Ethnobiology 24th Annual Conference, Durango, Colorado March 7-10.

Mack, C. A. and R. H. McClure. (2002). *Vaccinium* processing in the Washington Cascades, *Journal of Ethnobiology* 22(1):35-60.

Maffi, Luisa. 2001. *On Biocultural Diversity: Linking Language, Knowledge and the Environment.* Washington, DC: Smithsonian Institution Press.

Mark, David M., and Andrew G. Turk. 2003. Landscape categories in Yindjibarndi: Ontology, environment, and language. In *Spatial Information Theory: Foundations of Geographic Information Science*, eds. W. Kuhn, M. Worboys, and S. Timpf, 31-49. Springer-Verlag, Lecture Notes in Computer Science.

Mark, David M., Andrew G. Turk, and David Stea. 2009. Ethnophysiography of arid lands: categories for landscape features. In *Landscape Ethnoecology, Concepts of Biotic Physical and Space*, eds. Leslie Main Johnson and Eugene S. Hunn, pp. 27-45. New York: Berghahn Books.

Marsden, Susan. 2008. Northwest Coast *Adawx* study. In *First Nations Cultural Heritage and Law, Case Studies, Voices, and Perspectives,* eds. Catherine Bell and Val Naopleon, 114-149. Vancouver: UBC Press.

Martin, G. J. 1993. Ecological classification among the Chinantec and Mixe of Oaxaca, México. *Etnoecológica* 1(2):14-31.

Martin, Gary J. 1995. *Ethnobotany, A Methods Manual.* London: Chapman and Hall.

Matson, R. G., and Martin P. R. Magne. 2007. *Athapaskan Migrations, the Archaeology of Eagle Lake, British Columbia.* Tucson: University of Arizona Press.

Maxwell, B. 1997. *Responding to global climate change in the Arctic.* Canada Country Study: Climate Impacts and Adaptation, Volume 2. Environment Canada, Ottawa, Ontario, Canada; www.ec.gc.ca/climate/ccs/volume2.htm.

McClellan, Catharine, Lucie Birckel, Robert Bringhurst, James A. Fall, Carol McCarthy, and Janice R. Sheppard. 1987. *Part of the Land, Part of the Water, a History of the Yukon Indians.* Vancouver/Toronto: Douglas & McIntyre.

McDonald, James. 2005. Cultivating in the Northwest: early accounts of Tsimshian horticulture. In *Keeping it Living, Traditions of Plant Use and Cultivation on the Northwest Coast of North America,* eds. Douglas Deur and Nancy J. Turner, 240-273. Seattle: University of Washington Press and Vancouver: UBC Press.

McDonnell, Roger Francis. 1975. Kasini Society: Some Aspects of the Social Organization of an Athapaskan Culture between 1900-1950. PhD Dissertation, University of British Columbia.

McFee, R. D. 1981. Caribou fence facilities of the historic Yukon Kutchin. In *Megaliths to Medicine Wheels: Boulder Structures in Archaeology,* eds. M. Wilson, K. L. Road, and K. J. Hardy, 159-170. Proceedings of the Eleventh Annual Chacmool Conference, University of Calgary Archaeological Association, Calgary.

McGarigal, Kevin. 2003. NRS 223, Conservation of Populations and Ecosystems. University of Rhode Island on-line course materials, http://www.edc.uri.edu/nrs/classes/nrs223/readings/fragstatread.htm.

McNeary, Stephan. 1976. *Where Fire Came Down, Social and Economic Life of the Niska.* PhD Dissertation, Bryn Mawr College.

Merculieff, L. 2002. Linking traditional knowledge and wisdom to ecosystem based approaches in research and management: supporting a marginalized way of knowing. In *Ethnobiology and Biocultural Diversity,* eds. John R. Stepp, Felice S. Wyndham, and Rebecca K. Zarger, 523-531. International Society of Ethnobiology, Athens: University of Georgia Press.

Merlan, Francesca. 1982. A Mangarrayi representational system: environment and cultural symbolization in northern Australia. *American Ethnologist* 9: 145-165.

Metzler, Stephen, Julia Gold, and Preston Hardison. 2002. Using GIS to Integrate Traditional Knowledge into a Comprehensive Tribal Information System. Presentation, Proceedings of the Twenty-Second Annual ESRI User Conference.

Mills, Antonia. 1994. *Eagle Down Is Our Law, Witsuwit'en Law, Feasts and Land Claims,* Vancouver: UBC Press.

———, ed. 2005. *Hang On To These Words: Johnny David's Delgamuukw Evidence.* Toronto: University of Toronto Press.

Milton, Kay. 2002. *Loving Nature, Towards an Ecology of Emotion.* London, New York: Routledge.

Minore, D. 1972. *The Wild Huckleberries of Oregon and Washington—A Dwindling Resource.* USDA Forest Service Research Paper-143, Pacific Northwest Forest and Range Experiment Station PNW-261.

Minore, D., A. W. Smart, and M. E. Dubraisch. 1979. *Huckleberry ecology and management research in the Pacific Northwest.* USDA Forest Service, General technical Report PNW-193.

Money, Anton. 1975. *This Was the North.* Toronto: General Publishing Co. Ltd.

Moore, Patrick, ed. 1999. Dene Gudeji, *Kaska Narratives.* Watson Lake: Kaska Tribal Council.

————. 2000. Kaska Directionals. Paper presented at the American Anthropological Association Meetings, San Francisco, November.

————. 2002. *Point of View in Kaska Historical Narratives.* PhD Dissertation, Indiana University.

Moore, Patrick and Angela Wheelock, eds. 1990. *Wolverine Myths and Visions, Dene Traditions of Northern Alberta.* Dene Wodih Society, Compilers. Edmonton: University of Alberta Press.

Mora H., Eustaquio, Pascual Mora N., José Antonio Francisco, Francisco A. Basurto P., Rafael Patron S., Miguel A. Martínez A.1985, Nota etnolingüística sobre el idioma nahuatl de la sierra norte de Puebla. *Amerindia, revue d'ethnolinguistique amérindienne* 10:73-91.

Morice, A. G. 1904. *The History of the Northern Interior of British Columbia.* Smithers: Interior Stationery. Page references are to the 1978 edition.

Morphy, H. 1995. Landscape and the reproduction of the Ancestral past. In *The Anthropology of Landscape: Perspectives of Space and Place*, eds. E. Hirsch and M. O'Hanlon, 184-209. Oxford: Clarendon Press.

Morrell, Mike. 1989. The struggle to integrate traditional Indian systems and state management in the salmon fisheries of the Skeena River, British Columbia. In *Cooperative Management of Local Fisheries, New Directions for Improved Management and Community Development*, ed. Evelyn Pinkerton, 231-248. Vancouver: University of British Columbia Press.

Morrow, Phyllis, and Chase Hensel. 1992. Hidden dissension: minority-majority relationships and the use of contested terminology. *Arctic Anthropology* 29(2):38-53.

Moss, Madonna L. 1993. Shellfish, gender, and status on the Northwest Coast: reconciling archeological, ethnographic and ethnohistorical records of the Tlingit. *American Anthropologist* 95(3):631-652

Muir, John. 1912. *The Yosemite.* Berkeley: University of California Press. Page references are to the 1988 edition.

————. 1915. *Travels in Alaska.* San Francisco: Sierra Club Books. Page references are to the 1988 edition.

Müller-Wille, L. 1983. Inuit toponymy and cultural sovereignty. In *Conflict in Development in Nouveau-Québec*, ed. L. Müller-Wille. McGill Subarctic Research Paper No. 37, Center for Northern Studies and Research, McGill University, Montreal.

————. 1993. Place names, territoriality and sovereignty: Inuit perception of space in Nunavik (Canadian Eastern Arctic). *Schwiezerische Amerikanisten-Gesellschaft Bulletin* 53-54(1989-1990):17-21.

Mulrennan, M. E., and C. H. Scott. 1996. *Mare nullius:* Indigenous rights and interests in salt-water environments. Paper presented in the "Space and Place" symposium, American Anthropological Association Annual Meetings, San Francisco, November 19-24.

————. 2005. Co-management—an attainable partnership? Two cases from James Bay, Northern Quebec, and Torres Strait, Northern Queensland. *Anthropologica* 47(2):197-213.

Munn, Nancy. 2003. Excluded spaces, the figure in the Australian Aboriginal landscape. In *The Anthropology of Space and Place, Locating Culture,* eds. In Setha M. Low and Denise Lawrence-Zúñiga, 92-109. Malden, Maine: Blackwell Publishing.

Nabhan, Gary P. 2001. Cultural perceptions of ecological interactions, an "Endangered People's" contribution to the conservation of biological and lingujistic diversity. In *On Biocultural Diversity, linking language, knowledge and the environment,* ed. Luisa Maffi, 145–146. Washington and London: Smithsonian Institution Press.

Nadasdy, Paul. 1999. The politics of TEK: power and the "integration" of knowledge. *Arctic Anthropology* 36(1-2):1-18.

————. 2003. *Hunters and Bureaucrats, Power, Knowledge, and Aboriginal-State Relations in the Southwest Yukon.* Vancouver: UBC Press.

————. 2005. The anti-politics of TEK: The institutionalization of co-management discourse and practice. *Anthropologica* 47(2):215-232.

Nagy, John A., Denise Auriat, Ian Ellsworth, Wendy Wright, and Todd Slack. 2002-2003. *Ecology of Boreal Woodland Caribou in the Lower Mackenzie Valley: Work Completed in the Inuvik Region 1 April 2002 to 31 March 2003.* Gwich'in Renewable Resource Board, Inuvik, Northwest Territories. http://www.grrb.nt.ca/publications_author.htm.

Native Geography, Annual Magazine of the ESRI Native American/First Nations Program, Native Geography 2000 Web Version page 1, http://www.conservationgis.org/native/native1.html

Naveh, Zev, and Arthur S. Lieberman. 1994. *Landscape Ecology: Theory and Application.* 2nd ed. New York : Springer-Verlag.

Nazarea, Virginia, ed. 1999. *Ethnoecology, Situated Knowledge/Located Lives.* Tucson: University of Arizona Press.

Nelson, F. E., O. A. Anisimov, and N. I. Shiklommanov. 2002. Climate change and hazard zonation in the Circum-Arctic permafrost regions. *Natural Hazards* 26: 203-225.

Nelson, Richard K. 1983. *Make Prayers to the Raven, a Koyukon View of the Northern Forest.* Chicago: University of Chicago Press.

———. 1986. *Hunters of the Northern Forest, Designs for Survival Among the Alaskan Kutchin*, Second Edition. Chicago: University of Chicago Press.

Nyman, Elizabeth, and Jeff Leer. 1993. Gágiwduł.àt: *Brought Forth to Reconfirm, the Legacy of a Taku River Tlingit Clan.* Whitehorse and Fairbanks: Yukon Native Language Centre and Alaska Native Language Center.

Olwig, Kenneth R. 1996. Recovering the substantive nature of landscape. *Annals of the American Association of Geographers* 86(4):630-653.

Palmer, Andie Diane. 2006. *Maps of Experience, the Anchoring of Land to Story in Secwepemc Discourse.* Toronto: University of Toronto Press.

Parlee, Brenda, Fikret Berkes, and Teet'lit Gwich'in Renewable Resource Council. 2006. Indigenous knowledge of ecological variability and commons management: a case study on berry harvesting from Northern Canada. *Human Ecology* 34(4): 515-528.

Pentland, David H. 1975. Cartographic concepts of the northern Algonquians. *The Canadian Cartographer* 12(2)149-160.

People of Ksan. 1980. *Gathering What the Great Nature Provided.* Vancouver: Douglas and McIntyre.

Petersen, Robert. 1963. Family ownership and right of disposition in Sukkertoppen District, West Greenland. *Folk* 5:269-281.

Peterson, Nicolas, and Bruce Rigsby. 1998. *Customary Marine Tenure in Australia.* Sydney: Oceania Publications, University of Sydney.

Peuquet, D. J. 1988. Representations of geographic space: Towards a conceptual synthesis. *Annals of the Association of American Geographers* 78 (3):375-394.

Pickles, J., ed. 1995. *Ground Truth: The Social Implications of Geographic Information Systems.* New York, Guilford.

Ping, H. E. 1995. GIS Implementation Experience in Wisconsin Winnebago Nation. Abstract, ESRI User Conference Proceedings. http://gis.esri.com/library/userconf/proc95/to300/p293.html.

Pinkerton, Evelyn. 1998. Newsletter, Anthropology and the Environment, A Section of the American Anthropological Association, ed. Ed Liebow, September. For the Common Property Conference Highlights, Vancouver, BC, June 10-14. http://www.eanth.org/Newsletter.php?Id=63.

Posey, D. A., and W. Balée, eds. 1989. *Resource Management in Amazonia: Indigenous and Folk Strategies.* Advances in Economic Botany Vol. 7. Bronx: New York Botanical Garden.

Prince of Wales Northern Heritage Centre. Lessons From the Land, a Cultural Journey Through the Northwest Territories. Ɂdaà Trail. http://www.lessonsfromtheland.ca/IdaaHome.asp?lng=English.

Prince of Wales Northern Heritage Centre. Inuvialuit Place Names. Virtual Museum of Canada http://www.pwnhc.ca/inuvialuit/placenames/about.html.

Ray, A. 1985. The Early Economic History of the Gitxsan-Wet'suwet'en Territory. Unpublished report (revised 1987), on file at the Gitksan Treaty office library, Hazelton, BC 57p.

Rea, Amadeo. 1997. *At the Desert's Green Edge, An Ethnobotany of the Gila River Pima.* Tucson: University of Arizona Press.

Reichard, Gladys A. 1934. *Spider Woman: A Story of Navajo Weavers and Chanters.* Albuquerque: University of New Mexico Press.

Richardson, Allan. 1982. The control of productive resources on the Northwest Coast of North America. In *Resource Managers: North American and Australian Hunter-Gatherers,* eds. Nancy M. Williams and Eugene S. Hunn, 93-112. AAAS Selected Symposium 67.

Ridington, Robin. 1981. Beaver. In *Subarctic*, Volume 6, *Handbook of North American Indians* ed. June Helm, (general ed. William Sturtevant), 350-360. Washington: Smithsonian Institution.

———. 1990. *Little Bit Know Something, Stories in a Language of Anthropology.* Vancouver/Toronto: Douglas & McIntyre.

Rigsby, Bruce. 1982. Cape York Peninsula as a humanized landscape. *Seminar Papers. Conservation and Development: Australia in the Eighties.* Brisbane: Australian Studies Centre, University of Queensland.

Rigsby, Bruce, and James Kari. n.d. Gitksan and Wet'suwet'en Linguistic Relations. Report prepared for the Gitksan-Wet'suwet'en Tribal Council, on file, library, Office of the Hereditary Chiefs, Hazelton.

Roberts, Roma Mere, and Peter R. Wills. 1998. Understanding Maori epistemology: a scientific perspective. In *Tribal Epistemologies: Essays in the Philosophy of Anthropology,* ed. Helmut Wautische, 43-71 (Appendices 72-77). Aldershot: Ashgate.

Robinson, Cathy, and Nanikiya Manungguritj. 2001. Sustainable balance: A Yolngu framework for cross-cultural collaborative management. In *Working on Country, Contemporary Indigenous Management of Australia's Lands and Coastal Regions,* eds. Richard Baker, Jocelyn Davies, and Elspeth Young, 92-104. South Melbourne, Australia: Oxford University Press.

Roddan, Laura K., and Arlene C. Harry. 2000. Sliammon First Nation uses GIS to map traditional values. *Native Geography, Annual Magazine of the ESRI Native American/First Nations Program,* p. 4. Posted on-line at http://www.conservationgis.org/native/native4.html.

Rodman, Margaret C. 2003. Empowering place: Multilocality and multivocality. In *The Anthropology of Space and Place, Locating Culture,* eds. Setha M. Low and Denise Lawrence-Zúñiga, 204-223. Malden, Maine: Blackwell Publishing.

Roman, Frank, and David Carruthers. 2000. Aboriginal Mapping Network; after all, the border is artificially imposed, Networking the Aboriginal mapping community in British Columbia. *Native Geography, Annual Magazine of the ESRI Native American/First Nations Program,* p. 3. Posted on-line at http://www.conservationgis.org/native/native3.html.

Rosaldo, Renato. 1980. Doing oral history. *Social Analysis* 4:89-99.

Rosch, Eleanor. 1981. Categorisation of natural objects. *Annual Review of Psychology* 32: 89-115.

Rose, Deborah Bird. 2000. *Dingo Makes Us Human: Land and Life in an Australian Aboriginal Culture.* Cambridge: Cambridge University Press.

———. 2005. An Indigenous philosophical ecology: situating the Human. *The Australian Journal of Anthropology* 16(3):294-305.

Roseneau, D. 1974. Caribou Fences in Northeastern Alaska. Appendix A in *Proposal for Archaeological Salvage, Pipeline Corridor, Yukon and Northwest Territories,* by J.F.V. Millar. Archaeological Supplement to the Arctic Gas Biological Report Series.

Ross, John. 1999. Proto-historical and historical Spokan prescribed burning and stewardship of resource areas. In *Indians, Fire and the Land in the Pacific Northwest,* ed. R. Boyd, 277-291. Corvallis: Oregon State University Press.

Rundstrom, Robert A. 1990. A cultural interpretation of Inuit map accuracy. *Geographic Review* 80(2): 154-168.

———. 1993. The Role of ethics, mapping, and the meaning of place in relations between Indians and Whites in the United States. *Cartographica* 30(1):21-28.

———. 1995. GIS, indigenous peoples, and epistemological diversity. *Cartography and Geographic Information Systems* 22(1):45-57.

Sam, Donald. 2005. An Interactive Tribal GIS on the Flathead Indian Reservation. (Abs.) ESRI Library, Proceedings of ESRI User Conference, 2005. http://gis.esri.com/library/userconf/proc05/abstracts/a1405.html.

Scott, James. 1998. *Seeing Like a State, How Certain Schemes to Improve the Human Condition Have Failed.* New Haven and London: Yale University Press.

Sharp, Henry S. 1987. Giant fish, giant otters, and dinosaurs: "apparently irrational beliefs" in a Chipewyan community. *American Ethnologist* 14(2):226-235.

———. 2001. *Loon, Memory, Meaning, and Reality in a Northern Dene Community.* Lincoln and London: University of Nebraska Press.

Shepard, Glenn, H., Jr., Douglas W. Yu, Manuel Lizarralde, and Mateo Italiano. 2001. Rainforest habitat classification among the Matsigenka of the Peruvian Amazon. *Journal of Ethnobiology* 21(1):1-38.

Shepard, Glenn H., Jr., Douglas W. Yu, and Bruce Nelson. 2004. Ethnobotanical ground-truthing and forest diversity in the Western Amazon. In *Ethnobotany and Conservation of Biocultural Diversity, Advances in Economic Botany 15,* eds. Thomas J. S. Carlson and Luisa Maffi, 133-171. Bronx: New York Botanical Garden Press.

Sherry, Erin, and Vuntut Gwitchin First Nation. 1999. *The Land Still Speaks, Gwitchin Words About Life in Dempster Country.* Old Crow, Yukon: Vuntut Gwitchin First Nation Lands and Resources Department.

Sieber, Renée. 2008. The Role of GIS in Integrating Language in Landscape. Presentation at Landscape in Language Workshop, Thunderbird Lodge, Chinle Arizona. October 31, 2008.

Sillitoe, Paul. 1995. An ethnobotanical account of the plant resources of the Wola Region, Southern Highlands Province, Papua New Guinea. *Journal of Ethnobiology* 15(2):201-235.

———. 1996. *A Place Against Time: Land and Environment in the Papua New Guinea Highlands.* Amsterdam: Harwood Academic Publishers.

———. 1998. An ethnobotanical account of the vegetation communities of the Wola Province, Southern Highlands Province, Papua New Guinea. *Journal of Ethnobiology* 16(1):103-128.

Smith, Harlan I. 1997. Ethnobotany of the Gitksan Indians of British Columbia. Mercury Series Canadian Ethnology Service No. 132, eds. Brian D. Compton, Bruce Rigsby, and Marie-Lucie Tarpent. Hull, Quebec: Canadian Museum of Civilization.

Sterritt, N. J., S. Marsden, R. Galois, P. R. Grant, and R. Overstall. 1998. *Tribal Boundaries in the Nass Watershed.* Vancouver: UBC Press.

Stevenson, Marc. 1998. Traditional Knowledge in Environmental Management? From Commodity to Process. Edmonton: Sustainable Forest Network Centre of Excellence.

Strang, Veronica. 1997. *Uncommon Ground, Cultural Landscapes and Environmental Values.* Oxford: Berg.

Struzik, Ed. 2008. Guardian of sacred places. *The Province* March 1, 2008. Accessed from Canada Com, Where Perspectives Meet. URLhttp://www2.canada.com/ theprovince/features/saturdaymagazine/story.html?id=a32706ed-f852-4891-a728-09bf04a20207.

Sui, Daniel Z., and Michael F. Goodchild. 2003. A tetradic analysis of GIS and society using McLuhan's law of the media. *The Canadian Geographer/ Le Géographe canadien* 47(1):5-17.

Taller de Tradiccion Oral del CEPEC and Pierre Beaucage. 1996. La bonne montagne et l'eau malfaisante. Toponymie et pratiques environnementales chez les Nahuas de basse montagne (Sierra Norte de Puebla, Mexique). *Anthropologie et Sociétés* 20(3):33-54.

Terralingua website, About Terralingua http://www.terralingua.org/AboutTL.htm.

The Hagwilget (Tse-Kya) Band. 1995. *Tsë Cakh Wit'en, Hagwilget (Tse-Kya) People, Traditional Words and Texts from Band Members.* Hagwilget, BC: The Hagwilget (Tse-Kya) Band.

Thoreau, Henry David. 1854/1849. *Walden; and Civil Disobedience.* Page references are to the 1983 edition of both texts published together, Harmondsworth, Middlesex, England, New York, NY: Penguin Books.

Thornton, Thomas F. 1999. Tleikwaaní, the "berried" landscape: The structure of Tlingit edible fruit resources at Glacier Bay, Alaska. *Journal of Ethnobiology* 19(1):27-48.

———. 1997. Anthropological studies of Native American place naming. *American Indian Quarterly* 21(2) 209-228.

———. 2007. The cultural ecology of berries in Glacier Bay. In Proceedings of the Fourth Glacier Bay Science Symnposium, October 26-28, 2004, U.S. Geological Survey Scientific Investigations Report 2007-5047, eds. J. F. Piatt and S. M. Gende, 29-37.

————. 2008. *Being and Place among the Tlingit.* Seattle and London: University of Washington Press.

————. n.d. Relation and Revelation in Tlingit Landscape Perception. Unpublished manuscript in files of the author.

Tilley, Christopher. 1994. *A Phenomenology of Landscape, Places, Paths and Monuments.* Oxford and Providence, RI: Berg.

Tlen, Daniel. 2006. Conceptualizing Place and Identity: Southern Tutchone Directionals. Dene Languages Conference, Yellowknife NT June 12-15, 2006.

Toledo, Victor M. 1992. What is ethnoecology? Origins, scope and implications of a rising discipline. *Ethnoecologica* 1(1):5-21.

————. 2002. Ethnoecology: A conceptual framework for the study of Indigenous Knowledge of Nature. In *Ethnobiology and Biocultural Diversity,* eds. J. R. Stepp, F. S. Wyndam, and R. K. Zarger, 511-522. International Society of Ethnobiology.

Tom, Gertie. 1987. Èkiyi: Gyo Cho Chú, *My Big Salmon Country. Place Names of the Big Salmon River Region, Yukon Territory, Canada.* Whitehorse: Yukon Native Language Centre.

Topkok, Sean. 2000. Cultural Atlas: multimedia production as a pedagogy of place. Presentation at the 99th Annual Meeting of the American Anthropological Association, San Francisco, November 15-19, 2000.

Tracz, Boyan. 2006. May You Live in Interesting Times: Addressing Concerns Over the Impact of Cumulative Effects on Boreal Woodland Caribou in the Mackenzie Valley, NWT. Invited Talk to the Circumpolar Students Association, University of Alberta, November 28, 2006.

Trusler, Scott 2002. *Footsteps Amongst the Berries: the Ecology and Fire History of Traditional Gitxsan and Wet'suwet'en Huckleberry Sites.* MSc. Thesis, Environmental Studies, University of Northern British Columbia.

Trusler, Scott, and Leslie Main Johnson. 2008. "Berry patch" as a kind of place—the ethnoecology of black huckleberry in Northwestern Canada. *Human Ecology* 36(4):553-568.

Tsing, Anna Lowenhaupt. 2005. *Friction, an Ethnography of Global Connection.* Princeton and Oxford: Princeton University Press.

Tuan, Yi-Fu. 1974. *Topophilia, A Study of Environmental Perception, Attitudes, and Values.* Englewood Cliffs, New Jersey: Prentice-Hall, Inc.

Tulalip Tribes. n.d. Cultural Stories. Multimedia CD-ROM. Marysville, Washington: Tulalip Tribes.

Turk, Andrew. 2008. Exploring Philosophy of Place: Potential for Synergy Between Phenomenology and Ethnophysiography. Paper delivered at Landscape in Language Conference, Albuquerque, October 27, 2008.

Turk, Andrew, and Kathryn Trees. 2000. Facilitating community processes through culturally appropriate informatics: an Australian indigenous community information system case study. In *Community Informatics: Enabling Communities with Information and Communications Technologies,* ed. Michael Gurstein, 339-358. Hershey, PA: Idea Group Publishing.

Turnbull, David. 2003. *Masons, Tricksters and Cartographers*. London and New York: Routledge.

Turner, Monica Goigel. 1989. Landscape ecology: the effect of pattern on process. *Annual Review of Ecology and Systematics* 20:171-197.

Turner, Nancy J. 2005. *The Earth's Blanket, Teachings for Sustainable Living*. Vancouver: Douglas and McIntyre.

———. 1999. "Time to Burn", traditional use of fire to enhance resource production by aboriginal peoples in British Columbia. In *Indians, Fire and the Land in the Pacific Northwest*, ed. R. Boyd, 185-218. Corvallis: Oregon State University Press.

Turner, Nancy J., L. M. J. Gottesfeld, H. V. Kuhnlein, and A. Ceska. 1992. Edible wood fern rootstocks of Western North America: Solving an ethnobotanical puzzle. *Journal of Ethnobiology* 12(1):1-34.

Usery, E. Lynn. 1993. Category theory and structure of features in geographic information systems. *Cartography and Geographic Information Systems*. 20(1):5-12.

Vajda, Edward J. 2007. Siberian landscapes in Ket traditional culture. In *Landscape and Culture in the Siberian North*, ed. Peter Jordan, (unnumbered pre-print). London: University College London Press.

———. 2008. A Siberian link with Na-Dene languages. Manuscript prepared for Dene-Yeniseic Symposium, Fairbanks, posted at http://eres.uaf.edu/coursepage. asp?cid=919&action=of&f=2#14994 (password: Y-D).

Vitebsky, Piers. 2005. *The Reindeer People, Living with Animals and Spirits in Siberia*. Boston, New York: Houghton-Mifflin.

Wagner, Roy. 1977. Scientific and Indigenous Papuan conceptualizations of the innate: a semiotic critique of the ecological perspective. In *Subsistence and Survival, Rural Ecology in the Pacific*, eds. Timothy P. Bayliss-Smith and Richard G. A. Feachem, 385-410. San Francisco: Academic Press.

Warbelow, C., D. Roseneau, and P. Stern. 1975. The Kutchin caribou fences of northeastern Alaska and the northern Yukon. In *Studies of Large Mammals along the Proposed Mackenzie Valley Gas Pipeline Route from Alaska to British Columbia*, ed. by R.D. Jakimchuk, Chapter IV. Biological Report Series Volume 32. Renewable Resources Consulting Services Ltd.

Waterman, Thomas T. 1922. The geographic names used by Indians of the Pacific Coast. *Geographical Review* 12(2):175-194.

Wein, Eleanor E. 1994. The high cost of a nutritionally adequate diet in four Yukon communities. *Canadian Journal of Public Health* 85(5):310-312.

Wein, Eleanor E., and Milton M. R. Freeman. 1992. Inuvialuit food use and food preferences in Aklavik, Northwest Territories, Canada. *Arctic Medical Research* 51:159-172.

Weinstein, Martin S. 1992. *Just Like People Get Lost: A Retrospective Assessment of the Impacts of the Faro Mining Development of the Land Use of the Ross River Indian People*. A Report to the Ross River Dena Council, Ross River, Yukon Territory.

————. 1998. Sharing Information or Captured Heritage: Access to Community Geographic Knowledge and the State's Responsibility to Protect Aboriginal Rights in British Columbia. Presented at "Crossing Boundaries", the Seventh Annual Conference of the International Association for the Study of Common Property, Vancouver, British Columbia, Canada, June 10-14. Available as pdf at http://dlc.dlib.indiana.edu/archive/00000184/.

Williams, Nancy M. 1982. A boundary is to cross: Observations on Yolngu boundaries and permission. In *Resource Managers: North American and Australian Hunter-Gatherers. AAAS Selected Symposium 67,* eds. Nancy M. Williams and Eugene S. Hunn, 131-154. Boulder, Colorado: Westview Press.

Wintergreen Consultants. 2001a. Field Reconnaissance of Selected Wet'suwet'en Huckleberry Patches in the Bulkley Forest District: Case Study Summaries. Report submitted to the Prince Rupert Forest Region, Smithers B. C. Wintergreen Consultants, Telkwa.

Wintergreen Consultants. 2001b. "Footsteps Amongst the Berries" Field Reconnaissance of Selected Gitxsan Huckleberry Sites: Case Study Summaries. Report submitted to the Prince Rupert Forest Region, Smithers B. C. Wintergreen Consultants, Telkwa.

Wishart, Robert. n.d. *Walking Again on Terra Nullius.* Manuscript in the files of the author.

World Commission on Environment and Development. 1987. *Our Common Future.* Oxford: Oxford University Press.

Young-Leslie, Heather E. 2007. A fishy romance: Chiefly power and the geopolitics of desire. *The Contemporary Pacific* 19(2):365-408.

INDEX

A

Abies lasiocarpa. See subalpine fir
Aboriginal Mapping Network, 188, 191, 193
acoustic landmark. *See* landmark, acoustic
affordance, 13, 53, 177
agriculture/agricultural, 20, 44, 118, 173–174, 208
agriculture, swidden, 20
agroforestry, 19
alpine (zone), 30, 44, 57, 65, 68, 77, 81, 83, 87, 90, 93, 102, 137–140, 144, 147, 205, 216, 221n11
Amelanchier alnifolia (saskatoon), 72, 82, 144
anthropogenic, 8, 17, 24, 72, 173
Apache, 25, 65, 111, 134, 148, 209
archaeology, 144
Athapaskan / Athapaskan people, 7, 26, 36, 50–51, 53–54, 61, 65–67, 81, 94, 97, 118–119, 134, 140–141, 144, 150, 167–168, 180–181, 207, 209. *See also* Dene
Athapaskan language(-s), 5, 50, 55–56, 61, 64–65, 106, 111, 134–135, 154, 157, 162, 164, 167, 169, 181, 183, 223n5
Australia, 9, 17, 21, 24, 120, 154, 156, 176, 191, 203
avalanche (snowslide) / avalanche track, 20, 34, 36–37, 40, 43–44, 61, 63, 104, 170, 215–216. *See also* slide / slide area
axial orientation, 175
ayllu, 208

B

Basso, Keith, 9, 25, 41, 53, 62, 65, 111, 135, 148, 153, 156, 177, 209
berries, 20, 30, 40, 64, 68, 71–78, 81, 84–87, 89, 91, 93, 95, 102, 104–105, 107, 112, 115, 121, 132, 134, 144–145, 147, 152, 192, 206, 221n11
berries, yellow. *See* cloudberry
berry patch, 7, 32, 34, 36, 40, 44, 57, 68, 71–72, 74–87, 89–93, 107, 135, 139, 145–147, 154, 164, 170, 191, 216, 220, 220n2, 220n10, 221n11. *See also* trail, berry

black huckleberry, 71–76, 78, 79, 82, 84, 90–91, 93, 144–145, 147, 152, 220, 220n1
blueberry, 72–73, 75, 78, 89, 115, 144–145
blueberry, high bush, 89
blueberry, lowbush, 72–73, 75, 78, 144–145
boreal forest, 94, 106, 174, 214. *See also* forest
Bosavi, 208
boundaries/boundedness, 6–7, 27, 31, 42, 54, 62, 78, 84–85, 118, 131, 135, 138–139, 148, 154, 156, 162, 165, 170, 172–173, 178–179, 185, 187, 191–193, 198, 213, 215, 223n2 (chap. 10)
British Columbia, 4–5, 7, 13, 30, 50, 52, 71–72, 76, 91, 94–95, 134–135, 138, 142, 145–146, 173, 178, 187, 224–225n7
brush, 27, 40, 89–90
"brushland," 105
built environment, 9–10, 15, 17–18. *See also* environment; environment, social
Bulkley River, 50–51, 54, 59, 82, 146–147, 165, 220n5
burn / a burned place, 38, 43, 56, 62, 75–76, 90, 105, 128, 205–206. *See also* forest fire
burning, 40, 44, 67, 72, 74–78, 84–87, 89, 91, 145, 206, 221n11

C

camp, 15, 27, 32, 36–37, 38, 73, 76–78, 82–85, 96–97, 100–102, 105–106, 111, 113–115, 117–118, 130, 137, 145–146, 152, 164, 170, 175, 177, 201, 205, 208, 221n11
berry, 73, 76–78, 82–84
fish, 36–37, 84, 111, 113, 115, 117, 119, 123–124, 126, 145–146, 162
hunting or trapping, 38, 78, 100–101, 113–114, 127, 145
spring or fall, 111, 115, 122, 146, 154
summer, 111, 113, 115, 121, 141, 154
winter, 83, 111, 113–116, 121, 138, 146, 154, 162

248

Kaska language, 17, 54, 65–66, 94, 100,
102, 104, 106, 111, 135, 161–162,
164, 181, 204–205, 221n2 (chap. 6)
Ket, 150, 207
kind of place, 5, 36, 40, 44, 63, 67–68,
74, 100, 220n1 (chap. 5). *See also*
ecotope; place kind
kungax. See trail of song

L
lake, 27, 34–35, 51–54, 57, 59, 62,
64–67, 81, 83–84, 94–95, 97, 99, 101,
104, 107–108, 124, 126–128, 134–
135, 137–138, 140–143. 146–147,
151, 156–157, 161–162, 164, 174–
175, 177, 181, 197, 204, 221–222n1
(chap. 8)
land, the / the Land, 1–8, 10–11, 13–14,
17, 19, 22, 25, 28–29, 32, 36, 40–42,
44, 50, 53, 57, 61–62, 65–67, 73, 94,
96–99, 105–109, 111, 115, 117–122,
130–135, 137–138, 147–148, 150,
153–154, 156, 167–168, 170, 172,
174, 176–177, 180–181, 186–210,
212–214, 217 218n2 (chap. 2). *See also*
landscape
landform, 3, 5, 7, 11, 15, 17, 20, 52, 100,
109, 177, 203
land management, 7, 189, 196. *See also*
management
landmark, 4, 32, 53, 137, 147, 152, 156,
162–164, 170, 175, 177–179, 182,
185, 192–193, 208. *See also* icemark
landmark, acoustic, 208. *See also*
soundscape
landscape, 3–5, 7–27, 30, 32, 34, 40,
43–44, 51–56, 58, 60–62, 65–66,
71–73, 76, 78, 89, 96, 99, 104. 106,
108–109, 118–120, 122, 133–135,
137, 140, 148–151, 153–154, 156,
168, 170, 172–177, 179–182, 185–
187, 191, 195, 199–200, 203–214,
216, 218n1 (chap. 2), 218n3 (chap.
2), 221n1 (chap. 8), 222n5 (chap. 9),
224n1 (chap. 12)
and history, 11, 25, 29, 40, 99, 119,
170, 177

and mapping, 20–21, 27, 172–174,
179, 185, 187, 199, 214, 218n3
(chap. 2), 224n1 (chap. 12). *See also*
mapping
and power, 11, 17, 24, 27, 44, 98–99,
119–120, 148, 177, 199, 206–208
anthropology of, 8–10
archaeological perspecives of, 10
arid, 22–23
as medium, 4, 203
block diagram of, 106
boreal forest, 106
Bulkley Valley, BC, 52
concepts of, European, 15, 135, 185,
208
conversion of (to agriculture), 78
cultural. *See* cultural landscape
definitions of, 15–17
dynamic, 67,105 106, 148, 186, 206,
209, 222n5 (chap. 9)
European, 208
in geography, 15
in painting, 15
Navajo, 150–151
Northwest Territories (Canada), 54,
108, 132, 148, 186, 191
perception of, 4, 8, 11, 19, 24, 44,
53, 97, 135, 167, 174–175, 181,
206–208, 210
physical, 13, 22, 24, 168
sacred or sacral, 6, 11, 17, 29, 32, 44,
57, 147, 168, 171, 199, 205–208,
216. *See also* landscape and power;
place, sacred
seasonality and, 22–23, 107–109, 131,
133, 174, 186, 207, 215. *See also*
seasonality
sentient, 19, *67* 107, 118–119, 148,
168–169, 204
storied, 7, 24, 54, 98, 153, 168, 191,
198, 200, 206, 209, 211–212. *See
also* story; storyline
spiritual, 4, 17, 24–25, 28, 42, 62,
67, 147, 197, 206, 208, 214. *See
also* landscape and power; landscape,
sacred
urban, 173
Yukon, 96–97, 105, 140

Marquis Book Printing Inc.

Québec, Canada
2012